ANDRÉS (DREW) McKINLEY

I0121122

The Stories We Could Tell

Preserving the Historical Memory of El Salvador

Daraja Press

Published by Daraja Press
https://darajapress.com

© 2024 Andrés (Drew) McKinley

ISBN 978-1-998309-39-9

Cover art by Rafael Lemus Aleman

Library and Archives Canada Cataloguing in Publication

Title: The stories we could tell : preserving historical memory in El Salvador /
    Andrés (Drew)
McKinley.
Names: McKinley, Andrés, author.
Description: Includes bibliographical references.
Identifiers: Canadiana 20240539761 | ISBN 9781998309399 (softcover)
Subjects: LCSH: El Salvador—Biography. | LCSH: El Salvador—History—Civil
    War, 1979-1992. | LCGFT: Biographies.
Classification: LCC F1488.4 .M35 2024 | DDC 972.8405/30922—dc23

Daraja Press
PO BOX 99900 BM 735 664 Wakefield, QC J0X 0C2, Canada
info@darajapress.com
https://darajapress.com
EU Authorised Representative for GPSR: EAS www.easproject.com
For EU product safety concerns, please contact us at info@darajapress.com

CONTENTS

The struggle of man against power
is the struggle of memory against
forgetting.

– Milan Kundera

Acknowledgments

I offer my deepest gratitude to the following people without whom this book would not have seen the light of day: all of the amazing and profoundly admired friends who contributed their testimonies of courage and hope related to the civil war in El Salvador; Firoze Manji of Daraja Press for his trust, his willingness to take risks, his commitment to the defence of historical memory in Central America and his determined pursuit of building bridges in a troubled world; Ana Eugenia Marin, who has patiently edited and corrected my style for everything that I have written on Central America in the past 45 years; my beloved son, David Miguel, for sharing his creative skills and for telling me when I was wrong at any hour of the day; my beloved friend and confidant, Brian Murphy, for his endless revisions and excellent advice, saving me on numerous occasions from going down the wrong path; my boss and friend of many years, Omar Serrano, for his moral support, excellent editing and for providing most of the content for the final section on the Peace Accords; my longtime friend, Paco Alvarez, for being ready to help on any issue and for editing the Spanish version of this book; my deeply loved comrade in struggle from the days of the civil war, Rafael Lemus Aleman (Lito), for sharing his artistic skills in the preparation of the book's cover, as well as his personal testimony; Fatima Araceli Peña Fuentes for her ideas, vision and research for the final portion of the book; Fatima Alejandra Díaz for her logistical support and Xiomara Mariona Zepeda for her friendship and support of always, since my first days with the UCA. Thanks to you all!

Introduction

On January 16, 1992, a far-right political party (ARENA) representing the interests of one of the most powerful oligarchies of Central America sat down with a leftist anti-imperialist guerrilla insurgency (FMLN) and signed a series of accords that brought to a close twelve years of bloody armed conflict and generated hopes for a more just and democratic nation. It was a moment of national consensus regarding the urgency of a peaceful solution to the war and laid the foundations for an incipient democracy based on the separation of powers, citizen participation, respect for human rights and transparency. Nevertheless, almost three decades later, the current president of El Salvador is promoting rhetoric insisting that the civil war in El Salvador and the Peace Accords that brought it to an end were a "farce".

This troubling narrative was first heard in the midst of legislative and municipal elections on December 17, 2020, in an aggressive speech to promote the candidates of the president's party, New Ideas. It occurred in the village of El Mozote in the northern province of Morazan before a crowd of survivors and family members of victims of the worst civilian massacre of the war:

> *The war was a farce, they killed 75,000 people on both sides, including the thousand here from El Mozote, it was a farce, like the Peace Accords....Yes, I sully them because they were a farce, a negotiation between two leaderships.*

The speech caused outrage among the population of Morazan as well as the country's social movements, human rights organizations, victims' committees, academics and other sectors who had witnessed the cruel reality of the war and defended the democratic legacy of the Peace Accords.

El Salvador's president, however, knew that his speech would penetrate deeply and resonate with the majority of El Salvador's population who, following the war and the signing of peace, were confronting new manifestations of social violence in the form of violent street gangs and economic exclusion that continued to stifle attempts to lead a dignified and full life among the vast majority of the country's citizens. And the president's rhetoric appealed to this frustration.

The speech from El Mozote was widely disseminated via Twitter, and its historical distortions were repeated publicly on several occasions, including the 78th session of the General Assembly of the United Nations in 2023, when the intent to distort historical memory was once again evident in the president's words:

> *For decades we tried everything that others said was best for us… They made us fight a civil war for a cause foreign to our reality…. They made us sign false peace agreements which had nothing of peace, and which only served to allow the two sides in the war to share the spoils.*

The official narrative of the government continues to this day to distort and erase the significance of one of the most important periods in the history of El Salvador, rendering invisible a war and a set of Peace Accords considered by the United Nations to be the most successful experience of conflict resolution in its history. It is also an attack on a model for democracy established by the Peace Accords, a model that the current regime is actively attempting to neutralize and dismantle on its path from democratic to "hybrid" to populist authoritarian government.

The book that you are holding in your hands is a small grain of sand hoping to contribute to efforts to confront this challenge to our incipient and vulnerable democracy by speaking truth to power and defending historical memory in El Salvador.

Examples of post-conflict literature on El Salvador sometimes differ with each other on the emphasis given to the various causes of the war and the degree of influence that foreign powers had on its origins and evolution, but the vast majority of analyses coincide unquestionably regarding the reality of the war itself and its profound levels of cruelty. They recognize, further, the fact that the war was, in essence, a confrontation between two opposing national projects and that the principal causal factors had to do with the internal reality of the country.

Only those who benefited directly or indirectly from the situation of structural injustice existing in El Salvador at the time, generating intolerable levels of hardship and misery for the majority of the population, blamed the war on the expansionist interests of international communism in an attempt to divert the focus from chronic poverty and exclusion.

Today, more than 40 years after the formal beginning of the war and more than 30 years after it ended, the official narrative is attempting once again to deny the structural causes that gave rise to a bloody conflict that wracked El Salvador for more than a decade. Equally serious, the current narrative holds that the war itself was a farce and sullies the Peace Accords for having been part of that farce, affirming that the war was the product of foreign powers within the context of the Cold War following a script to benefit themselves at the cost of the bloodshed of thousands of Salvadorans. (Like many falsehoods, this narrative contains an element of truth, especially as it relates to the role of the United States with its anticommunist rhetoric during the years of Ronald Reagan, but in no way explains the origin of the civil war in El Salvador.)

Although this narrative is not new, what is new (and dangerous) is that in the context of El Salvador today with a vast majority of the population supporting the current president, his narrative is finding receptivity among large sectors of the society.

Denigrating the war and sullying the Peace Accords is not the ultimate goal of the current regime, however. The underlying purpose of the current narrative on the war and Peace Accords, as mentioned earlier, is to erase the historical memory related to one of the most important periods of El Salvador's history in an effort to gradually dismantle the incipient democracy that the war and the Peace Accords achieved, concentrate power and consolidate a populist authoritarianism. This dangerous regression establishes a situation that, in many ways, resembles the country in the period leading up to the war.

The Spanish philosopher Manuel Reyes Mate dedicated much of his life to studying the political dimension of memory, arguing that memory is a key prerequisite for achieving justice. From this perspective, memory does not consist simply of recovering a detailed and meticulous version of what happened; memory is a vision of the past through an ethical lens. It is a "moral reading of the past, [which] not only wants to tell the facts but also seeks their meaning, a meaning that the past must have for us."[1] Those who seek to bury the past, rendering invisible the true

---

1 Mate, Manuel E. (2015), "Historical and ethical memory of the victims" in *Pensamiento Crítico*, January – February 2016. http://www.pensamientocritico.org/manrey0316.htm

causes of the war and the impact of the Peace Accords, are seeking to erase memory.

We saw something similar to this happen in El Salvador in March 1993 when the report of the Truth Commission investigating serious human rights violations during the armed conflict was published. The right-wing ARENA government, in power at that time, shelved the report by applying the attractive language of "turning the page", "cleaning the slate", and "forgiving and forgetting", but with the underlying motives of protecting the perpetrators while ignoring the urgency of doing justice for the victims. And this history of impunity continues in El Salvador today.

The current government does not recognize the Peace Accords and does not celebrate their signing. It remembers, instead, the victims of the war. But the best way to recognize the rights of victims would be to support their search for the truth about what happened to family members and who was responsible. Nevertheless, the present government, like governments before it, has continued to refuse access to military files that could clarify many of the violations of that time. In addition, it has ignored a proposal for a National Reconciliation Law that would put the country on the path to justice for the victims of armed conflict and end the impunity of perpetrators who remain untouchable. Memory is the path to justice because it leads to truth. Silence, on the other hand, is the path to impunity.

The contents of the Peace Accords are largely unknown to many Salvadorans today. And the powers that be are trying to render invisible this historic accord that successfully brought the war to an end after twelve bloody years of confrontation, contributing to the birth of a new nation built upon participative democracy, respect for human rights, transparency and truth.

The Stories We Could Tell is an attempt to push back on current strategies to distort and erase historical memory. It begins, appropriately, with the memory of Rufina Amaya, a poor peasant woman and sole survivor of one of the worst civilian massacres in modern times, vilified, ridiculed and discredited by the Salvadoran and US governments in her desperate attempts to reveal the truth about the rape, torture and slaughter of close to 1000 men, women, children and elderly in the village of El Mozote between December 11 and 12, 1981.

The book continues with a brief account of the war itself and its causes, including the role of the United States in prolonging the suffering and augmenting the costs of the war for El Salvador and its people. In this same section, the book traces the persistent efforts of key actors promoting a peaceful solution to the war through a long and arduous process of dialogue and negotiations.

This section is followed by the heart of the book, consisting of testimonies of courage and hope from key protagonists in the struggle for a more just and democratic nation, demonstrating the levels of persistence and commitment in a people's war of a thousand trenches.

The book ends with a summary analysis of the Peace Accords and their historical contribution to building a new nation and a sustainable peace, calling upon the new generations of El Salvador to accept the challenge of defending these accords, offering a pathway to democracy in El Salvador in the name of those who suffered and sacrificed for a utopian dream 40 years ago.

Omar Serrano
Assistant Dean for Social Projection
Central American University, José Simeón Cañas (UCA)

Note to the reader

This book is an effort to contribute to the preservation of the historical memory of El Salvador. It describes the tragedy of a civil war that lasted almost two decades and took the lives of over 75,000 people, gives voice to key actors of that period, a complicated task for people unaccustomed to talking about themselves and analyzes the hopes of the Salvadoran people for a new nation and a durable peace.

The book is dedicated in a special way to Rufina Amaya, a poor peasant woman born in the small village of La Guacamaya in the northern province of Morazan, who lost all that she loved on December 11, 1981 in the massacre of El Mozote, considered at the time to be one of the worst crimes against humanity in the western hemisphere. The book is also dedicated to all of the people of El Salvador and from other nations, from all social sectors, ages and creeds, who suffered from the horrors of that violent period. May it serve as a light for those still living and as proof to the generations to come that hope still lives in El Salvador.

Andrés (Drew) McKinley
San Salvador, September 10, 2024

Prologue

"My name is Rufina Amaya. I was born in the La Guacamaya, part of the village of El Mozote [in the northern department of Morazan]. On December 11, 1981, a large contingent of government soldiers arrived in our village at about six in the afternoon and locked us up in our homes. Others, including small children, were then taken from their houses and made to lie face down on the ground, where the soldiers proceeded to confiscate everything of value from each person, especially money and the simple jewelry that the people wore. Then, at about seven o'clock that night, they took the rest of us out of our homes, some of whom they killed.

At approximately five o'clock the following morning, the soldiers made us form two lines in the village square, one line of men and one line of women, and they kept us there until around seven am. The children were crying from hunger and from the cold because we had nothing to shelter us. I was in line with my four children; my oldest son was nine years old, my daughter, Lolita, was five, another daughter was three, and my youngest was only eight months old. We all wept together.

At seven in the morning a helicopter landed near to where we were gathered in front of Alfredo Márquez's house. A large group of soldiers got down from the helicopter and came over to where we were standing. They carried large, two-edged knives and pointed their rifles at us. Then they carried the men away and locked them in the hermitage by the convent, and some of us began thinking that maybe we would not be killed.

We could see through the window of the hermitage and observed how the soldiers had tied up and blindfolded the men, stepping on some of them. Others had already been killed, and these they beheaded and threw the remains into the convent next door. By twelve o'clock that afternoon, the soldiers had finished killing all of the men and began taking the young girls out into the hills. The mothers wept and screamed at the soldiers not to take their daughters away from them, but they were beaten with rifle buts by the soldiers. The children who cried the loudest and who made the most noise were the first ones to be taken away, never to return.

At about five that afternoon, they came for me and approximately 22 other women. I was the last in line and was breastfeeding my youngest daughter when the soldiers suddenly ripped her from my arms. As we passed the home of Israel Márques, I could see the mountain of dead in the process of being machine-gunned by the soldiers. The other women with me were holding onto each other, screaming and crying. I fell to my knees, thinking of my four children, and, at that moment, with no one looking, I suddenly saw a nearby fruit tree and leaped behind it.

The soldiers finished killing the remaining women in my group without realizing I had escaped and proceeded to bring another group of women into the square to continue the killing. By approximately seven that evening, no men or women remained alive, so the soldiers sat in the street to rest just a few meters from my hiding place. At that moment, I heard their conversation, one soldier saying to another, "We are done with the old men and women now, only this big group of children that we have locked up remains. They are beautiful children; we don't know what we are going to do." Another soldier responded, "The order we bring is to leave no one alive because these people are collaborators with the guerrillas, but I do not want to kill children." Still, another soldier said, "If you're done killing the old people, go burn their cadavers."

The soldiers then went off to set fire to the homes of the dead. The flames quickly approached the small tree where I was hiding, frightening me, so I had to move. You could hear the cry of a child trapped in the fire – they had by then begun to kill the children – and I heard another soldier say, "Go on, you haven't killed that son of a bitch." The soldier moved off, and minutes later, shots were heard.

I heard the soldiers comment that they were from the Atlacatl battalion. I even knew some of them, as they were local recruits. One was the son of Don Benjamín, who was an evangelical. Don Benjamín was also killed along with 15 other family members in their home. The son must have seen it because he was right there when they killed him along with another local named Nilo.

One of the soldiers said, 'Look, there were witches here, and they can come out of the fire.' As the soldiers talked, one of them sat almost at my feet. I couldn't breathe out of fear, and I heard him say, 'We have finished killing all of these people, and tomorrow we are going on to La Joya, Cerro Pando...'

Around one o'clock in the morning, one said, 'Let's go eat something at the store,' and later I heard the sounds of bottles clinking.

I had to move, but the area was full of soldiers. I spent about an hour thinking about how to escape. Animals are attracted to light, and there are a number of cows in our village, so several calves and dogs began approaching the fire. I asked God to give me an idea about how to get out of here, and then I found the way. I tied my dress, which was half white and crawled on the ground through the legs of the animals to the other side of the street into a large orchard of fruit trees. I dragged myself under the fence, like a dog would do, and sat for a bit on the other side, waiting to hear gunshots, but there were none. The only sound was the children screaming, my children yelling, 'Mama, they are killing us, Mama, they are strangling us, Mama, they are sticking a knife into us!'

I longed to go back to save my children because I recognized their screams. But then I reflected. I knew that they would kill me too. I said to myself, 'Maybe they're afraid, and that's why they're crying. Maybe they won't kill them, maybe they'll take them away, and one day I'll see them again. I knew little about war and thought that perhaps I could see my children again in some other place.

'My God,' I thought, 'I can escape from here, but if I go back, I will surely die, and there will be no one to tell this story. There is no one left but me,' I said to myself. So, I continued my efforts to escape...."

Testimony of Rufina Amaya (deceased), survivor of the massacre of El Mozote on December 11, 1981. Museo de la Palabra y la Imagen, https://museo.com. sv/2011/07/rufina-ayala-la-verdad-sobre-el-mozote/

PART ONE
When Madness Reigned

Monument to Memory and Truth in honor of the innocent victims of the war in El Salvador

In the majestic and pristine beauty of northern El Salvador, the towering mountains reach for the sky with the persistent hope of touching the heavens, symbolizing a people's heroic struggle for a more just and democratic nation of nearly half a century ago. And in the surrounding towns and villages, once part of highly contested war zones, the generations struggle to keep the memory alive of some of the worst crimes against humanity of the twentieth century.

During the decade of the 1980s and the early 1990s, two of the most powerful and antagonistic political and economic projects in the history of El Salvador were intertwined for more than 12 years in a bloody civil war seeking, on the one hand, to perpetuate almost 50 years of military dictatorship in defense of an oligarchic economic model of exclusion and, on the other, to lay the foundations of participatory democracy with a more just and equitable model of sustainable development for all. It was a conflict driven by two opposing political/military forces with differing world views and irreconcilable visions of nationhood determined to triumph by any means.

The accords that finally brought an end to the war in January 1992 established a Truth Commission coordinated by the United Nations to investigate the crimes committed by both parties to the conflict with the aim of contributing to reconciliation and a lasting peace, as well as freeing El Salvador from the cyclical violence that had plagued the country for centuries.

The Commission's final report, "From Madness to Hope," conceived of as a vehicle for preserving historical memory based on truth, objectivity and transparency, found that the vast majority of serious human rights violations during the conflict were committed by government forces (85%). It revealed as well, however, that an undisputable level of violations had been carried out by the guerrilla insurgency of the FMLN, including forced recruitment, the slaying of civilian mayors and attacks on unarmed U.S. military personnel. It also provided a clear image of the dimension, complexity and horror of one of the most significant periods in the history of El Salvador.

> *Between 1980 and 1991, the Republic of El Salvador in Central America was engulfed in a war which plunged Salvadorian society into violence, left it with thousands and thousands of people dead and exposed it to appalling crimes... The violence was a fire which swept over the fields of El Salvador; it burst into villages, cut off roads and destroyed highways and bridges, energy sources and transmission lines; it reached the cities and entered families, sacred areas and educational centers; it struck at justice and filled the public administration with victims; and it singled out as an enemy anyone who was not on the list of friends. Violence turned everything to death and destruction, for such is the senselessness of that breach of the calm plenitude which accompanies the rule of law, the essential nature of violence being suddenly or gradually to alter the certainty which the law nurtures in human beings when this change does not take place through the normal mechanisms of the rule of law. The victims were Salvadorians and foreigners of all backgrounds and all social and economic classes, for in its blind cruelty violence leaves everyone equally defenseless.* [1]

In the history of the civil war in El Salvador between 1980 and 1992, one can find good as well as evil, human solidarity as well as betrayal, hope as well as desperation and joy as well as suffering. It took the lives of over 75,000 people, left 350,000 people wounded, drove over a million rural peasants from their communities of origin, left over eight thousand

---

1 Introduction to the report of the UN Truth Commission, 1993

disappeared and thousands more physically and emotionally incapaci-
tated, with an economy in ruins. Nevertheless, it produced one of the
most successful experiences of conflict resolution in the history of the
United Nations, engendering hope for a new nation with an incipient
democracy based on citizen participation, transparency, respect for
human rights and sustained peace. In his book *El Salvador's Civil War*,
published in 1996, author and analyst for the Washington Office on
Latin America (WOLA), Hugh Byrne, insists:

> *It is a great tribute to the participants in El Salvador's long
> conflict, as well as a hope for the future and an example for
> those involved in similar struggles, that an exit was found that
> did not necessitate the destruction of one or the other side but
> provided the conditions for peaceful political competition.* [2]

For 12 years, the war confronted Salvadoran with Salvadoran, brother
with brother, neighbor with neighbor, wealthy with poor and poor with
poor, tearing apart the fabric of society and leaving the country with levels
of polarization, anger and resentment unresolved to this day. Perhaps the
greatest tragedy of all, however, is that it could have been avoided.

If the poverty, hunger and desperation of El Salvador's disenfranchised majorities had not been so deeply and profoundly rooted
throughout history from the time of the Spanish Conquest, if the ruling
classes had had ears to listen, eyes to see and hearts to feel, permitting
a minimum of reform to reduce human suffering and if politicians had
been more honest and committed to resolving the needs of the people,
the war need not have happened.

If military leaders had been less corrupt, less repressive and less
consumed by their ambition for power; if the United States had been
less ruthless in its exercise of hemispheric hegemony; if the forces of
evil had not eliminated, in the precise moment that they were most
urgently needed, key figures like Rutilio Grande, Archbishop Oscar
Arnulfo Romero and so many others promoting justice and peace; if
right wing death squads had not terrorized and disappeared so many
committed young students, union organizers, human rights activists
and other Christians, the contradictions of Salvadoran society could

2 Byrne, *El Salvador's Civil War*, 1996. P. xi

have been managed without violent confrontation. But that is not the way it was.

The civil war was perceived as the final option by desperate men, women, youth and aged for overcoming centuries of injustice and oppression. It followed decades of failed attempts to modify an unsustainable reality through non-violent means but gradually became accepted as the only viable path for change.

The specific causes of the war are more than evident. They leap off the pages of any objective historical account of the country, grab you by the throat and shake you until your eyes finally open to the undeniable truth of landlessness, endless poverty, a lack of basic political freedoms, over fifty years of military dictatorship, electoral fraud, foreign intervention, and ever-increasing levels of state-sponsored repression.

The costs of the war were immeasurable, terrible and tragic, but the gains of the confrontation were also significant, turning the page on half a century of military dictatorship, igniting a light in the darkness and hope where only madness and despair had reigned.

The year 1980, with the slaying of Monsignor Romero, is generally considered to mark the formal initiation of civil war in El Salvador, although the armed conflict actually began a decade earlier as students and landless peasants, along with workers, slum dwellers and other traditionally marginalized social sectors, became more radicalized and politically active.

During that same period, right-wing death squads were organized and controlled by members of the security forces with names like the White Hand, the Union of White Warriors, the Secret Anticommunist Army and the Maximiliano Hernández Martínez Anticommunist Brigade. Their goal was to immobilize social protest through a reign of selective terror aimed at any person or group perceived as opposing the regime.

It was state-sponsored terrorism in its purest form and left the country strewn with decapitated and cruelly tortured corpses for all to see along highways, in open fields and in the ravines around towns and villages as a warning to all who might consider joining the struggle. Another eight thousand people, in the majority youth, were disappeared without a trace.

In spite of the fear that permeated society during that period, the political slogan that guided the process in the streets was: *In the face of growing repression, more organization and struggle.* Broad-based multi-sectoral coalitions were formed, joining peasants, students, workers, slum dwellers and other sectors with names like the *Bloque Popular Revolucionario* (BPR) (Popular Revolutionary Block); *Ligas Populares 28 de Febrero* (LP-28) (Popular Leagues, February 28); *Movimiento de Liberación Popular* (MLP) (Popular Liberation Movement) and the *Frente de Acción Popular Unificada* (FAPU) (Front for United Popular Action).

On January 11, 1980, these coalitions joined with opposition political parties to form the *Coordinadora Revolucionaria de Masas* (CRM) (Revolutionary Coordination of Masses) and, on the 22nd of that month, mobilized over 200,000 people in repudiation of the military dictatorship in power at the time and demanding a halt to repression. This process reached its pinnacle on April 1, 1980 with the formation of the *Frente Democrático Revolucionario* (FDR) (Democratic Revolutionary Front), a political/diplomatic initiative proposing, as an alternative to war, the formation of a popular democratic and revolutionary government through a participative process of dialogue and negotiation.

In October 1981, FDR presented its proposal to the General Assembly of the United Nations, but it was quickly and decisively rejected by the government, the military and their right-wing supporters in El Salvador, convinced of the need and the viability of winning the war through military means. Then, on November 27 that year, the death squad, Maximiliano Hernández Martínez Anticommunist Brigade, kidnapped, tortured and killed all five members of FDR's national directorate, including its president, Enrique Álvarez Córdova.

Córdova was from a wealthy family of the oligarchy who had left a life of luxury and privilege to join the cause of the poor. He was considered by other members of the oligarchy as a traitor to his class, and his cruelly tortured corpse displayed the profound hatred and the special attention he had received from his executioners. Also among the dead were Juan Chacón, leader of the Bloque Popular Revolucionario (BPR); Humberto Mendoza, leader of the Movimiento de Liberación Popular (MLP); Manuel Franco, leader of the Unión Democrático Nacional (UDN) and Ernesto Barrera, leader of the Movimiento Nacional Revolucionario (MNR).

In the face of growing political violence, highly clandestine guerrilla organizations, founded and operational during the 1970s but moving in the shadows for almost a decade, began gaining in strength as the option of armed struggle became increasingly accepted by broad sectors of society. And on October 10, 1980, these organizations came together to form the *Frente Farabundo Martí para la Liberación Nacional* (FMLN) (Farabundo Martí National Liberation Front), a force that would become the undisputed vanguard for revolutionary struggle in El Salvador for the remainder of the war and for years afterward.

The primary motor force in the struggle for change in El Salvador was a traditionally divided and voiceless peasant population that gradually evolved into one of the strongest and most belligerent social movements in all of Latin America. The change was quantitative as well as qualitative, built upon decades of oppression and the arduous efforts by priests, nuns and lay promotors of the Catholic Church, together with other committed social activists, determined to dismantle the historical structures of injustice in the country and empower the poor with a sense of their own dignity.

This process of accumulated popular force, with its growing demand for land reform, proposed as a basic step toward ending poverty, was perceived by the strategic alliance between the oligarchy and a corrupt military as a threat to the profoundly embedded interests of the dominant classes. The response of the security forces and death squads was to target the Church and its supporters with vehemence, circulating flyers in the wealthy neighborhoods urging the population to "Be a patriot, Kill a priest"!

Rutilio Grande was the first priest murdered on March 12, 1977 for his work with landless peasants and heavily exploited cane cutters in the parish of Aguilares. His death was followed by the assassination of father Alfonso Navarro on May 11 of that same year; by father Oviedo Ernesto Barrera Motto on November 28, 1978; by Octavio Ortiz on January 20, 1979; by Rafael Palacios on June 20 that same year; by Alirio Napoleón Macias on August 4, 1979 and by the much-loved "voice of the voiceless", Monsignor Oscar Arnulfo Romero, on March 24, 1980.

Following this horrific chain of events, on December 2, 1980, national guardsmen kidnapped, raped and killed three North American Catholic nuns and a Catholic lay missionary (Maura Clark, Ita Ford, Dorothy Kazel and Jean Donovan) accused of being guerrilla sympathizers for their work with families displaced from their villages of origin by the indiscriminate bombing of the Salvadoran Air Force and frequent and bloody incursions by government infantry.

From the first years of the armed struggle, the Salvadoran government, its Armed Forces and its North American mentors demonstrated their willingness to apply strategies and tactics of the cruelest nature in order to halt the advances of a popular movement that was increasingly united and determined on its path to liberation. In May 1980, just two months after the assassination of Monsignor Romero, the National Guard, together with right-wing paramilitaries, aggressively attacked several hundred civilians from villages in the northern department of Chalatenango, traditionally one of the poorest regions in the country.

Eyewitnesses to the event describe the desperate attempts at escape on the part of men, women, children and elderly fleeing a military bent on their annihilation. Most of the villagers ran towards the Sumpul River, marking the border with Honduras, in hopes of finding refuge in that country, but the Honduran military met them on the other side of the river, firing indiscriminately into the crowd as helicopters flew overhead, contributing to the slaughter.

Children and the elderly, many unable to swim, were torn violently from the arms of family members and carried downriver in the turbulent waters to drown. Some children, according to witnesses, were thrown into the air, caught on the bayonets of the soldiers and chopped to pieces. The consensus is that between 300 and 600 unarmed civilians were killed on that tragic day that became known as the Sumpul Massacre.[3]

The incident marked the initiation of counterinsurgency strategies and tactics brought by U.S. military advisors from the war in Vietnam and produced the first massive flight of Salvadoran refugees to Honduras, where they would later congregate in three large refugee camps under

3 Armstrong and Shenk, *The Face of Revolution*, 1982, p.162

the control of the United Nations. The strategy being applied on the ground in El Salvador was referred to as "scorched earth" and, together with the indiscriminate bombing of peasant villages, was designed to isolate FMLN guerrillas from their strategic social base and life support system. It was considered a key strategy for winning the war by "drying up the sea to kill the fish."

The Sumpul massacre was followed by another equally horrific massacre in December 1981, this time in the villages in and around El Mozote in northern Morazan. It was considered to be one of the worst crimes of the 20th century in which somewhere between 800 and 1000 men, women, children and elderly were systematically raped and slaughtered by the infamous Atlacatl battalion, formed and trained by the United States. The Salvadoran government and the U.S. Embassy vehemently denied both of these incidents until independent investigators uncovered the bones, presenting the world with undeniable evidence.

Along with El Sumpul and El Mozote, a long list of additional tragic incidences was documented over the years, including the Lempa River massacre in March 1981, the Las Hojas massacre in February 1983, the massacre in Tenango and Guadelupe at the end of February 1983; the massacre of Copapayo and San Nicolas in November 1983 and many others of lesser dimension, all considered by the UN Truth Commission to be crimes against humanity and all of which went unpunished.

In spite of the blatant brutality of U.S.-sponsored counterinsurgency strategies in El Salvador, it was evident in the early years of the war that the FMLN maintained the political and military initiative, and by the beginning of 1984, almost a third of the countryside was under FMLN control. In these "liberated zones", local governments, called Local Popular Powers (PPL in Spanish), were established to experiment with new ways of governing at the local level based on participatory democracy and responding to the unique challenges of a people at war.

The PPLs promoted a mixed economy with individual as well as collective production of food, clothing, footwear, kitchen utensils, honey and other strategic necessities of general use by the civilian population and by guerrilla forces. There was also a system of "popular stores" operating throughout the fronts on the barter system. It was an effort to begin the process of building a new society in the midst of war.

In military terms, the guerrilla forces of the FMLN were capable of defending their ever-broadening territories, rendering it almost impossible for the armed forces to sustain a permanent presence or even temporary large-scale incursions into guerrilla-controlled zones. The FMLN was also capable of concentrating its forces at any given moment to attack strategic military targets outside of their controlled areas, demonstrated by the attack on the Ilopango air base in 1982, the overrunning of government troops in the town of Tenancingo in 1983, the overrunning of the Fourth Infantry Brigade at El Paraiso in Chalatenango that same year; the destruction of the strategic Cuscatlan Bridge over the Lempa River, essentially dividing the country in two between east and west, in 1984; the overrunning of the military training center in La Union in 1985 and the constant harassment of important military bases in San Miguel, Chalatenango, San Francisco Gotera, Morazan, and even the installations of the Joint Chiefs of Staff in San Salvador.

During the later phases of the war, the strategies and tactics of the insurgency in El Salvador were heavily influenced by a complex struggle to repopulate thousands of peasant families who had been forcefully displaced from their communities since the early years of the war. Internally displaced families throughout the country had been returning to their homes silently on an individual basis over several years, but a more formal, massive and public process was begun in 1986, motivated, designed and coordinated by the displaced population itself with support from organizations like the Christian Committee for the Displaced of El Salvador (CRIPDES) and the CORDES Foundation.

This process included the return of thousands of refugees who had fled to neighboring countries, like Honduras, Nicaragua, Costa Rica, Panama, Australia, Canada and the United States and changed forever the dynamic of the war, transforming the role of the displaced population from that of frightened victims into highly-organized and politicized defenders of the right to reside in their communities, even in the midst of war, as established by the Geneva Convention.

Throughout the process, the army continued to harass the returning civilians with efforts to block resettlement in areas under FMLN control, accusing the population of being terrorists and FMLN supporters.

Nevertheless, the process continued into the 1990s and became a transparent and non-violent assertion of sovereignty and agency among the civilian population most affected by the war, serving as a bulwark in the face of continuing military aggression and repression.

It also served as a kind of buffer between the forces of the state and the forces of the FMLN. It was a brilliant and unprecedented strategy that opened up the war fronts to international eyes, inhibiting the ongoing efforts of the military to "dry up the sea in order to kill the fish." It offered new opportunities and platforms (many international) for demanding respect for basic human rights and strengthened direct access of newly populated communities to reconstruction and development aid from international cooperation.

With all of this, the repopulation process became a turning point, introducing a new and dynamic element in the tension between waging war and waging peace, signifying a transition in existing relationships among popular movements, the Salvadoran government, the 'international humanitarian community, the political/military structures of the FLMN and its constituent parties.

The role of the US in prolonging the war

Unlike its involvement in other countries of Latin America, up until the 20th century, the United States paid limited attention to El Salvador unless bananas or coffee were involved. This changed abruptly with the overthrow in 1979 of the Nicaraguan dictator, Anastasio Somoza Debayle, whose family had been placed in power by U.S. marines in the 1920s.

The people of Cuba had also overthrown the dictatorship of Fulgencio Batista – another strong ally of the U.S. – in 1959, and the United States had suffered a shameful defeat in Vietnam in 1975. The popular victory in Nicaragua was seen as one more serious blow to American power at a time in which the seeds of rebellion were taking root throughout Central America. The U.S. saw its hegemony threatened, not only in its own "back yard" but throughout much of the developing world and, once again, aligned itself on the wrong side of history.

The people's struggle in El Salvador was portrayed as international communist aggression intent on establishing a beachhead in

the western hemisphere. In El Salvador, the government began referring to poverty-stricken peasants struggling for land as "terrorists."
Workers and union organizers demanding fair wages, students struggling for democracy and church activists following the message of Jesus
in defense of the poor were referred to as "subversives", "delinquents,"
and "communists".

It was madness, but it was an essential part of the plan to justify the
provision of more than six billion dollars in military as well as "non-mili-
tary" aid to prop up a failing regime and a brutal and repressive military
that were systematically demonstrating a willingness to slaughter their
own population.

As a result, a war that, according to most experts, should have lasted
less than three years was prolonged for nine years more, dramatically
augmenting costs in terms of human suffering, the loss of life and the
destruction of the country's infrastructure. It also meant the rending of
an already-torn social fabric and lost opportunities for experimenting
with new social, economic and political paradigms that might have freed
the Salvadoran people from poverty.

In the late 1970s, U.S. President Jimmy Carter was proclaiming his
concerns for human rights in countries around the world. When it came
to Central America, however, it became clear that human rights came
second to defending U.S. interests. In February 1980 , as repression was
growing in El Salvador, Archbishop Romero (now Saint Romero of the
Americas) sent a letter to Carter requesting that he curtail all military aid
to the country. One month later, in a sermon that ultimately led to his
death, Romero confronted the Salvadoran military directly, demanding
a halt to the repression and instructing soldiers to disobey orders to kill:

> In the name of God and in the name of this suffering people,
> whose laments rise to heaven each day more tumultuous, I beg
> you, I beseech you, I order you in the name of God stop the
> repression!

He was assassinated the following day while celebrating mass. Nevertheless, the U.S. Congress, a few days later, approved a package of
military aid for El Salvador that would continue to increase over the
remaining years of the war.

With the arrival of Ronald Reagan to the presidency, the U.S. commitment to the Salvadoran government and its military deepened. Reagan and his followers openly criticized the human rights policies of the Carter administration, accusing the ex-president of having been weak and ineffective in the struggle to halt the expansion of communism around the world. The Reagan administration saw Central America as a key battlefield in this effort and defined the conflicts in the region in terms of a threat to the security of the United States, a threat that the U.S. was willing to confront at all costs.

Aware of the risk of supporting a government accused of systematically violating human rights, the U.S. Congress conditioned its aid to El Salvador through a system of biannual reporting to verify advances made in human rights and the consolidation of democracy. This requisite, nevertheless, was not an obstacle for Reagan, who complied with the presentation of reports every six months without fail, minimizing or ignoring altogether the abuses of human rights committed by the Salvadoran authorities against their own people.

The day before the first certification report was due, U.S. and world media reported the rape and slaughter of almost a thousand unarmed civilians in villages in and around El Mozote in the northern province of Morazan, perpetrated by the US-trained and equipped Atlacatl battalion. Reagan responded by sending his Undersecretary of State for Interamerican Affairs, Thomas Enders, to the region to investigate the reports.

Upon his return to the U.S., Enders, without having visited the site of the massacre, reported that the U.S. Embassy in San Salvador, which also had not visited the site, insisted that there was no evidence to sustain reports of the massacre in question. Hence, U.S. military aid to El Salvador continued to increase without interruption.

The strategic objective of economic and military aid to El Salvador during the 1980s focused on strengthening the Salvadoran state and ensuring the capacity of the Armed Forces to attain a definitive victory against an insurgency that was perceived as strong, capable and committed, but not invincible. In order to attain this objective, it was necessary to strengthen the military, on the one hand, and build a participatory democracy on the other, overcoming in the process the political and socioeconomic conditions that continued to drive the population to war.

The intervention of the United States in El Salvador changed the dynamic of the war in important ways, especially during the period of Reagan with his strong emphasis on the military dimension. U.S. advisors promoting new strategies and tactics of counterinsurgency warfare brought from Vietnam initially confronted significant levels of resistance on the part of the Salvadoran High Command. However, embarrassing defeats on the battlefield ultimately convinced the officer corps of the urgency of making changes in organizational structures and strategies.

Five special infantry units called Immediate Reaction Infantry Battalions (BIRI in Spanish) were designed, trained and equipped for the new strategies of counterinsurgency warfare. The first BIRI was Atlacatl, formed in 1980, trained in the United States and sent into action in March 1981, just nine months prior to the massacring of hundreds of innocent men, women and children in El Mozote. The second BIRI was Atonal, formed in December 1981 and followed by the BIRI Ramon Belloso, formed that same year. The last two BIRIs, Manuel José Arce and Eusebio Bracamonte, were formed in 1983.

During this same period, Long Reach Reconnaissance Patrols (PRAL in Spanish) were also formed. These were smaller and more agile units of approximately six men who could infiltrate deep into guerrilla-controlled territories to locate guerrilla camps, and direct air or ground strikes against them. The U.S. Pentagon, with its military advisors, "essentially undertook the task of converting El Salvador's 9-to-5, five-day-a-week garrison-bound Army into an unconventional and aggressive war-fighting machine."[4] To strengthen the ground war further, between 1984 and 1989, the Salvadoran infantry grew from 17,000 to 60,000 troops, assuring an advantage of 10-to-1 over guerrilla forces while also improving its equipment and training.

However, it was the strengthening and modernization of the Air Force that contributed most to the efforts to detain guerrilla advances at the national level. During the early phases of the war, the Air Force would bomb and machine-gun peasant communities indiscriminately,

---

4 Klare and Kornbluh, *Low Intensity Warfare*, 1987, p. 116

principally in the northern regions of Chalatenango and Morazan and around the Guazapa volcano in the central part of the country. These operations had tragic consequences for the rural population but had a limited impact on the guerrillas. By 1984, however, the air war had become a key component in the overall strategies of the Armed Forces, permitting the government to carry the war into the most remote areas within guerrilla fronts at the national level.

After a small guerrilla force penetrated the air base at Ilopango in 1982, destroying a large part of the government fleet, the United States sent a large number of replacement aircraft, including A-37 jet bombers, reconnaissance aircraft and helicopter gunships armed with rockets and high caliber machine guns capable of riddling a soccer field with bullets in seconds. All of the new aircraft came equipped with modern communication systems, making it easier to communicate with ground forces during combat.

In the mid-1980s, U.S. military advisors also introduced the concept and tactics of civic action based on the experience of *"strategic hamlets"* in the war against Vietnam. It was a strategy designed to win the hearts and minds of the civilian population and dispute the social base of the FMLN by bringing development and public services to the target population. The initiative, however, was mired in confusion and unable to demonstrate the difference between sustainable development and counterinsurgency. Hence, it had only minor success in distancing the population from its revolutionary vanguard.

The final component of U.S. strategies consisted of strengthening trust in the electoral process by embarking on a process of democratization through elections. This strategy was intended to convince the world (and the U.S. Congress) that U.S. aid was making an important contribution towards winning the war and eradicating some of its root causes.

As part of this strategy, several elections were held for the presidency, for the national assembly and for municipal mayors, all funded and promoted by the United States. With the country completely militarized, a state of siege and curfew in effect, a political opposition that was being systematically decimated and excluded and a general population living in fear, it was difficult to convince anyone that the essential elements of true democracy existed anywhere in the country. Under such conditions, elections smelled more of propaganda and counterinsurgency than an authentic strengthening of citizen participation.

Taking all of these initiatives into account: the modernization of the Armed Forces of El Salvador, the gradual convincing of the High Command in favor of more effective counterinsurgency strategies and tactics, the development of smaller and more agile military units specialized in anti-guerrilla warfare; the modernization and strengthening of the Air Force; the design and execution of civic action initiatives to win hearts and minds and the promotion of electoral processes to create an image of building participative democracy, it is clear that, despite their weaknesses, the United States' influence and impact on the war was definitive.

In 1993, President Bill Clinton clarified even further the degree of U.S. involvement when he declassified close to twelve thousand documents related to the war in El Salvador, revealing the enormous amounts of intelligence information U.S. advisors had possessed during the war about the violation of human rights and responsible parties, the frequency with which U.S. advisors had participated directly in ground and air operations and the systematic filtering of U.S. intelligence and special operations agents across the borders with neighboring countries to carry out operations in El Salvador.

The long and difficult road to peace

At the beginning of the decade of the 1980s, with the logic of war displacing nonviolent options for change and the armed struggle dominating national reality, dialogue and negotiation were perceived by a significant proportion of Salvadoran society – principally sectors of the far right – as synonymous with betrayal. The idea of a negotiated peace remained in the shadows as both parties to the conflict held tightly to the conviction that a military victory over their adversary was legitimate, necessary and feasible.

In this radicalized environment, early initiatives pursuing peace through dialogue and negotiation tended to respond to more tactical goals of winning hearts and minds, building alliances and isolating the opponent rather than promoting a sincere search for the resolution of the underlying causes of the war. It required years of failed attempts and much bloodshed for the parties in conflict to finally understand the strategic and central role of negotiations for building a more just and democratic society and attaining a sustainable peace through ideas rather than bullets.

Nevertheless, eventually, through creativity and persistence over many years, an ultra-right political party whose hymn promised to bury the "reds" in El Salvador and whose founder was one of the lead actors responsible for the death squads (and for the assassination of monsignor Romero), ultimately came to the table and signed a peace agreement with one of the most radical and anti-imperialist guerrilla movements in Latin America.

The difficult path that led to that moment in early January 1992 was a process that, not even in its final days, escaped the armed confrontation raging throughout the country. While representatives of the government and the FMLN, together with the Democratic Revolutionary Front (FDR in Spanish), sustained their meetings in search of peace, the blood continued to flow.

The first initiative in favor of dialogue came in October 1981 when the FMLN/FDR presented its proposal to form a popular democratic revolutionary government through dialogue and negotiation to the General Assembly of the United Nations. The absence of adequate political conditions in El Salvador, along with the continued emphasis of both sides in the conflict on pursuing a military victory, led to the failure of this proposal and, a short time after its presentation, a right-wing death squad captured, tortured and killed its leadership closing the door to further initiatives for several years.

The strategy of the United States for winning the war did not include, until the final years, negotiations with the FMLN due to the fact that any negotiated solution to the war would obviously lead to a formula for sharing power and, in the view of the Reagan administration, that would be equivalent to defeat. In spite of this obstacle, the FMLN/FDR, in February 1984, presented a second proposal that included again the formation of a provisional government, but in the new proposal neither side would dominate. The new government that resulted would be "the expression of the ample participation of all political and social forces in the country" dedicated to the "elimination of the oligarchic dictatorship" and the "rescue of national sovereignty and independence."

On the theme of international relations, the proposal of the FMLN/FDR suggested a "policy oriented toward the conservation of peace, in opposition to the arms race and to nuclear weapons in defense of "the principles of passive co-existence, self-determination and non-intervention." Regarding relations with the U.S., the proposal suggested the formulation of a set of "special accords" that would guarantee the interests and security of both nations.

The political content of the proposal actually coincided to a notable degree with the Peace Accords that were finally signed eight years later in Chapultepec, Mexico, ending the war. It was widely supported by the Catholic Church, academic institutions, unions, peasant organizations, human rights organizations and the majority of other social forces in the country, but in 1984, the government of El Salvador and its Armed Forces continued betting on total victory.

Later that same year, the leadership of the FMLN directed a communique to the high command of the Armed Forces of El Salvador in an effort to circumvent the resistance of the politicians, focusing on the direct protagonists of the war who were shedding their blood on the battlefield:

March 13, 1984

Members of the High Command, Chiefs of Staff, Officers and Soldiers of the Armed Forces:

We direct ourselves to you at this historic moment in the life of our nation. Two positions have been clearly put forth, one by those who wish to continue with the war and one by those who seek a political solution to the conflict. The battlefield is stained with the blood of Salvadorans in a civil war between families, brothers, friends, companions from work and study. The military solution is unviable, as demonstrated by eight years of war in which thousands of intelligent and brave young people have died for the motherland on hoth sides of the confrontation. But it is completely possible to find a just, dignified and independent solution among Salvadorans.

It is indispensable that we exercise flexibility, since maintaining a closed position will only prolong this war – which with each coming day becomes a more lucrative business for others at the expense of our lives. The opportunities for peace and the structural changes necessary to build social justice and a lasting peace are in the hands of those of us who possess the weapons, [and] between you and us, we can decide without the consent of Washington or of the oligarchy. In the current situation in which we are living, we both are the real powers of the country....

Let us talk; let us dialogue. We have common enemies in the form of injustice, misery and dependence which we can battle together....

Let us build the peace, applying the warrior spirit inherited by our people from the legendary ancestral heroes, Atlacatl, Atonal and Anastasio Aquino, in an effort to consolidate that peace and build a new future. Attaining this goal requires making concessions on both sides, including building a new Armed Forces dedicated to true democracy, social justice and national sovereignty....

Our people want peace, our revolutionary forces want peace and we are sure that the majority of officers and soldiers of the Armed Forces also want peace....

Commanders: Francisco Jovel, Eduardo Sancho, Salvador Sanchez Ceren, Shafic Jorge Handal, Joaquin Villalobos

The initiative was spurned by the High Command of the Armed Forces. When Napoleón Duarte was elected to the presidency two months later, on June 1, 1984, however, dialogue finally found its place on the policy agenda of the government. Duarte entered the presidency committed to putting an end to the war as quickly as possible, but his intent was continually blocked by a High Command who perceived him as a leftist, indecisive and soft on communism. Nevertheless, in October of that year, in a speech before the General Assembly of the United Nations, Duarte called upon the FMLN/FDR to join him in a process of dialogue in search of peace and, on the following day, the FMLN/FDR accepted.

With the support of the Episcopal Conference of the Catholic Church, social movements and even several people in the U.S. State Department, the parties in conflict came together for the first time on October 15, 1984, in the tourist town of La Palma in Chalatenango with the mediation of the Catholic Church. Participating for the government was the president, Napoleon Duarte, with members of his administration, including his Minister of Defense. The FDR was represented by Guillermo Ungo and Rubén Zamora, while the FMLN was represented by Facundo Guardado and Ferman Cienfuegos.

A second meeting was held on November 30 in a retreat center of the Catholic Church named Ayagualo, located in Zaragoza, department of La Libertad. With the FMLN/FDR pursuing profound reform while the government and Armed Forces insisted on pacification through disarmament, neither of these meetings had much chance of producing significant accords other than an agreement to continue talking.

A third meeting, proposed for September 19, 1986 in the small eastern town of Sesori in the department of San Miguel, was canceled at the last minute by the FMLN for a lack of security for its representatives and the failure to agree on an agenda. With this, the process of dialogue was interrupted again.

During the eight years of the Reagan administration, the emphasis of the United States was focused on attaining a military victory with limited concerns about human rights or a negotiated peace. With the arrival of George Bush in 1989, however, U.S. policy towards El Salvador changed, presenting new opportunities for dialogue and negotiation. Nevertheless, during the first months of that year, death squads continued attacking anyone who publicly promoted peace-through-dialogue, bombing, kidnapping and assassinating leaders in an attempt to derail any initiative for a negotiated settlement to the war.

In the face of growing repression, dialogue remained a small glimmer on a distant horizon until the election in 1989 of right-wing oligarch and millionaire businessman Alfredo Cristiani. Cristiani, unlike Duarte, had the trust of the business class as well as the Armed Forces and was convinced of the urgency of putting an end to the war in order to rebuild the economy. There were many in his party who continued to oppose dialogue and negotiation with "communists", but they also recognized that the war, now in its ninth year, was an obstacle to economic recovery and growth.

The FMLN, for its part, in spite of its participation in the process of dialogue with the government, remained committed throughout the 1980s to its original strategy of popular insurrection, encouraged by the experience of Nicaragua in 1979. At the same time, victories on the battlefield were considered essential to strengthening the weight of proposals at the negotiating table.

Some on the right, especially within the military, perceived the apparent willingness of the FMLN to participate in negotiations (even if only tactically) as a sign of weakness, leading the military to hold onto the hope of a military victory or a negotiated peace without having to cede much. Both of these factors contributed to the decision of the FMLN in late 1989 to move forward with their plans to mount a major offensive at the national level.

On November 11, FMLN forces occupied positions in all of the major cities of the country and held them for several weeks in spite of the desperate and fragmented efforts of a shocked military to dislodge them (including the indiscriminate bombing of densely inhabited urban communities). It was a clear and convincing demonstration to a doubtful world that the FMLN remained strong and militarily invincible.

Five days into the offensive, on November 16, with a government curfew and state of siege in effect, a platoon of the Atlacatl battalion penetrated the installations of the Central American University (UCA), killing six Jesuit priests, the wife of their gardener and her daughter. Among the dead was Father Ignacio Ellacuría, dean of the UCA and recognized nationally as well as internationally as a principal promotor of a negotiated settlement to the war. This event shook the world, including the United States, and strengthened the sense of urgency for ending the war through dialogue and negotiation.

At the same time, a new generation of civil society organizations arose out of the ashes of nine years of civil war, joining human rights groups with NGOs, workers, peasants, a recently-formed network of women's organizations, churches and international allies in a united cry for a sustainable peace through broad citizen participation in the negotiating process. On November 9, 1989 the world had also witnessed the fall of the Berlin Wall, essentially ending the Cold War and reducing the geopolitical importance of El Salvador. In this new context, the United States began to push both sides to recognize a stalemate and negotiate an end to the war.

On December 6, Salvador Samayoa and Ana Guadalupe Martínez of the FMLN met with a delegate of the Secretary General of the United Nations in Montreal, Canada and proposed the urgent need for the UN to begin to play a mediating role in the Salvadoran peace process. Advisors of Alfredo Cristiani preferred the mediation of the Organization of American States (OAS), considered to be more conservative and susceptible to U.S. influence. Nevertheless, after the events of November, especially the grave and unforgivable crime of slaying the Jesuits, the Cristiani government was forced to cede, accepting the General Secretary of the UN, Perez de Cuellar, as mediator and allowing negotiations to begin again.

Over the next two years, with UN mediation, negotiations continued their slow and painful path forward, frequently threatened by a military bent on disarming the FMLN without any significant reform. Nevertheless, in a new round of talks in May 1990, with heavy combat raging throughout the Salvadoran countryside, the two parties finally agreed to an agenda for negotiations that included a) the reform of the Armed Forces, b) human rights, c) judicial reform, d) electoral reform, e) constitutional reform, f) social and economic issues and g) UN verification.

The reform of the Armed Forces continued to be the thorniest issue on the agenda throughout the process, given the resistance of a military that had essentially been in power for five decades and which had been bolstered and privileged through years of U.S. military aid and support. It wasn't until September 1991 that the first agreements were reached on the vetting of the military, a reduction in its size and the modification of military doctrine.

In October 1991, parties accepted the FMLN proposal to dissolve the security forces most responsible for years of impunity, repression and the violation of human rights. This included the National Police, the Revenue Police and the National Guard. In response, the FMLN, in a gesture of good faith, offered a unilateral ceasefire.

An increasingly cornered and desperate military rejected the offer and initiated its own offensive in November 1991, provoking the FMLN to respond in kind with attacks on the country's already vulnerable infrastructure in San Salvador, Usulután, Chalatenango, San Miguel, La Paz, La Libertad, Cuscatlán and Morazán until Mexico and Canada, with the support of the UN General Secretary and other actors, intervened, pleading with both parties to avoid putting the peace process at risk once again.

The year was coming to an end, and the term of UN Secretary-General Perez de Cuellar was in its final days as tensions continued to rise. In desperation, Pérez de Cuellar decided to transfer the negotiations directly to UN headquarters in New York City, where, by the end of December, the parties were finally able to untangle and resolve pending issues on the agenda. Final discussions came to an end at two in the morning on the day of January 1, 1992.

What became known as the "Peace Accords" was signed by all parties on January 16, 1992, establishing a series of unprecedented measures to reform the mandate and reduce the size of the military; separate national defense from public security; promote respect for human rights; promote juridical and constitutional reforms and build an incipient participative democracy. Forced recruitment would be ended, and the five counter-insurgency battalions (BIRI), built and strengthened by U.S. advisors, would be dismantled, along with the National Guard, National Police and Revenue Police, responsible for the majority of human rights violations during the war.

The FMLN would be recognized as a legal political party, while a Supreme Electoral Tribunal would be established to assure universal suffrage along with a long list of additional measures. The social and economic agenda was left to a separate process to begin in the months that followed the signing, a worrisome reminder that El Salvador still had a distance to travel in its effort to resolve many of the most important underlying structural causes of the war (for more detail, see the Epilogue on Peace Accords at the end of this book).

The signing ceremony in Chapultepec Castle in Mexico City was attended by over 200 invited guests, including heads of state, media, the new General Secretary of the UN, Boutros Boutros-Ghali and the

Secretary General of the Organization of American States (OAS), João Baena Soares.

Following the signing, President Alfredo Cristiani, a millionaire oligarch, a symbol of capitalism and big business in El Salvador, kissed his wife and stepped away from the VIP table to personally greet the signers of both parties. He then turned his attention to the invited guests and TV cameras and, with a degree of humility, statesmanship and objectivity that few would have anticipated, recognized that the civil war in El Salvador "did not come out of nothing," that it was rooted in the historical political, economic and social conditions of the country. He ended by asserting, "If we can attain this peace which has seemed so impossible, then nothing should be denied to us in the future."

It was a noble gesture intended to unite a still-divided country. But it left many pondering about the uncertainties on the horizon. In the cities, towns and villages of El Salvador, citizens took to the streets to celebrate, but the obstinate divisions that had characterized the society during 12 years of civil war were still evident, even in this moment of shared joy and hope.

In San Salvador, the supporters of the right-wing ARENA government and its Armed Forces occupied the Plaza La Libertad with speeches, music and dancing, while supporters of the FMLN and other progressive forces occupied the Plaza Cívica in front of the National Cathedral. As the title of the UN Truth Commission's final report presented in 1993 expresses, the country had come through a long and difficult process, from madness to hope. But the challenges of the future were significant and worrisome in order not to return to the madness.

PART TWO

Testimonies of Courage and Hope

Introduction

Despite the frightening levels of state-sponsored repression in the 1980s and early 1990s, both in the cities and in the countryside, with its tactics of terror and scorched earth, thousands of men and women joined in the struggle for change in El Salvador. Many were direct victims of poverty, exclusion and persecution who formed the motor force of guerrilla columns, taking up arms in their own defense or working on the war fronts in a supportive role such as healthcare, communications, logistics, propaganda, cooking, media and other strategic areas. Others consciously chose a life in solidarity with the poor and the oppressed, working clandestinely with FMLN-linked organizations in areas of the country under government control or through legal, institutional spaces to promote the revolution.

Many worked with the churches, especially the Catholic Church, motivated and guided by the principles of liberation theology, preaching the preferential option for the poor. Still others worked with national as well as international institutions dedicated to human rights, humanitarian aid and sustainable development. Finally, there were the masses of people who were not integral to the revolutionary movement but who did what they could when an opportunity presented itself, or necessity demanded, bravely and persistently, in hope and in fear. They did not perceive themselves as guerrillas or even revolutionaries, but their lives and actions were intrinsic to the struggle.

All shared a utopian dream for a better future and, in many cases, a willingness to give their life for that dream. They made choices based on love for their fellow man that guided them along a path of struggle and self-sacrifice, accepting the physical and emotional consequences of their decision and unsure of any reward except the dignity of the struggle itself. The struggle became their lives, and their lives became the struggle.

Some were heroes. Others were martyrs, but most were just everyday people opting for battle in the face of evil and looking for goodness along the way. The violence and tragedy that characterized the period were accompanied by uncommon levels of human solidarity, creativity, hope and love in the face of tremendous odds - a David and Goliath struggle, some would say.

Of the thousands of Salvadorans and non-Salvadorans who dedicated their lives, or part of their life, to make El Salvador a more just and democratic nation, this author was blessed to have known and admired many over the years. The testimonies that fill the pages that follow reflect the diversity as well as the attributes held in common by all in terms of valor, persistence and hope in a war that, in its darkest days, seemed eternal:

1. **Rubén Zamora** was a lawyer and opposition politician of the Christian Democrat party who played a key role in the search for a negotiated solution to the war as president of the Revolutionary Democratic Front (FDR).

2. **Jorge Meléndez (Jonás)** was an aspiring actor studying arts at the National University who became a guerrilla commander and head of the northeastern front of El Salvador.

3. **Isaías Alas Sandoval** was a peasant farmer and delegate of the word of the Catholic Church who became a guerrilla commander and postwar mayor.

4. **Rosario Chicas** was a young peasant woman who helped her family grow hemp to make ropes and harvest basic grains on the steep mountain slopes of Morazán who served the revolution first as a messenger, then as a combatant and, finally, as a highly-skilled radio operator.

5. **Ana Menjivar** was a young domestic worker from a rural village in the picturesque region of Lake Suchitlán near the town of Suchitoto forced by a repressive military and local death squads to join the guerrilla movement, serving bravely throughout the war as a non-combatant.

6. **Roberto Cruz** was the director of the well-known aid and rescue organization Comandos de Salvamento, working to provide humanitarian assistance, emergency medical care and evacuation support to civilians and combatants alike prior to and during the civil war in El Salvador.

7. **Salvador Orellana (Chamba)** was a high school student in San Salvador, forced into exile in Costa Rica, who joined the guerrillas as a political cadre working on the war fronts with the civilian population.

8. **Lorena Martinez** was a young peasant woman who picked coffee on the slopes of the volcanoes of Usulután province prior to the war to finance her basic education and, like Ana, finally joined the guerrilla movement as a young non-combatant, eventually assuming a leadership role in a national organization supporting civilian families displaced by the war.

9. **Orlando Netiyo** was a university student of architecture who fell in love with photography and eventually joined the guerrillas in the war zones of Chalatenango and Cuscatlán, working with the guerrilla radio and as a photographer.

10. **Janeth Rodriguez** accompanied her mother as a domestic worker in the middle-class neighborhoods of the capital city and then in the rural areas of Usulután, who ended up serving in the war fronts of Morazan as a guerrilla radio operator.

11. **Rogelio Poncel** was a Catholic priest from Belgium who lived and preached in the urban communities of Zacamil in San Salvador until death threats forced him to flee, finding his way to the war fronts of northern Morazan, where he accompanied the guerrillas as a non-combatant priest during the 12 years of war.

12. **Rafael Lemus Aleman (Lito)** was an impoverished young art student at the National Academy of Arts in San Salvador who spent the war years in the northeastern front responsible for guerrilla propaganda.

13. **Mirna Perla** and her husband, **Herbert Anaya Sanabria** (assassinated by security forces in 1987), were law students at the National University and later human rights activists with the Salvadoran Human Rights Commission. In the post-war, Mirna served as a judge on the Supreme Court.

14. **Francisco Alvarez (Paco)** was an analyst and researcher at the Jesuit University, UCA, and his ex-wife, **Paty**, worked with the Legal Aid office of the Catholic Church until she was captured and disappeared by the security forces of El Salvador.

15. **Ana del Carmen Alvarez** was a university professor and writer who managed the church-sponsored radio for monsignor Romero until it was bombed by right-wing death squads, forcing her into

exile in Costa Rica returning to El Salvador just before the massacre of the Jesuits.

16. **Brian Murphy** was a member of a Canadian international human rights organization working in solidarity with the Salvadoran people during and after the war.

If these individuals had the opportunity to address the future generations of El Salvador, who will likely know little of the war and this significant period of their country's history, here are a few of the stories that they could tell.

Rubén

Introduction

In El Salvador's political history, from the moment of our independence in 1821 until the signing of the Peace Accords in 1992, the military has played a key role in government. Wealthy *caudillos* with their private armies ruled the country for a period until President Francisco Dueñas (1869-1871) formally established the Armed Forces as an institution of the state, giving rise to the political dichotomy of "Civil Society and the military," which has characterized El Salvador up through the modern era.

In 1931, General Maximiliano Hernández Martínez became the first president to address the people "in the name of the Armed Forces". He received the presidency from the hands of 12 high-ranking military officers who made up the Civic Directorate and structured the model of political governance for the country on the basis of an alliance between the Armed Forces and the oligarchy of the bourgeoisie, leaving politics in the hands of the military while the oligarchy controlled the economy. It was an arrangement for distributing economic power to one and political power to the other with a guarantee that both would have the power of veto if one of the two considered that the other's actions were harmful to their interests.

The 60-year period between 1931 to 1992 was, without a doubt, a period of much political gyration with moments in which the relations between the Armed Forces and the oligarchy were problematic and conflictive, but I leave that detail for another time, focusing here on the most relevant political events of the 1970s, since this is period which serves to explain the rise and role of one the most important political spaces for citizen participation and social struggle in the history of El Salvador, the Revolutionary Democratic Front (FDR), of which I was a part.

The decade of the 1970s

By the 1970s, the Armed Forces had achieved broad control of the state apparatus in El Salvador, gaining control of government ministries, the legislative assembly and many autonomous institutions. This situation led them to believe that they successfully confronted the oligarchy at the center of its economic power: agriculture, and, with the intention of providing an escape valve for the growing pressure in the rural sectors of the country for land reform, proposed the idea of the country's first "agrarian transformation zone" on June 29, 1976. The response of the oligarchy, however, was not long in coming. Supported by numerous private business associations, it launched a radical campaign on July 8 of that year, arguing that, while it was not opposed to the specific reforms put forth by the military, it was against "state interference, in a negative way in the economic and social life of our country." On October 20, President Molina announced changes in the law that had been developed to promote an urgent if minimal reform of the agrarian sector, essentially freezing the initiative, but the alliance between the military and the oligarchy that general Martínez had structured 50 years prior had been shattered.

In the meantime, revolutionary political-military organizations were being formed, promoting armed struggle as the only viable means of taking power in the face of diminishing non-violent options for change. These were:

- The Popular Liberation Forces (FPL) formed in April 1970,
- The People's Revolutionary Army (RPA) formed in March 1972,
- The National Resistance (RN), formed in May 1975,
- The Revolutionary Party of Central American Workers (PRTC), formed in January 1976 and
- The Armed Liberation Forces of the Salvadoran Communist Party who decided to join the armed struggle at the end of 1979.

In addition to the above, the Second Vatican Council (1962 to 1965) constituted the basis for important modifications in the position and actions of the Salvadoran Catholic Church, leaving aside the Church's traditional role of blindly supporting the government in power. Thus, two bishops from the Episcopal Conference, numerous priests, nuns and lay people began opting for the defence of the neediest sectors of society based on the Gospel, the orientations of the synods of the Latin American bishops and the new Liberation Theology spreading throughout Latin America along with the creation of Christian Base Communities operating as the organizational expression of this new church. At the same time, the guerrilla organizations were dedicating their efforts to organizing civilian groups to denounce the situation of the poor, promoting processes of organization and mobilization in peaceful demonstrations against the injustice plaguing the nation. All of this led to the growth of an increasingly strong and emboldened civil society with the decision to become actors and agents for change through the political process.

By the middle of the decade, the situation of the country was becoming more critical every week. The oligarchy/Armed Forces alliance was paralyzed; the number of guerrilla organizations had increased from two to five; civil society organizations were growing quantitatively as well as qualitatively with more and more citizens incorporating into the political struggle against the existing regime; internal conflicts were deepening within the official party, PCN, as well as within the Army itself; opposition parties were confronting growing violence from the police and an Electoral Tribunal was denouncing electoral fraud with increasing vehemence.

The democratic and non-violent path to power was rapidly closing in the face of growing repression against all opposition voices. The most viable path in the eyes of the military had always been through brute force applied with increasing frequency against the civilian population and with no respect for constitutional rights. They had the full support of the U.S. government at a time in which it was prioritizing a halt to communism in Latin America, "communism" being a term applied to all opposition.

To assist in this task, the military created the ultraright wing paramilitary Nationalist Democratic Organization, ORDEN, which eventually grew to have more than 100,000 members, including former army officers and reservists, to assure against a peasant uprising as had occurred in 1932. The then president, General Carlos Humberto Romero, supported these repressive measures by enacting the "Law for the Defense and Guarantee of Public Order", referred to by its victims as the "Law for a License to Kill."

The government of Romero and the National Forum

In the context of the growing chaos and violence, a group of businessmen and professionals, anguished and frustrated by the growing loss of authority on the part of President Romero, proposed the creation of a National Forum with the aim of "strengthening democracy" while avoiding the exclusion of any sector or citizen group. President Romero accepted the proposal, but without the participation of guerrilla organizations and, in his speech announcing the new Forum on May 17, 1977, he made this point clear: "... We will not give in in our struggle against the forces of anarchism."

For the civilian opposition, the decision to participate in the National Forum or reject the offer was delicate, requiring much analysis and internal discussion. Given the challenge of remaining faithful to the struggle against military domination and the lack of democracy in our country, achieving clarity and consensus required an intense process of meetings between various groups in an effort to unite a wide and varied organizational force, bringing together organizations holding different political ideologies and tactics.

The final decision of the civilian organizations involved in this complicated process was to reject the government's offer to participate, a position that was announced initially by the National Opposition Union (UNO in Spanish), made up of the three opposition political parties–Christian Democrats (PDC in Spanish), National Revolutionary Movement (MNR in Spanish) and the Nationalist Democratic Union (UDN in Spanish) – plus the Central American Unionist Party. This response had a substantial impact on non-party civil society organizations trying to decide on their own participation. It accelerated an alternative process of organization and resistance among civil society groups distrustful of the government's efforts to manipulate us.

In addition to the process of meetings for reflection on whether or not to participate in the government's National Forum, other important events were occurring at the time, which had a strong influence on the decisions being made by civil society organizations. Among these was a vicious attack by the National Guard on a peaceful street protest, resulting in 14 deaths and a large number of wounded on May 29, 1977.

In the face of growing repression, a simple refusal to participate in the National Forum was not enough. Citizens needed a broad-based political actor providing a more authentic space for civil society participation, shared analysis and discussion on strategies and tactics. As this need became increasingly apparent, four opposition parties, along with seven workers' confederations, a national association of peasants, an independent trade union and three revolutionary organizations, presented a proposal for a **popular forum** on September 2, 1978, as an alternative to the government's initiative.

Archbishop Romero had repeatedly called for such a forum to permit dialogue and unity in the search to avoid a civil war in El Salvador. It is the reason that he was assassinated in March 1980. Unfortunately, this elusive goal of building unity around a shared vision for El Salvador could only be attained after monsignor Romero's death and 12 years of bloody conflict when opposing parties finally understood that a political solution was the only way to begin to build democracy and sustainable peace that the people yearned for so strongly.

The coup d'état and the People's Forum

On October 15, 1979, a coup d'état ousted then-president Carlos Humberto Romero. The following day, a delegation of the coup perpetrators requested a meeting with the Popular Forum, asking us to propose a civilian candidate to participate in the Junta that would be made up of three civilians and two members of the Armed Forces to lead the new "Revolutionary Government." They also requested suggestions from members of the cabinet of the new government. Our response, once again, required a process of analysis and reflection. The proclamation presented by the perpetrators of the coup, all young military officers supposedly more educated in civics, not only recognized the violations of human rights, the corruption and the submission to the oligarchy of previous military governments but also proposed concrete measures to achieve peace, true democracy and respect for human rights. It was also emphasized to us that the composition of the new Revolutionary Government Junta, for the first time in history, would have a majority of civilians. They were seeking our support and proposals, arguing that their Proclamation coincided with the fundamental objectives of the Popular Forum.

The members of the Popular Forum had no problems with the specific text of the Proclamation of the military coup, and we knew that to reject the offer to participate in the new government, where we could continue the struggle for our ideals and vision for El Salvador, would be seen by many as cowardice or ideological weakness. We were keenly aware, however, that the military was leading the process, even if they were young and more modernized in their thinking, and that we had no guarantee that efforts would continue to move in a positive direction.

The leadership of the Popular Forum made up of five comrades and myself, met for several hours with two of the young colonels who had led the coup. They tried to convince us that this coup was different from others throughout the history of El Salvador since it was led by youth, including col onels, captains and even sergeants. They informed us as well that they intended to release all political prisoners, that the military would no longer be involved in the control of strikes or other issues within the labour sector and that "… we seek to implement a democratic scheme that brings structural changes to El Salvador."

Our reaction to that first meeting was mixed. The presentation of the young officers left us with the impression that they did not have great clarity regarding the immediate needs of the country and that they felt isolated from society. They needed our participation in order to confront the chaos of the moment: an Armed Forces internally divided and isolated from the people, state-sponsored repression on the rise, political parties in crisis, a growing guerrilla movement and an economy in shambles. The panorama was not hopeful nor easy, but precisely for this reason, we considered it our duty to help construct a workable and positive alternative. This had to be done, however, by establishing the necessary conditions that would permit authentic participation.

After serious consideration, the organizations of the Popular Forum reached the following consensus: "… we are ready to collaborate with the

Revolutionary Junta under the following conditions: ... that participatory meetings will be held at least biannually with the Junta to evaluate progress in pursuit of the goals established in the coup's Proclamation and to present our own proposals for action; that orders be given by the Junta to its ministers assuring an open door policy allowing for the resolution of specific problems or issues that came up in the field."

We presented these conditions to the two colonels on the Junta. We were quickly informed that they were in agreement and that they urgently needed our recommendations for civilian participation in the Junta and other areas of the government. They told us that the business sector had already decided on its representative, as had the academic sector, and this forced us to expedite our decision-making process to identify our candidate. Our unanimous choice was Dr. Guillermo Manuel Ungo. During that same period, we began to look as well for candidates for ministers and heads of Autonomous entities. We succeeded in convincing more than 20 professionals to leave their current jobs to participate in the government. All of these candidates were honest, democratic men and women with the necessary preparation and ability to effectively manage the specific thematic areas to which they would be assigned without concern for ideological or political inclination, something that had never occurred previously in the history of government in El Salvador.

During October and November 1979, when the Provisional Government began to operate, human rights violations began to decline, civil society organizations increased their numbers, and the organizations of the revolutionary movement increased their presence on the political scene, giving rise to a process of agglutination. But this brief respite, bringing a sense of freedom and security to the people, did not last. The systematic violation of fundamental human rights of peasants, opposition party members, human rights and church activists defending the people, along with bloody attacks on peaceful demonstrations, began to increase again with even greater frequency and intensity.

The members of the Popular Forum responded by requesting an urgent meeting with the Provisional Government to present our concerns about all that was transpiring in violation of our initial agreements. We presented a document analyzing the violations committed by security forces and the military and proposing to halt all unconstitutional acts immediately.

The military's response was disappointing. It was limited to denouncing the actions of revolutionary organizations. At the same time, the civilian members of the Junta assured us that they would investigate the specific cases of violations we had presented. It was not a constructive meeting. Days later, during the plenary session of the Popular Forum, it was agreed that if conditions did not improve over the following two weeks, we would withdraw our support of the government.

In December, while the three civilian members of the government Junta and senior government officials were gathered at the presidential palace to celebrate the approach of Christmas with a typical lunch, an officer of the Armed Forces (who served as Minister of the Presidency) approached me to inform me that the High Command of the Armed Forces was celebrating in another large hall of the presidential palace and that it seemed to him that it would be good to take advantage of their presence to meet together following lunch. I quickly consulted the proposal with my comrades, and we agreed to meet.

Upon entering the hall, we found about 60 officers gathered on one side of the large room while our group of approximately 30 civilians gathered on the other side. Our meeting began cordially, but it didn't take long for the issue of human rights to be raised by several government ministers, pointing to a series of concrete cases of serious violations committed by police and soldiers. One of the colonels present responded by blaming the guerrillas. The dynamic of the meeting quickly began to heat up as the interventions on each side became stronger and stronger until the colonel in charge of the National Guard (one of the most violent abusers of human rights in the country) stood up and said to us: "Remember that if you are in those government positions that you currently hold, it is because we put you there." The comment was followed by total silence while the civilians present left the premises.

The changes that we had hoped to attain through our participation in the new government never occurred. On the contrary, the military and the security forces intensified the repression throughout the country with the massacre of peasants and the slaying or disappearance of all opponents. The membership of the Popular Forum determined that it would be unethical to continue our participation in the government under these conditions. The people who we had recommended to fill the positions of government informed us that they were going on strike until the Junta resolved the issues that had been put forth to the military leadership, and the Popular Forum issued an urgent statement that ended by saying: "If these events continue and there is not an adequate solution to this crisis, we (the Forum) will be forced to reconsider our participation in the government."

Faced with this situation, the Popular Forum met in plenary session the day after Christmas. It concluded that it was impossible to continue in alliance with the Junta. Our next step was to inform the civilian members of the Junta, and they replied that they had come to the same conclusion. We agreed that they would be the first to resign and that we would follow suit. On January 3, 1980, Dr. Guillermo Ungo and Mr. Ramón Mayorga publicly announced their resignation from the government and explained the reasons why. For our part, we agreed to make our resignation public as well but decided to meet first with senior government officials whom we had proposed, arguing that it was their right to choose to leave or stay without being considered a traitor.

That evening, I visited Archbishop Romero to inform him of the decision that we had made and explain to him our reasoning. I could see the anguish on his face as I spoke and then listened as he said to me: "Rubén, you don't realize that if you withdraw, the only thing left is the civil war", to which I responded, "Monsignor, it is my conscience, as a Christian, that is telling me that it is unethical to participate in a government that is murdering more and more innocents every day." He then looked at me and said: "My son, you must always act as your conscience tells you." Unable to let go of his hopes for peace, he asked me, "Rubén, do you not consider it possible to overcome this situation by reaching an agreement between the Forum and the colonels?" I replied that I thought it would be difficult but that I would raise the option of further talks with the leaders of the Forum and, if they agreed, I would let him know by phone.

Upon consulting with the members of the Popular Forum, however, the decision remained that it was too late for further talks. Nevertheless, because Monsignor Romero had requested it, people expressed their willingness to try again in a meeting that was held in the offices of the archbishopric days later. But this final attempt was a repetition of the previous one, perhaps with the absence of so many insults. We looked like two giant blocks of iron, cold and useless, colliding in the night. The only thing that remained clear was that the civil war was coming upon us.

The birth of the Revolutionary Democratic Front

With the systematic abuses of the security forces and the police, the urgent need for a broad-based political front to organize the citizenry and advance the struggle for democracy became more evident with each passing day. With this goal in mind, the Revolutionary Coordination of Masses (CRM in Spanish) was formed in 1979 with the participation of the Unified Popular Action Front (FAPU in Spanish), which had emerged in 1974, the Popular Revolutionary Bloc (BPR in Spanish), formed in 1975, and the "February 28" Popular Leagues (LP-28 in Spanish), formed in 1977. Later, the Nationalist Democratic Union and the Popular Liberation Movement also joined.

For their part, the democratic organizations of the Popular Forum and a large majority of the people who had been participating in the new government decided to continue their struggle for democracy through a new configuration that we decided to call the Salvadoran Democratic Front (FDS). They were eventually joined by the Independent Movement of Professionals and Technicians of El Salvador (MIPTES), the National Revolutionary and Popular Social Christian Movement, a group of union federations, small business owners, a sector of retired dissident military officers with the country's two universities, the UCA and the UES, as observers.

On April 18, 1980, the FDS and the CRM unified under the name of the **Revolutionary Democratic Front** (FDR in Spanish). It was the most significant expression of civil society unity in El Salvador's history. The FDR was not a political party. It was a broad-based instrument of political struggle that integrated a wide variety of ideological and political positions in opposition to the current regime. At the same time, it was a response to the urgent need to advance an agenda that would lead to a more just and humane society, free from the systematic violations of the human rights of the population with an economy and a society at large that placed the human person at its center. Its objectives were:

a. To put an end to the long history of governance by the military-oligarchy alliance in El Salvador and assure compliance with the separation of powers established in the constitution

b. To curtail the systematic violation of human rights

c. To build a new society with an economy centred on the human person and respect for Mother Earth

d. To inform and mobilize the international community and multilateral organizations in the pursuit of peace.

Salvadoran historian Roberto Turcios, in his essay on the FDR, summarized the process in the following way: "The creation of the FDR and the role it played as a representative force in the struggle of the Salvadoran people was of great importance both nationally and internationally. Its efforts were focused for more than a decade on the conduction of the social/political struggle, obtaining strong political support from the people and governments of other nations, which translated into material aid for the insurgent forces..." To the above, I would add that all of our efforts during that key period were directed at attaining a political solution to the conflict, respecting at all times and recognizing the fact that, without the essential component of the guerrilla struggle led by the political/military forces of the FMLN, it would not be possible to obtain our objectives, nor would we be able to attain the most profound social, political and economic changes in the history of our nation that we were proposing.

The Political Landscape and the FDR:

The FDR began its work in the midst of the most serious political crisis in the history of the country, with a political landscape that was utterly unfavorable. Its leadership, including myself as its president, following the assassination by death squads of our original leader, Enrique Alvarez, was forced to operate semi-clandestinely in a political environment with the following characteristics:

a. Massacres of the civilian population were on the rise, especially in the rural areas of the country, as U.S. strategies of "scorched earth" were applied indiscriminately. As part of this strategy, the right-wing paramilitary organization, ORDEN, was strengthened to attack all opposition. The Truth Commission formed by the UN at the end of the war studied 29 cases of massacres ranging from 10 people to more than a thousand victims. The report estimated that in the 12 years of civil war, no less than 75,000 people were killed, of which 80% were civilians. The collective murders carried out by the death squads, linked to the police and the military, increased with military officers providing the lists of names and details of the people to be tortured and killed.

b. The High Command of the military, in spite of having signed on to the Proclamation of the younger officers following the coup, continued their tactics of brutal repression against civilians.

c. The alliance between the military and the oligarchy was broken, and the ruling party (PCN) was divided. There were no options for resolving the crisis.

d. The U.S. government began to perceive the limited military capacity of the Salvadoran Armed Forces to win the war, causing a U.S. officer to state at one point, "... The Salvadoran military believes that a war of this type can be won by operating eight hours a day with two days of rest per week." In response, the U.S. launched a two-and-a-half-year program in its military bases, through which all officers passed, with the aim of transforming the military into a more effective force. The same process was extended to train soldiers and to integrate five Immediate Reaction Infantry Battalions (BIRI in Spanish) that began to operate at the national level with increasing levels of brutality and violence against the civilian population. To build social support, the U.S. State Department contacted a group of Salvadoran professionals led by Napoleón Duarte of the Christian Democrat party (of which I was a member). It offered them an opportunity to govern in alliance with the Armed Forces, which they agreed to behind the back of the party leadership, causing several members, like myself, to resign from the party and form the Popular Social Christian Movement, a member of the FDR. During this period, the U.S. government proposed to the military's high command that it abandon its traditional links to the PCN party and that it establish an alliance with the PDC. The military had no alternative but to accept. and thus, the alliance was celebrated: Armed Forces and PDC. The party presented the military with a set of economic changes similar to those of the coup Proclamation, and the military initially accepted. Nevertheless, a short time later, they insisted that the priority of winning the war militarily would not permit them to focus on reforms.

e. In the meantime, the FMLN's guerrilla struggle continued to consolidate and spread, making the armed struggle the primary component of seeking change in El Salvador.

The second path of the FDR:

Upon my arrival in Mexico, where we established a humble center of operations for the FDR, I was greeted by FDR comrades and Jorge Castaneda Jr., a senior official of the Mexican Ministry of Foreign Affairs, who had played an important role in the preparation of the Franco-Mexican Declaration recognizing the FMLN/FDR as a legitimate actor in the efforts to negotiate a peace settlement in El Salvador.

My first job was to learn, on the one hand, how the Ministry of Foreign Affairs of Mexico operated and, on the other, the progress to date of our comrades in terms of raising awareness about our struggle. I was assisted in the former by Jorge Castaneda Jr., who informed me about the political situation and the role that the government of Mexico was playing in gaining international support for our struggle for democracy and peace; in the second area, I was surprised by the extensive interest in the situation of El Salvador on the part of politicians, universities, research centers and the media from Mexico and other countries; however, I perceived that our comrades were not operating under the single banner of the FMLN-FDR alliance but rather under the individual banners of each of the five guerrilla organizations of the FMLN.

This situation generated problems for an efficient and unitary approach to strengthening our international work. To overcome the problem of sectarianism, we established the single office of the FMLN/FDR alliance, provided and furnished by the Mexican government. We then formed a joint Steering Committee composed of three FMLN leaders and three FDR leaders with their respective alternates. In this office, the mechanisms of liaison between our work and our comrades operating in the interior of El Salvador and around the world improved, permitting us to highlight more effectively what was occurring in our struggle and the need for support at the diplomatic level.

Once installed and operational, we began to analyze how to distribute the work better in order to achieve results more efficiently as well as attend to the civil society organizations who supported us as well as the exiled Salvadorans residing in Mexico. At the same time, we developed a scheme of priorities among the variety of countries that we were focusing our diplomatic efforts on, with Mexico and the United States at the top of the list, Germany, Italy, the Vatican and Sweden at the second level of importance and France, the Netherlands, the European Union and the United Kingdom at the third level of importance. Finally, we defined the colleagues who would be assigned to each country responsible for communication with our office in Mexico. From the beginning, we saw that this structure had to be flexible because we were dealing with various nations with different societal norms in Europe and America.

To conclude, I would simply add that FDR continued to operate and serve the Salvadoran people throughout the years of the civil war, that we were an essential part of the struggle for democracy and respect for human rights and that we were able to contribute, together with thousands of other comrades, the best of ourselves to achieve our objectives. If it were possible to go back to those years, knowing what we went through, I would not hesitate to relive them but modify some things and acts that could be improved.

Jonás

I present this testimony with profound respect for the Salvadoran people, the true authors of a grand and historical moment filled with heroes and martyrs. I am aware that this brief essay, focused on the aspect of the process, more specifically, the development of the popular military forces of Morazan, is a pale and insufficient homage incapable of recognizing in all of its profoundness the thousands of men and women involved, nor the numerous virtues that merit being highlighted. Nor does it reflect, or pretend to reflect, the richness and complexity of the period alluded to.

In the decade of the 1970s, Morazan was considered to be one of the poorest and most remote departments in El Salvador, marked by low levels of development, particularly in the north, and with only one paved highway, referred to by locals as the "black road".

Its economy was built upon the production of corn and beans, while in the higher mountainous areas, coffee and timber were produced.

The majority of the population was made up of small peasant farmers, generally owning a small plot of infertile land with limited productive capacity, and inhabitants tended to be politically conservative, holding tight to their traditions while supporting the official party of the military.

The Christian Democrats, the principal opposition party in El Salvador at the time, were beginning their presence in the region and towards the end of the decade, the Catholic Church began organizing Christian Base Communities (CEB in Spanish) with a program based on awareness raising and founded on the precepts of liberation theology with its preferential option for the poor.

By the end of 1979 and into 1980, large military incursions of government troops were being launched into the areas of El Salvador in which landless peasants had begun to organize, especially in the northern departments of Chalatenango and Morazan. In the process, entire families were slaughtered or forced to seek refuge away from their home villages in order to avoid being captured or killed.

It was in this context of poverty, incipient peasant organization and growing repression that we began to build one of the strongest revolutionary armies in the history of Latin America with the goal of overcoming military dictatorship and advancing an agenda of profound change in favor of the poor and traditionally marginalized of our country.

Following a decade of clandestine life in the urban areas of El Salvador, where I was focused on consolidating and strengthening politically as well as militarily our guerrilla organization, the People's Revolutionary Army, I arrived in Morazan for the first time in my life on January 8, 1981 to help coordinate a national offensive of the FMLN. Our hope at that time was to bring our revolutionary struggle to a quick and decisive victory and avoid a long and bloody struggle, an unrealistic and naïve aspiration, to say the least.

My arrival in Morazan required 24 hours of exhausting walking through the mountains and ravines of the northeastern part of El Salvador, a painful task for one more accustomed to the comforts of an urban setting and with only one question in mind: "How much further before reaching our objective?" And the famous answer of the experienced guerrilla fighters who were guiding us, "Just one more mountain to scale."

Supposedly, I was in relatively good physical shape. But, by the time we reached our final destination at the Sapo River in the mountainous region of northern Morazan, I was no longer living inside my body. A comrade had carried my overweight knapsack from our starting point in Santa Rosa de Lima near the gold mines of San Sebastian, but I was totally exhausted.

A group of comrades awaited us, many of whom I recognized from earlier years of our struggle, including commander "Memo", who at that moment was in charge of the guerrilla front of Morazan, and "Mario Chocho", who came to us from the insurrection in Nicaragua that drove the dictator, Anastacio Somoza, from power. All were focused at that moment on the magic date of January 10th when our guerrilla forces would attack the military installations in the city of San Francisco Gotera while sister organizations of the FMLN attacked military positions in other cities.

I was temporarily out of action from the walk; hence, the comrades gave me the opportunity to bathe, eat and rest. Later we met to analyze together the overall situation where I was informed of the number of our combatants and how they were divided among our zones and subzones of Morazan. These include La Guacamaya, where we were presently located; the central zone, where our best and most experienced fighters were concentrated; the subzone of Cacahuatique and, with fewer combatants, the subzone of Hecho Andrajos in Santa Rosa from where I had just walked. There was also a subzone located in the village of Agua Blanca in the municipality of Cacaopera, considered part of the zone of La Guacamaya.

Our total attack force consisted of fewer than 400 combatants, principally due to a tremendous shortage of weapons. Along with this, we wanted to leave sufficient forces behind to defend the civilian communities of our front, given the proximity of National Guard posts and paramilitary groups.

Our arms consisted primarily of M-16 rifles captured in battle from the army. Along with these, we had a number of FALN rifles of Belgian manufacture, a few bolt-action Mousers, M1 and M2 carbines from the Second World War, 22-caliber rifles, shotguns, a browning machine gun, a 30-caliber machine gun, three RPG-7 rocket launchers and numerous homemade grenades, a danger to the enemy but also to our less experienced troops, given the ease with which they exploded on contact.

Later, our attack plan was explained. I didn't know the city of San Franciso Gotera or the location of the military fort, so it was a bit difficult for me to follow the discussion and express my opinions on the designated routes for the advance of our troops, but I quickly began to admire the capacity and the self-assurance with which our comrades in charge were able to explain what to me appeared like a highly complex operation compared to my urban experience where simpler maneuvers and fewer combatants were employed. I trusted my comrades completely since many of them had participated in the war in Nicaragua, and our plan seemed logical, at least on paper, so our meeting consisted more of an explanation than a discussion.

The advance on the military fort would proceed from three directions: one from the southeast that would be led by forces concentrated in Cacahuatique and would come down from the shoulders of the Cacahuatique mountain. The other direction of attack would be from the north, passing through the landing field of Chilanga, and the third direction would come from the northeast, leaving from La Guacamaya and advancing toward the entrance of the city of San Francisco. Needless to say, I was in no shape to participate in this operation. Those who were doing the explaining would be the commanders who would lead it.

When the meeting ended, our guerrilla forces of La Guacamaya were concentrated in military formation in a large clearing and I had the opportunity to direct a few words to our combatants in preparation for their departure. I explained the strategic importance of our offensive at the national level as well as the important contribution we would be making through our attack on the fort in San Francisco Gotera.

It was nightfall when I finished speaking, and our troops were ready for departure with the field commanders shouting "columna firme… alinear… por la izquierda a paso columna marcha", then leading their columns of combatants off into the darkness in route to their "encounter with destiny", knowing that many might not return.

I could observe the young men and women as they marched, and some not so young, slowly disappearing into the night. I was aware that few had uniforms. Each wore different colored clothing, some with sombreros, others with baseball caps, a few with camouflage shirts or pants, and all of the commanders with blue jeans and tan shirts, the official uniform of the People's Revolutionary Army (ERP in Spanish) at that time. Nevertheless, I felt proud and amazed at the sight of our incipient revolutionary force and saddened at the same time not to be accompanying them. It was January 1981, and our heroes were marching off to the first general offensive of the FMLN.

Our communications in the war fronts during those early years relied on young messengers ("correos") who moved from one guerrilla camp to another or among our troops in battle, always trying to evade enemy soldiers, carrying messages and orders from one guerrilla commander to another. We also utilized the few short-wave radios that we had, brand Spiltburg, with an orange color for which we referred to them as the "orange radios". They were simple devices that produced lots of interference with horrible receptivity, but it was all we had at that time.

On the contrary, government soldiers had Access to PRC-77 radios of high resolution, permitting better coordination and information. They also had the support of artillery with 60- and 81-millimeter mortars; M-60 and 50 caliber machine guns; 20-mm canons with unlimited ammunition; the support of aviation, including A-37 jet bombers from the war in Vietnam, and helicopters armed with rocket launchers and machine guns capable of riddling a soccer field with bullets in seconds.

With such an enormous advantage, it should be no surprise that the Armed Forces overpowered us on the battlefield, and our general offensive was defeated at the national level. Our troops throughout the country were forced to retreat, returning to the limited areas under guerrilla control at that moment.

We had naively promoted the idea among our combatants that this would be a final offensive, hence, with the retreat of our forces, many of our combatants considered that the war was over and that we had been defeated, deciding to return to their homes, weapons and all. Some returned to our guerrilla camps hidden in the mountains, but most went missing. Hence, the following three or four days had to be spent in search of our combatants in order to explain to them that the struggle continued, although, after a week or so, most began returning to their respective camps upon realizing that they were still intact.

It is important here to clarify that our troops never returned to their homes with the idea of surrendering to the army of the dictatorship. They were simply aware that they needed to continue their lives of survival under the same difficult conditions under which they had always lived.

Understanding this situation helped us understand as well that we were not dealing with a classic guerrilla army but rather a mass of peasants who had felt threatened by the military and who had incorporated into the struggle massively as a mechanism of self-defense. This perception was even reflected in the language of our combatants. For example, whenever the army invaded our zones, instead of talking of a military incursion, our combatants would say, "The repression is coming."

It was repression, especially against the peasant population organized in Christian Base Communities of the Catholic Church or in other forms of popular organization, that had forced peasant families to leave their homes to hide in the mountains and ravines of the department in the 1970s before we had a guerrilla army to defend them. This reality also made us reflect more on our methods for building and consolidating our guerrilla fronts, especially on the political, social and cultural challenges we had to take into consideration in this complex process.

The repression of the military had nothing to do with confronting international communism. This argument could never justify the horrible practice of genocide against the civilian population by a military regime that had lost the support of its own people and that was attempting to weaken and flatten these same people in order to perpetuate a dictatorial, militaristic regime in defense of the interests of an elite oligarchic minority.

After the failed offensive of January 10, I assumed the political and military leadership of the northeastern front of Morazan with the challenges of building and preparing a strong guerrilla army for a long and difficult struggle. We began by attempting to obtain smaller military victories, carrying out attacks on nearby National Guard posts, but these also ended in defeat. We always knew, however, that we had a number of elements in our favor that we needed to take better advantage of in order to help us to grow and strengthen our forces.

Among these were almost ten years of accumulated military experience in urban guerrilla warfare, with a profound mystique among our combatants leading them to prefer death to defeat in battle. Secondly, the mission, for our combatants, was sacred, and nobody would desist from completing it, even if it meant the loss of life. Thirdly, our discipline was incomparable, and, finally, every man and woman of the guerrilla army was an exceptional, highly-trained combatant.

These characteristics were clearly expressed in the attack on San Francisco Gotera on January 10. When our advance against the military fort was stalled, and our combat became poorly coordinated with the offensive in other regions of the country failing, I was informed that we had sustained more than 35 dead and dozens of wounded. There was a notable lack in our communications on the ground and we didn't know the exact situation of each guerrilla column.

At that moment, I had given the order to retreat, but the response from our battlefield commanders was, "And the offensive?" Our comrades preserved in their hearts and minds to need to continue fighting with whatever and whoever remained in order to contribute our part to the general offensive being played out at the national level. I had to insist with force in order to be heard and obeyed so that all of our commanders understood the seriousness of the order I was giving.

A similar incident occurred several days later with another of our field commanders, who was leading a guerrilla column in the Conchagua volcano. From Morazan, we heard the constant explosion of the bombs and artillery, day after day, without communication. Finally, I was able to get a radio message to our commander in charge of the operation and he informed me that he and his troops were surrounded and being pushed towards the mouth of the volcano.

It was evident that if they became penned in, the aviation and artillery would cause enormous damage, and the final outcome would be a disastrous defeat with the annihilation of him and his combatants. Making matters worse, his ammunition was running out. Again, I ordered him to withdraw but immediately received a reply saying, "My mission is the army fort in La Union." My next message to him was simple: "If you remain where you are, our forces will be overrun and annihilated, and you will not be able to complete any mission. Your priority now is to save yourself and your men."

Even after this exchange, our commander and his men fought through the rest of the day. Then, in the late afternoon, they hid themselves as best they could under leaves and earth as the army advanced on their position, but, finding no one, moved on, allowing our forces to slip through the military encirclement and escape.

Another advantage was the anger and resentment caused by "la platada", the peasants' term for obligatory military service in the army of the dictatorship or forced recruitment. Having participated in the army, many of our guerrilla combatants, even before joining us, possessed a high level of knowledge of military procedures and the ability to handle a wide variety of weapons. They were also highly disciplined and, in some cases, experienced, like me, in urban guerrilla warfare. We also had the advantage of having several commanders who had participated in the insurrection in Nicaragua, some of whom had earned the grade of commandant in the Sandinista army.

Another key strength came from the incorporation of several officers of the Salvadoran army at the beginning of the war, including Lieutenant Colonel Navarrete, Captain Cruz and Captain Mena Sandoval, all professionals who shared their knowledge and experience through courses to our combatants. They also designed and implemented a special school for squad and platoon leaders. But perhaps their greatest contribution was to share their profound knowledge of the functioning of the Armed Forces of El Salvador. Of course, all of this was a process that would take time under normal circumstances, but given the urgency of our need to strengthen our forces, it was accelerated to respond to the concrete demands of the war.

When we captured the first PRC-77 radio, we thought that by acquiring others, we could create our own communications capability, but Captain Cruz insisted instead that we use this first radio to improve our military intelligence by listening in on government communications, so we organized and developed a unit that would provide us with one more unmatched advantage over our enemy.

A final advantageous element for us was the amazing resource provided by our guerrilla radio, "Radio Venceremos", broadcasting live from guerrilla-controlled territories in Morazán. Broadcasts were twice a day, at 6 a.m. and another at 6 p.m. and were generally received by audiences at the national and even international levels. Their unbroken signal was evidence of our control of the northeastern front of Morazan.

The radio had a political as well as an emotional impact on the population and on our combatants – political because it served as a source of information directly from the guerrilla organizations themselves and emotional because the live transmission was coming from a military force in the act of trying to overthrow a dictatorship and its repressive military machinery.

That emotional force was multiplied by the genius and mystique of "Santiago", a comrade of Venezuelan origin who had previously collaborated with "Radio Sandino" in Nicaragua during the insurrection in that country. Santiago's voice resounded with strength, enthusiasm and heroism, lifting our spirits from the very moment he began to speak.

With all of the aforementioned, we gradually began to build a fighting force that was physically, intellectually and morally strengthened and impossible to defeat.

The response of the dictatorship to the advances of the guerrilla struggle at the national level was the strategy of "scorched earth" with the objective of "taking the water away from the fish", based on a phrase of the Chinese leader Mao Tse Tung, who stated, "... the guerrilla moves in the village like a fish in water." For the Salvadoran army, it was a matter of taking the people away from the guerrillas through massacre and terror.

In December 1981, the army of the dictatorship began an operation with several battalions in the areas of Agua Blanca, Las Mesas, El Junquillo, Cerro Pando, La Guacamaya and El Mozote in Morazán. In the villages of Las Mesas, El Junquillo and Cerro Pando, where they passed through under the command of Captain Napoleón Medina Garay, they slaughtered without mercy children, elderly men and women.

The testimonies of the people who survived by hiding helplessly nearby, where they were able to observe the actions of the military against their own family members, are heartbreaking, grotesque and difficult to believe, given the level of extreme evil. Months-old children were thrown into the air by Medina Garay himself and received on the tip of the bayonet of his rifle.

Women and young girls were raped in front of their parents, and orders were finally given to kill everyone. To some of his more hesitant troops, Medina Garay was heard screaming, "Idiots, don't you see that they are communists? Those you leave alive will one day have your heads cut off. Kill those sons of bitches." And the soldiers proceeded to obey orders.

Later, the "little angels from hell", as the Atlacatl battalion has been referred to, arrived at the village of El Mozote under the direct orders of Colonel Domingo Monterrosa Barrios, and here the story was the same. They locked all of the women and children in a church and then proceeded to put them to death. They killed every human they found, scattering their corpses along the roads and hillsides, together with the remains of cattle and domestic animals, even birds. All that was left was the smell of death that penetrated everywhere.

The most tragic thing about the El Mozote massacre is that we had warned the people that the army was coming and told them to evacuate to the nearby town of Arambala, three kilometers away. But their leaders refused, arguing that they were evangelical Christians, that the army knew that they were not guerrillas nor supported the guerrillas, that they had talked with the army colonel of Gotera who had assured them that they were not in any danger and that they could remain calmly in their homes. So, these people trusted the army. But, on that fateful day of December 1981, more than a thousand people, including over seven hundred inhabitants of El Mozote proper, were slaughtered.

Little by little, our small-scale battles in Morazán grew into large-scale battles, and our troops began to gain confidence and enjoy the satisfaction and pride of victory. In March 1981, in preparation for a major battle with government troops planning an incursion into our territories, our "engineers" established an extensive line of fire, building eight kilometers of trenches extending across our zone of control to help us resist enemy forces. We also hid a large contingent of combatants behind enemy lines in the area of La Esperanza, who would attack the army from the rear, seeking to annihilate it or, at least, create enough havoc to assure our victory.

This battlefront extended along the banks of the Sapo River, Cerro Pando and La Guacamaya. Only one more ingredient was necessary: the courage and heroism of our guerrilla fighters and the ability to endure massive artillery bombardments without abandoning our positions, moving from trench to trench, from foxhole to foxhole, under enormous stress.

An infantry company from San Francisco Gotera sent a patrol through the village of El Junquillo in the direction of Cerro Pando and got bogged down in combat with our forces. They sent another company of 180 men, and they got bogged down as well. The fighting continued into the following day when the rest of the government battalion arrived and also got bogged down. Then they sent a second battalion from

Gotera, and a third battalion from San Miguel, and these three battalions were bogged down, fighting for their lives for ten days, in spite of the constant support of intense bombardment and artillery attacks against our positions.

Radio Venceremos was transmitting the battle and utilizing a new language that applied new concepts, like "controlled zone", "line of fire", "battlefront," and "enemy casualties". It was the broadcast of a real-life war novel: the confrontation of a popular army against the army of the dictatorship. It was a new reality. It was "The war in El Salvador!" in all of its glory.

Two battalions of paratroopers were eventually added in support of those who remained bogged down, and the battle continued. And it went on like this for 22 days. Finally, the Armed Forces sent the Atlacatl battalion, which they said was made up of only "shucas" (veteran soldiers fighting for pleasure).

In the first combat against Atlacatl, we were able to ambush them, cause their retreat and recuperate a large part of their arms. What is more, we extended our northeastern front of Morazan by fourteen kilometers. In the end, we decided to halt the siege and withdraw our troops, leaving the army to fight alone in the area for two more days after we had gone.

The results of the battle demonstrated that we had been able to maintain our positions against the maximum offensive capacity of the Salvadoran army for 22 continuous days, sustaining a minimum of losses. We also recovered rifles and large quantities of ammunition and caused almost 250 government casualties between dead and wounded.

Following several additional and similar battles, we became more confident. The phrase "the repression is

coming" disappeared forever from our rhetoric, and the Armed Forces became more convinced that sending its troops into our controlled zone with less than an entire battalion was inadvisable. In the meantime, our guerrilla-controlled front continued to grow and consolidate.

The rest of 1982 was one of learning and development, resisting and advancing. In Morazán, we overran every military post north of the Torola River, and our troops scored numerous victories from east to west, from west to east, from south to north and from north to south.

With the formation of our Rafael Arce Zabla Brigade (BRAZ in Spanish) at the end of that year, the popular army of the ERP became an unstoppable force equipped with enormous firepower, maneuverability, and experienced fighters with high morale. From an army of torn pants and bare feet emerged the People's Revolutionary Army of the FMLN.

Isaías

My name is Isaías Sandoval Alas. I am a peasant by origin from a poor community in central El Salvador. In my youth, I served for several years as a "delegate of the word" in the Catholic Church, working under the slain Jesuit priest Rutilio Grande. When the war came, rendering our lives impossible, I joined the guerrilla movement and served for 12 years as a commander in hopes of overcoming the poverty, injustice and dictatorship that had plagued our nation for decades. After the war, I served four terms as the mayor of Suchitoto and am currently the owner of a small tourist center on the shores of the beautiful Lake Suchitlán in the department of Cuscatlán.

I was born and raised in the small village of El Tablón in the municipality of El Paisnal, department of San Salvador. My father's name was Felipe Sandoval Umaña, and my mother was Feliciana Alas Umaña. We were nine siblings, consisting of seven brothers and two sisters.

Our village was made up primarily of our extended family with great-grandparents, grandparents, uncles, cousins, etc. We were a large, well-knit, supportive and hardworking family, always promoting and participating in efforts aimed at solving communal needs in our village and its surrounding areas.

I have only beautiful memories from those times, living in peace and enjoying the warmth of relatives where the young respected the elderly and the adults provided only positive lessons in an effort to ensure that we grew up with values and principles for a healthy and harmonious coexistence with others.

Our mornings were filled with hard work in the fields or with studies when we were attending school. In the afternoons, we would gather together to play soccer or go to the river to bathe, fish and bring the cattle to graze. At night we would get together at our great-grandparents' house to play the games popular with rural peasants during that period. We were a large group of young children and teenagers enjoying a healthy life and dreaming of eternal youth. We knew nothing about firearms at that time or other forms of violence. Our lives were happy and peaceful, without conflict.

In El Tablón, we attended a small adobe school with tile roofing, but without water and without electricity. It only had two grades, however, so formal education ended there for most of us. The population of our village was primarily Catholic, and my great-grandfather contributed a small piece of land and some trees in order to build a simple church so that the parish priests of Aguilares could come to celebrate mass. We all helped with the construction and attended mass every Sunday together with people from nearby villages.

Our tranquil and joyful coexistence lasted until 1973, the year that I turned 17. My father had been a member of the "Adorers of Christ the King", a group within the Catholic Church, for many years. This group was frowned upon by the local authorities because of its critical position on social justice, led locally by the parish priest at that time, Rutilio Grande.

Complicating this situation further, our family, being poor itself, was known for being sensitive to the suffering of others, for sharing what little we had with people who were poorer than ourselves and for providing support to workers of the local haciendas when they were mistreated or overexploited by owners. What was worse, we participated in the Christian Democratic Party, which opposed the military dictatorship of that time.

After the meeting of the Conference of Catholic Bishops of Latin America in Medellín, Colombia, a new theology was promoted in the Catholic Church in all of the countries of Central America referred to as Liberation Theology. It preached a preferential option for the poor, questioned inequality in our society and promoted social action in the name of justice.

It was in this context that a group of Jesuit priests associated with Rutilio Grande began to arrive in our area with the goal of awakening the conscience of rural peasants and promoting a praxis of empower-ment by analyzing the reality of our lives, identifying the causes of our poverty and taking action to resolve those causes. They formed catechists and delegates of the word among the laypeople who guided this effort, and my older siblings (Mariano, José María, and Juana) and I began to participate under the tutelage of Father Grande.

In this way, we began to deepen our knowledge and our awareness of the injustices in our country causing endless suffering to poor families due to the overexploitation of workers by the owners of the large farms. As our awareness deepened, our commitment to the poor increased, and we began to look for ways to organize ourselves to push for change.

At first, we joined Ecclesiastical Base Communities (CEB in Spanish) being formed by the Jesuits and other progressive elements of the Catholic Church. When popular organizations began to emerge with a stronger focus on social struggle, such as the Christian Federation of Salvadoran Peasants (FECCAS), however, my older brothers and I joined and quickly became leaders, first at the local level and then at the national level.

As people continued to organize in the name of justice and democ-racy, the repression of the dictatorship increased, and from 1976, our family became the object of persecution. The time came when my older siblings and I had to separate ourselves from our parents and younger brothers and sisters (Felipe, Margot, Bartolo, Hugo and Candelario), at first because of our work as catechists in the Church and members of the CEB, and later because of our militancy in FECCAS.

Rutilio Grande, in 1976, convened an assembly with all the catechists of the parish of Aguilares, which included the municipalities of El Paisnal, Aguilares and Suchitoto. For that meeting, he asked for the presence of his great friend and auxiliary bishop of San Salvador at the time, Monsignor Oscar Arnulfo Romero. (Several months later, Rutilio would invite my brother and me to the ceremony in San Salvador celebrating the appointment of Romero as archbishop of San Salvador.)

The objective of the assembly was to give the catechists of the parish the opportunity to present to the bishop all of the obstacles that we were facing in our attempts to promote a program of evangelization based on an objective analysis of the reality of the country and on the example of

Christ during His days on earth. At the same time, we criticized the close friendships that some priests maintained with the military and with the economically powerful, hiding in their sermons and in their actions the injustices being perpetrated against peasant communities and charging for church services, such as baptisms and marriages.

It was a highly productive assembly. For many of us, it was the first opportunity that we had had to address the hierarchy of our Church. Father Rutilio remained silent for the duration of the assembly, simply observing how Romero focused so strongly on all that we were saying.

At the end of the event, Monsignor recommended that we continue with our evangelizing work based on liberation theology in spite of the obstacles but advised us to be careful in the face of possible repercussions with the threat of being persecuted, arrested or even disappeared or assassinated. He assured us that he would never abandon us, however, that he would always be with us and that he would not leave us alone. At the end of the meeting, Father Rutilio looked happy with the result we had obtained.

After the assembly of catechists, in a symbol of his preference for the poor, Rutilio took down the images of the saints in the church of Aguilares, leaving only the image of the crucified Christ. The altar was decorated with ornaments of corn husks and sugar cane instead of shiny metal objects, and the bronze tabernacle was replaced by a small, more rustic structure of cane and corn to house the chalice and the hosts. Our evangelization program continued to focus on the precepts of liberation theology with faith in God, in monsignor Romero and in Rutilio Grande.

From there, it wasn't long before the first catechist of our group was murdered. Rutilio left the routine of the parish and traveled immediately to the village of the slain catechist to accompany his suffering family and offer them a week of prayer and religious ceremony in their home. And many of us from nearby villages also came to offer our solidarity, following the example of our beloved pastor.

In all aspects of life, Rutilio was humble and dedicated to the Church. He had no material possessions. Nor was he attached to this life on earth. I remember on one occasion when he came to celebrate mass in our small church in El Tablón how, in the middle of his sermon, he looked at us with a smile and told us, "If one day I am assassinated, you must not weep or be sad. Carry me to my burial place with joy, with music, with praise to God for allowing me to die for the gospel, as He wanted." Rutilio, like Monsignor Romero, knew that his death was imminent and inevitable, and, in the years that followed, I would come to better understand this great lesson in all of its depth.

On March 12, 1977, the words of Rutilio Grande came back to us all as we received the tragic news that he had been ambushed and murdered that day by National Police and the National Guard in route to celebrate mass in the town of his birth, El Paisnal. That fatal day should have been a time of great joy for me and for my family as I had planned to marry and was awaiting in our small church in El Tablón in my best suit of clothes for the arrival of another Jesuit priest, Marcelino, to conduct the ceremony.

Rutilio was the first of many Catholic priests to be assassinated by government security forces or ultra-right death squads for their commitment to the poor, and from the day of his death, things began to change drastically for the worst in our region. State-sponsored repression increased dramatically, forcing most of us to leave our homes each evening with all of our family members to sleep in the nearby hillsides around our villages for security.

Our vision of struggle had always been peaceful. We had organized to fight against injustice without a thought of violence. The landowners were treating their workers as slaves, paying starvation wages and refusing to provide even a small plot of land to plant for their families. When desperate workers protested, they were quickly fired and driven from the small shacks where many had lived for decades despite having children, pregnant wives and disabled elderly who were hungry, sick and with nowhere else to go.

The electoral process in El Salvador was controlled by the economically powerful aligned with the military and fraud was a common occurrence. Even so, we never thought, in the first years of our struggle of using violence, especially those of us who were associated with the Church.

Rutilio Grande and monsignor Romero were not guerrillas, as they were accused of being. They were opposed to the use of violence and in favor of the peaceful resolution of conflicts. I knew that very well about both of them. They never advised nor condoned the use of violence. Rutilio told us at one point that the parish would never allow a gathering of people who applied violent means. Both of these men were assassinated for denouncing injustice, not for promoting violence, and for their commitment to defend the poor.

The problem was that the government, the economic elite and the military were unwilling to cede in the face of our demands for justice and democracy. It was the State that opted for violence through its security forces, the army and civilian followers organized in armed patrols.

Death squads, such as the "Mano Blanco" (White Hand), began to repress the peaceful meetings, rallies and marches of the population and to persecute people in their homes, in their workplaces or in their places of study. They captured and disappeared or murdered innocent people, starting with the massacre of students at the National University in 1975.

After that incident, it became common to find the tortured and often headless bodies of students, union organizers, peasant leaders, human rights advocates and members of the Church in almost any part of the national territory, in the streets or in the fields, many of whom had no membership or participation in the popular organizations.

The first military takeover in our parish of Aguilares was carried out by the army, the National Guard and the Treasury Police. It occurred in the early morning one day in 1976 as Father Rutilio was leaving the church. He was met by a horde of government troops pointing their rifles at him, threatening him and ordering him back inside. But he paid them little attention, and the people of the parish joined him while a stunned military stood watching, unable to prevent him from carrying out his priestly duties.

After Rutilio's death, the army took over Aguilares again, this time with more aggressive force. They arrested and beat any priest they came upon and threatened them with death if they didn't leave the parish. On that occasion, one of our fellow catechists trained by Rutilio Grande, upon seeing that the soldiers were occupying the church and the convent, climbed to the bell tower and began to ring the bells as a warning to the people. The army could only bring him down with a bullet and ended up murdering him.

Those of us working with FECCAS were gradually becoming more radical in our views and actions. In May 1979, I accompanied a peaceful demonstration of the Bloque Popular Revolucionario (Popular Revolutionary Block), an alliance of peasants, students, workers, church activists and other sectors, of which FECCAS was a member. Our purpose was to demand the release of several of our leaders who had been arrested by the police several days earlier, in late April.

I had been assigned the task of defending our group from Paisnal and Aguilares, who had traveled by bus to the capital city to participate in the event and, for the first time, I was carrying a small 38 special revolver. As we gathered in front of the National Cathedral, we were suddenly attacked by members of government security forces. My first reaction was to throw myself to the ground on the steps of the Cathedral, but in minutes, there were bodies piled around me, so I joined others who could still move and ran up the steps into the Cathedral as a hail of bullets continued to rain down upon us.

Inside the Cathedral, a large number of seriously injured comrades lay dying in large pools of blood, now covering the floor. Between the dead on the steps and the wounded who later died inside the Cathedral, we lost 25 comrades that day.

I positioned myself at the front door, waiting for government forces to rush the Cathedral. My plan was to shoot the first soldiers who came to the door and save the last bullet to take my own life. This was the first time in this war that I realized that I was willing to die for our struggle.

The government troops chose not to enter, and, in the afternoon of the next day, with the intervention of the International Red Cross, we were able to leave and find our way out of the city. I arrived home two days later to find my older brother standing in the doorway of my father's house in El Tablon, waiting for me with a look of astonishment at finding me alive. Later, he took me aside and, with a smile, told me, "You're not going to die in this war."

The options for non-violent change were quickly disappearing in El Salvador, and we were being pushed toward more violent means to advance our struggle. It became increasingly apparent that the only option remaining was to take up arms, so we began, slowly at first and then massively, to join the guerrilla organizations operating at that time in the region of Aguilares.

Following the massacre of the Cathedral in San Salvador, I joined the Popular Liberation Militia, the first seed of armed guerrilla struggle in our area and part of the Popular Liberation Forces (FPL in Spanish), the largest member organization of the Farabundo Martí National Liberation Front (FMLN in Spanish). And I was quickly moved into a command position.

By 1980, I was serving with the local guerrilla columns being consolidated in the subzone of Guazapa around the Guazapa volcano. Later, when my older brother was ambushed and killed by the army in the nearby village of La Loma, I was assigned to replace him as commander of these units.

My father, upon learning of the death of his first child, began to comprehend better the danger to our family that this approaching storm implied and lost all control. Between tears and screams of anguish and pain, he began swinging his machete and chopping at the wooden pillars of our house while yelling, "I told you that this was going to happen at any moment!"

In January 1981, the guerrilla organizations of the FMLN called for a nationwide offensive mistakenly named the "Final Offensive," given the hope that it would provide us with a rapid victory or at least bring us closer to winning the war. At that moment, I was responsible for two guerrilla columns assigned with the task of taking and holding the highest peaks of the Guazapa volcano, an area referred to as El Roblar and located strategically about 40 kilometers from the capital city. The task was key to our success in the offensive as it had been determined that the command structures of the FPL would be based there in order to direct our forces during the fighting.

As is well known, the offensive did not bring the successes that we had hoped for, first because of a shortage of weapons and, second, because of failures in coordination among the five FMLN organizations. Also, our combat experience at the time was minimal. Hence, it did not mark the end of the war as we had proposed, but rather the beginning of the war with the formation and consolidation of guerrilla fronts around the country where our combat forces could prepare for the long and difficult road ahead.

In mid-1981, I was located in the newly formed Felipe Peña Front, which consisted of the Radiola subzone (municipality of Cinquera), the Guazapa subzone (the slopes of the volcano and the surrounding lowlands) and the subzone of Piedra (municipality of Paisnal). One day, I was called by the commander of our front, Susana Peña, sister of one of the founders of the FPL, Felipe Peña, at which time I was assigned to head up the guerrilla forces in the subzone of Piedra (my area of origin) and its periphery, including Apopa and Nejapa. At that time, my war name was Sebastián.

The subzone to which I was being assigned was presenting difficulties at that time due to the fact that the army was entering from all sides and harassing the civilian population, accompanied by paramilitary patrols made up of people from the subzone who served the military for money or other benefits. They were particularly dangerous because they knew the terrain and the people who lived there and served as spies and informants against their own former neighbors.

Our objective was to consolidate the subzone under our control. Those who had been in command of this region had shown too much weakness and cowardice in the face of army incursions. They did not want to fight but rather fled in "guinda" (forced retreat) along with the civilian population every time government troops arrived. It was a difficult situation.

My father, my mother and my younger siblings still lived in the subzone in our village of El Tablón. My first daughter, Eva, born in 1979, also lived there. Like the rest of the population, they were vulnerable and at great risk of falling victim to a government and a military that had already demonstrated its willingness to slaughter its own people and had no respect for women, children or the elderly. A few months after my arrival in command of local guerrilla forces, I paid the enormous price for not having resolved this dilemma.

Several times, I had advised my family to take steps to protect themselves. Together with my father, we built a well-hidden tatu (underground tunnel) where they could hide when the soldiers came. I gave my father a new machete and bid him to carry it always in order to have some minimal degree of self-defense, but my father rejected all of this, insisting rightly so that "it would be useless since the soldiers were all well-armed."

One day, an infantry battalion from the First Brigade, along with an artillery battalion and civilian patrols, entered our subzone with force. In the village of Natividad, the population had refused to flee their homes when the approach of the soldiers was detected. They were confident that nothing would happen to them because they were from a conservative evangelical church, but the men were badly beaten, women were raped, and all were ordered to abandon their village immediately.

On the following day, our combatants, now better prepared, better armed and ready to fight, ambushed the government soldiers, causing a large number of casualties. In their anger and frustration, the soldiers moved on to my village of El Tablon, where they dealt me the most painful blow that I would sustain in this horrible war by attacking my home and family and killing my beloved father after a member of the civilian patrols identified him as the father of a guerrilla commander. It was September 1981, and the only reason for his death was the fact that I was his son.

Upon arriving in my village, the people informed me that my father had been wounded by the soldiers and had tried to escape while my mother hid in the nearby brush. The soldiers pursued him, following the traces of blood, and finally caught up with him, collapsed on the ground weak, bleeding heavily and clearly dying.

He had been carrying the new machete I had given to him, and the army used the machete to cut off his head. Afterwards, they took the head, carrying it by the hair, to the house of my uncle, a brother of my mother, to show him what they had done, and there they threw the head to the ground. My youngest brother, seven years old at the time, was there and saw how the eyes moved in my father's head, leaving him totally traumatized and requiring many years of therapy to overcome his nightmares.

Later, the soldiers carried the head to the National Guard headquarters in the town of El Paisnal, where they kept it for several days in the street, kicking it as if it were a soccer ball each time they passed by, shouting with joy that this was the head of the father of the guerrilla commander of El Paisnal.

At that time, my war name was still Sebastian, and, in a future incursion of the Atlacatl battalion, formed and trained by the U.S. and now famous for its civilian massacres, the soldiers were said to have been inquiring among the population for the guerrilla commander, Sebastian. In response, it was suggested that I change my name, so I took the name of my father, Felipe, remaining with that sacred name for the rest of the war.

By 1982, we had consolidated our subzone with a growing guerrilla presence more capable of controlling the territory and defending the population. It had become another "liberated zone" of the FMLN. But I never overcame the cruel irony of my father's death, assassinated with the machete that I had given to him and buried quickly one night by myself and others in the underground tunnel that we had dug together for my family's safety.

I have never cried as I did on that occasion when we collected the remains of his body, knowing the cruelty he had endured at the time of his death and the fact that he owed nothing. Following that incident, we transferred my mother and younger siblings out of the subzone along with my daughter, Eva, who was two and a half years old at the time.

At the end of that year, I received notice that the guerrilla forces of the FPL had taken a strategic leap forward in terms of structure and strength with the formation of the Vanguard Zonal Units, bringing together our best military resources (combatants, weapons and equipment). And I was ordered to incorporate into this structure. Shortly afterwards, I was sent to the northern department of Chalatenango to incorporate into the Vanguard Units at the national level.

In reality, the Vanguard Zonal Units were being concentrated into a single force in Chalatenango, with our best fighters and weapons captured over the years in combat against the army. The objective was to carry out a military campaign in the department to "cleanse" the area of all government presence, leaving only the larger military installations in the city of Chalatenango and in El Paraiso.

My brother, José Maria, was in command in Guazapa at the time of my departure for Chalatenango and happy with my new assignment, declaring jokingly as I was preparing to leave that I would have to return to the Felipe Peña Front when we had finished cleaning up in the north in order to eliminate the government positions in this front.

We formed the first battalions of the Vanguard Units soon after my arrival to Chalatenango, and I was assigned to command the third detachment of one of those battalions with almost 300 combatants, along with logistics personnel, cooks, medical staff and radio operators.

With our new military structures in place, we quickly became engaged in some of the most strategic battles of the war, driving the military out of large towns, overrunning key military installations throughout Chalatenango and destroying command posts of the National Guard. Through it all, we celebrated a long chain of victories and caused enormous casualties among government troops, but we always respected the lives of soldiers who surrendered in battle and handed them over to the International Red Cross or the Catholic Church.

Our policy was always to try to convince soldiers to surrender in battle, promising to respect their lives, and the word quickly spread among government infantry troops in the field that the FMLN honored this practice, rendering government troops less likely to fight to the end, especially when they found themselves surrounded, with wounded and dead.

Every day, we became stronger with higher morale, armed with better weapons and with more accumulated experience. Nevertheless, the sight of dead and wounded soldiers brought us no satisfaction, and the death of our own comrades was deeply felt by all.

During my stay in Chalatenango, my brother, Nelson, assigned to the subzone of Cinquera (Radiola), sent me a letter that, among other things, informed me that he was going to bring his wife and small son to the front. He also wanted to bring my daughter, who was between five and six years old at that time, but I told him categorically not to bring her despite the enormous desire I had to see her.

Conditions at the front were difficult and dangerous. In addition, we were planning a new military operation in those days to overrun the army post on the El Limon bridge on the road to Chalatenango city. I told my brother that it would be better for my daughter to remain with my mother, who lived in Apopa at the time. Despite my advice, Nelson proceeded to bring his own wife and young son.

At that time, we had an important visitor in our front. Her name was Marianela García Villa, and she was a member of the Salvadoran Human Rights Commission residing in exile in Mexico. The purpose of her visit was to investigate and corroborate information on the indiscriminate bombing and "scorched earth" tactics being applied against the civilian population, including the army's use of "white phosphorus" bombs. My brother was a member of the political-military command responsible for this front and was assigned the task of accompanying her and ensuring her safety during her visit.

On March 14, 1983, the guerrilla column that was transferring Marianella from the subzone of Guazapa to the subzone of Radiola (Cinquera) with abundant testimonies, photos and other evidence was ambushed by a company of government soldiers in the hacienda La Bermuda. Marianella, along with my brother, his family and about 25 other comrades, were killed in the fighting.

One of our commanders in Chalatenango, Jesús Rojas, a soft-spoken Nicaraguan and ex-Jesuit seminarian serving in the guerrilla ranks of El Salvador (he was killed in an ambush just before the war ended) approached me the next day to inform me personally of my brother's death.

I initially fell into a state of denial and replied to Jesus that perhaps my brother was among the few survivors, but he confirmed the death, leaving no room for doubt and, afterwards, asked me gently how I felt and if I was going to be able to accompany the military operation that we had planned for this day. I responded that I was fine, although that was far from the truth, and that I would join my detachment, already concentrated in military formation and getting ready to depart.

Throughout the war, the army carried out some of its largest and bloodiest operations in the sub-zones of Cinquera and Guazapa, involving the indiscriminate bombing of civilian communities along with large incursions of infantry troops supported by artillery in an attempt to annihilate or force the displacement of civilians from our controlled zones. On February 28, 1983, a month before the death of my brother and Marianella García, the army sent several thousand troops into the Felipe Peña Front and massacred more than 150 people, including women, children and elderly, who were fleeing communities in Guazapa and seeking temporary refuge in the abandoned villages of Tenango and Guadelupe in the subzone of Cinquera.

Following our successes in the department of Chalatenango, we began to move our battalions of the Vanguard Units south, across Lake Suchitlán to the Felipe Peña front, just as my brother had jokingly predicted on the day of my departure more than a year before. How sad it was to return to this subzone with him dead, knowing that he would never see our proud columns of young combatants, experienced and armed to the teeth, arriving with the task of clearing the subzones of this front.

When I arrived at Cinquera with the detachment under my command, I went straight to the Bermuda hacienda, where my brother had been ambushed and killed. When I arrived at the site, I could see the remains of bodies still in place without knowing which one was my brother's. I also passed through Tenango and Guadelupe and found the streets leading into these villages strewn with the remains of the massacred population.

A few days after our arrival, we carried out our first military maneuver, which consisted of the capture of Cinquera and several army positions in the elevations around Tejutepeque and Jutiapa. After that, we launched a second maneuver against military positions in Zapote, Azacualpita and Coyote Hill, peripheral to Tejutepeque.

On September 23, 1983, we attacked army positions in the town of Tenancingo, capturing more than 60 soldiers with several officers who had cornered themselves in the town church when it became clear that we were about to overrun them. In desperation and panic, the officers had ordered the air force to bomb the town in an effort to halt our advance and eliminate our forces. They were willing to kill as many civilians as it took to do that and ended up killing many. They also killed 35 townspeople with a 500-pound bomb dropped squarely on the site where volunteers from the Green Cross had concentrated survivors of the first bombing in preparation for evacuation.

When I entered the first houses at the entrance of the town, I encountered a tragic scene. One of the houses had been serving as a public health clinic, and six women, some of whom were pregnant, lay dead on the floor in puddles of their own blood. I also found a seriously injured young boy of about eight years of age whom I helped to leave the destroyed building and join a group of civilians who were in the process of leaving the town. I realized years later that this moment was filmed and reported by CNN.

With these operations, the subzone of Cinquera was left free of government presence, another "liberated territory" under the control of the revolutionary forces. And so our Vanguard Units returned to Chalatenango, where we began to focus our sights on several larger and more strategic targets.

On December 30, 1983, we overran and seized the military fortress of the Fourth Brigade in El Paraíso (an installation that U.S. advisers had assured would be impossible to defeat). At the same time, we attacked the military barracks in the city of Chalatenango in order to ensure that reinforcements could not be sent to El Paraíso. With these important victories, we were demonstrating to all that there was no military target in the country that we could not defeat.

In the installations of El Paraíso, there was a huge warehouse of weapons, munitions and other military equipment, so all of us took advantage of the opportunity to exchange our aging and well-used equipment (M-16 rifles, ammunition and uniforms) for new ones, frustrated by the fact that we had to leave behind almost two-thirds of the supplies in storage. We also captured about 250 soldiers, who were later handed over to the International Red Cross.

Our victories were significant, but our losses were high as well. The fighting was fierce, and, on several occasions, I witnessed the tragic scene of seriously wounded young combatants grabbing their rifles and taking their own lives, overcome by depression at having been left without arms, legs, hearing or sight, or with partial paralysis.

In spite of the suffering, however, our morale was generally high, and life began to improve. Our territories under guerrilla control grew and became more stable and more difficult for government troops to penetrate. It became easier to obtain access to food, medicines and inputs for production, and our contacts with the civilian population on the margins of our fronts became more frequent.

Following all of these operations, our Vanguard Units were dispersed as we began to operate again in smaller units in standard guerrilla style. My detachment was placed under the command of another comrade, and I was assigned to the political-military command of the subzones of Cinquera, Guazapa and El Paisnal, a position that had belonged to my brother before his death.

In 1989, I resumed command of a military unit with which I participated in the second guerrilla offensive at the national level, "Hasta el
Tope" ("Until the End"). Similar to our first national offensive in January
1981, we had planned this strategic initiative, coordinated among all of
the five organizations of the FMLN, in an effort to bring the war to an
end and force a negotiated solution to our struggle. On this occasion,
however, we were much stronger and better prepared with accumulated
experience and the lessons of a decade of war.

After several weeks of fierce fighting, we were again unable to win our
definitive victory, primarily due to a lack of adequate weapons (especially
surface-to-air missiles to confront the air war of the government). Nevertheless, we demonstrated to the world that we were invincible and forced
a more serious effort to reach a negotiated solution to the conflict.

I spent those days in the San Salvador Volcano just south of the
capital city, along with our high command. The Air Force attacked us
daily and, on one occasion, bombed from five in the morning until six in
the afternoon. It was under these circumstances that we lost our beloved
comrade and head of the Vanguard Units, Dimas Rodríguez. My radio
operator and wife since 1986 was with me and frequently commented
that, either from the bullets or shrapnel from the bombs, we were all
surely going to die.

Shortly after the offensive of 1989, I received the sad news of the death
of my younger brother, Felipe, who was living in Apopa at the time. He had
not joined the guerrillas as a youth but had become a small businessman
instead and, one day, was shot dead by a gang of thieves who arrived at his
store to rob him. A few years earlier, my older sister, Juana, who had joined
the guerrillas in the eastern part of El Salvador, had returned gravely ill to
my mother's house and died there as well. With the death of both siblings,
I instructed my mother, along with my remaining brothers and sisters, to
leave Apopa and move to Santa Tecla or Santa Ana. The constant "guinda"
(forced retreat) of my family was not over yet.

In 1991, as a negotiated solution to the war began to appear more
feasible, I was sent to Cuba for surgery on both of my knees, destroyed
by so many years of climbing and descending mountains. And my wife,

Isabel, accompanied me. We were there for six months, and on the way back, we passed through Nicaragua, but my short stay in that country left me disappointed at the sight of so many of our comrades, especially directors at the national level, accommodating themselves to a bourgeois lifestyle while in the war fronts of El Salvador, young revolutionaries were still suffering and putting their lives at risk to build a more just and democratic nation. There was good news also, however. My wife informed me that she was pregnant.

By the time we returned to El Salvador and the subzone of Cinquera (Radiola) in the Felipe Peña Front, peace had been signed, and our guerrilla forces were in the process of disarmament and demobilization. The end of the war was being celebrated by all, but I was concerned to find our combatants in a lethargic state of exaggerated inactivity, sleeping through much of the day.

There was great uncertainty about the future, especially for our younger fighters who knew only war. They had no experience of life under "normal" conditions. They felt insecure and overwhelmed by concerns for their security, wondering if the army would respect the Peace Accords or if they would begin to pursue and kill guerrillas again.

For my part, I had always been deeply moved by the sight of so much suffering on the part of the civilian population in our zones of control, and I recalled now with great sadness the long columns of civilians fleeing in "guinda" from their communities of origin while we provided security and guidance to them and helped them slip through the enclosing circle of government troops in search of temporary refuge.

My mind returned frequently to the images of exhausted peasant women walking silently through the night and carrying young children, domestic animals and other household items that they knew would be killed or destroyed if the army found them. I also remembered the old people walking with the help of family members, but most of all, I remembered the small children, barefoot, malnourished with their rib cages protruding, who, if given the opportunity to draw, could only produce images of planes dropping bombs, helicopters machine-gunning communities and soldiers killing family members.

I remembered the cases of young babies suffocated by their own mothers or fathers if they began to cry when the army was nearby, and all of the children lost to the powerful currents of the rivers people were forced to cross in order to escape certain death at the hands of the military. And I asked myself, "Where are these people today? The people who supported us informed us when the enemy was close by, who sent their youth to fight in our ranks and helped us to sustain the dream. Will they have survived this war?"

With the signing of the Peace Accords, the FMLN became a legal party, and I was appointed as secretary general for the department of Cuscatlán, where I had served as a guerrilla. Then, in 1994, I was elected mayor of Suchitoto, one of the most important cities in the department, and served for four terms in that office, administering the affairs of the municipality and promoting sustainable development projects for the communities in the jurisdiction of Suchitoto.

Strategies and tactics for winning the war were traded for initiatives to strengthen local government and resolve the needs of the population without ideological or religious bias. All of my energy became focused on resolving the challenges of the day in the municipality and assuring access to clean water, electrical power, good roads, adequate housing, sanitation, education, the promotion of tourism and culture, the repopulation of communities displaced by the war and getting legal documents of all kinds in order.

Our activities were guided by a concern for citizen participation and transparency, for which the experiences that I had accumulated during my days in social movements before the war proved useful.

My role as mayor led me to establish and maintain contacts with people and entities with whom I had been in confrontation during the war, including the U.S. embassy in El Salvador and representatives of the State Department in Washington, D.C., thinking always how curious and ironic life can be if one is open to change and the new challenges it can bring.

Today, together with my wife and comrade of so many years, Isabel, I operate our small tourist business on the shores of the beautiful Lake Suchitlán, a lake that we crossed frequently in small boats during the war to move our troops between the Felipe Peña front where I am currently located and the Apolinario Serrano front in Chalatenango to the north and to transfer our wounded combatants to hospitals in the north for treatment.

There are people in the world who consider those of us who went to war as terrorists or delinquents. They believe that we liked carrying weapons and liked to kill. The truth is that we hate all of these things, and none of this explains our reasons for going to war. The truth is that we saw no alternative in our country to armed struggle and that we perceived our struggle as just and motivated by love for the poor.

It was a battle to eliminate social inequality and build a more dignified life with true participative democracy. It was a necessary effort to defeat militarism, to halt repression and the overexploitation of disenfranchised workers, and to assert our rights. That is why we fought and that is why we sacrificed ourselves to the point of giving our lives. Someone who does not have a social conscience or feel love for others could never have endured the sacrifices that we made.

In the guerrilla movement, we had a document called "The 15 Principles of the Guerrilla." One of those principles was respect and love for the people. Any violation of this principle was punished.

We accept that the war led us to deviate from these principles at certain moments, even to commit crimes against humanity, as revealed in the UN Truth Commission report of 1993, but it was not our common practice.

Forty years later, I remain here among my people, enjoying the natural beauty of the landscape of El Salvador and the hardworking and struggling men and women around me. I am still in this territory, famous now for its tourism, culture and history of which I am a part. Lake Suchitlán greets me each morning, and the slopes of the Guazapa volcano remind me of the dreams as well as the failures of the past, while China Mountain, off to the west, throws its shadows over the village of my birth, El Tablon, where my social conscience took root under a beloved pastor, Rutilio Grande, and the dreams of utopia began to occupy my mind.

Rosario

Anecdotes from war

My name is Rosario and I am originally from the town of Meanguera in the mountains of northern Morazán province. I am the sixth born of a family of nine siblings, making a living by working the land, planting henequen to make rope, raising a few heads of cattle, producing basic grains (corn, beans, rice) and marketing all of these products.

During my early childhood, I studied during my early years in Meanguera, but our school only went to third grade; so, in order to continue, I had to move to the nearby town of Osicala, where I lived with an uncle and cousins until reaching ninth grade in 1980.

Since the 1970s, my older brothers had participated in the clandestine guerrilla cells being formed in that area, so it should not be surprising that, between my studies, household chores and farming, I began to support the activities of the revolutionary movement by doing surveillance and warning whenever the National Guard or the Police were nearby.

When security forces were detected advancing on our communities, we set off small explosive devices called "papas" to warn the population and our guerrilla fighters of their coming. This was before we had radios for communication, so I also collaborated as a "correo" (messenger), carrying information and orders (or sometimes explosives) from one guerrilla camp to another.

One day during the 1980s, while I was in class, one of my brothers came to inform me that I needed to carry out an important task that involved traveling to Villa del Rosario, a town of some distance, to meet one of our commanders who was returning from Nicaragua to join our forces in northeastern El Salvador after having participated in that country in the insurrection to overthrow the Somoza dictatorship. My task was to meet him and guide him to one of our "safe houses" in San Miguel, ensuring that he arrived safely.

He was a quiet and serious man, speaking little as we walked the trails of the rugged countryside leading from Villa del Rosario, passing through Torola and the village of Carrisal and arriving finally at the town of Carolina, where we were able to catch a bus for San Miguel. I then left him in the designated "safe house" and returned home alone to resume the routine of my life, my studies and my daily chores, mission completed.

Little by little, my incorporation into the revolutionary struggle was intensified, not only because of the participation of my brothers but also because of the growing repression against the humble peasant families of Morazán, along with the army's policy of compulsory recruitment of young people and the sexual harassment of young women by military authorities.

I remember to this day, while living in Osicala, being awoken one morning in my uncle's house to the sound of army trucks passing by en route to Meanguera, Jocoatique, Mozote and the other villages north of the Torola River. I ran to the top of a nearby hill, and from there, I could see that the trucks were full of soldiers. I could also see my family's house, where my mother lived with my siblings, and, at that moment, smoke was rising into the air in that area, so I shouted to my uncle, "I'm leaving because they are burning our house", and I left Osicala on foot for Meanguera as fast as I could run.

I ran with all my strength on the "black road" (as we referred to the only paved road in the area) that leads to Perquín and arrived at the town of Meanguera at one in the afternoon. Trucks with soldiers were still passing on the same road, and an old man from the town who was a friend of my family stopped me and said, "Where are you going? There are only soldiers ahead, and they are going to kill you if they see you. Come and hide until this is over." I resisted going with the old man, but he grabbed my arm and forced me to hide in an old storage bin for corn, where I spent the next five days.

The soldiers showed no signs of leaving, so one morning, at about two am, I escaped from the storage bin and went out in search of my family. I was told that the families of the town had taken refuge nearby in a place called La Guacamaya, so I hurried there and found my family. Following this incident, I didn't return to my uncle's house but remained in the guerrilla camps around Meanguerra and Guacamaya.

My first mission, as a young guerrilla, was to accompany the political cadres of our organization in the task of carrying out a census of families residing in the Torola River basin in the areas of Agua Blanca, Cacaopera and Joateca. My other mission continued to be carrying messages among the guerrilla camps, covering the area of the Guacamaya to the Villa el Rosario Lagoon, from the camps called La Curva, El Tablón to the area of Corinto, Sociedad, to a camp called Hecho Andrajo and to the mining area of San Sebastián de Santa Rosa de Lima in the province of la Union.

I traveled at times on horseback but more commonly on foot. In the area of the mines of San Sebastián, I was sent one day to pick up a European named Rogelio Poncel, a Belgian priest who came to the front to accompany our struggle. I remember that we had to walk all day with him sweating profusely and turning red like a tomato.

Later, when the camps were formalized, and the guerrilla forces were better organized, I met up again with the commander whom I had taken months before to his meeting in the "safe house" of San Miguel. On this occasion, however, he was more talkative as we were beginning to plan the Final Offensive of January 10, 1981, coordinated with all of the guerrilla organizations at the national level.

I had been selected to be part of his communications team for the main attack on the military barracks in San Francisco Gotera. At that time, we had a few radios, but they were unreliable and rarely functioned, so messengers like me were required to cross through large stretches of battlefields with bullets and mortars flying over our heads and bombs exploding everywhere in order to ensure communications among our field commanders.

The attack on the military barracks in San Francisco Gotera, the first strategic military operation for many of our combatants, went badly for us, finally forcing us to retreat with a deep sense of failure. At that decisive moment, I had to cross the line of fire again to deliver a handwritten note to Commander Carmelo with orders to withdraw.

They were dangerous times filled with dangerous tasks that could lead to death at any second, but our lives since before the war, scratching out a living on the infertile hillsides of Morazan, had taught us not to be too attached to life, and I am proud to say that I was always able to overcome my fears and fulfill my duties to the best of my abilities.

As we returned from the battle, I met up with several other of my comrades on our way out of the city of San Francisco Gotera and received the tragic news that one of my brothers had been killed during the fighting. I felt so heartbroken that I went into an abandoned house to cry alone. While I was inside the house, I found a small doll that was so beautiful I could not resist sticking it in my backpack and carrying it with me when I left.

On the way back to our camps, I was still crying about the loss of my brother, but when we arrived at our scheduled meeting point, I became filled with joy to find all of my brothers present and well. No one in my family had died. It had been a mistake. And my joy was even greater as I recalled that, for the first time in my life, I had a doll.

After the failed attack on the San Francisco Gotera barracks, other battles of a lower scale followed. Our forces continued to train in the tactics and techniques of war with both theoretical and practical, even ideological, preparation supported by two former officers of the government army, Mena Sandoval and Marcelo Cruz Cruz, who had rebelled against the dictatorship, together with all of their troops, during the first days of the January offensive and had joined the revolutionary struggle.

The war was not always a serious or tragic affair. It also brought moments of humor capable of bringing light to the dark night and breaking the routine of horror and sacrifice. One such incident occurred during an attack we carried out against government troops stationed in my village of Meanguera in 1981.

I was assigned to carry mortars for an RPG-7 (Chinese-made mortar launcher) while another comrade carried the cannon. The mortars were large and heavy, and I could barely hold them along with my own M-2 carbine.

Our squad was also accompanied by a journalist from our Radio Venceremos, who we called Maravilla, and I asked him to help me with one of the mortars, but he responded negatively for fear that they might explode in our hands. Later that day, during an intense battle with the army, Maravilla was still by my side in the trenches when we suddenly heard a loud noise coming in our direction through the tall elephant grass, and my first thought was that an entire company of government troops was coming at us.

We all tensed up, and Maravilla shouted, "Here come the cuilios" (the name given by the guerrillas to government security forces). "Hurry! Shoot! Attack!" At that moment, we loaded a mortar into the cannon, and I was aiming and ready to fire when a large and terrorized pig came charging out of the grass and into the open. In the midst of our relief and the raucous laughter of my comrades, I could not stop thinking about the mess we would have caused for this poor animal if we had hit it with an RPG-7.

By the end of 1981, our communications systems had improved greatly, and I was assigned to train as a radio operator ("radista") for operational as well as strategic communications (for larger military maneuvers). It meant that I would still be accompanying our troops into combat, assuring effective radio communications, but I would no longer be involved in the act of combat itself. The truth is that I loved being a combatant – and we had a number of women comrades filling this role along with the men – but orders were to be obeyed, and I remained in this position for the remainder of the war, accompanying our commanders in all of their military operations.

In all of those years, death was always lurking, even with the simplest of tasks, like the day at the beginning of the rainy season in 1983 when we planned a simple operation on the margins of our controlled zone in an effort to retrieve several plastic tarps off passing trucks to serve as protection against the heavy rains that were coming.

By five in the morning, we had set up a checkpoint on a lonely stretch of highway from Cacaopera to Lolotiquillo, where trucks covered with tarps frequently passed. There was a local National Guard post in the nearby town of Cacaopera, so we stopped almost all of the cars and checked IDs on the lookout for military personnel, although few of our comrades knew how to read.

About 15 minutes into the operation, a pickup full of men suddenly arrived. Adonay, the comrade in charge of our operation and I were busy reviewing the IDs of a group of villagers who were passing by when the men in the pickup suddenly began to uncover G-3 rifles (weapons of choice of the National Guard) that were hidden in the bed of the truck and began shooting at us at close range.

Adonay yelled for me to drop to the ground, and I threw myself immediately against the hard dirt just as a loud blast took his life. The other comrades got away, and I was left alone, knowing that the guardsmen would want to capture me more than kill me, so I ran as fast as I could over the rugged terrain through the sparse forest and the thick underbrush with bullets whizzing over my head until I finally found myself in more familiar terrain. All that day, the army sent troops and helicopters to search the area, but I managed to get away unharmed and reach a previously agreed meeting point where the rest of my comrades were waiting.

In 1983, '84 and '85, I was assigned as a radio operator to our elite combat force, the Rafael Arce Zablah Brigade (BRAZ), with whom I accompanied strategic military operations throughout eastern El Salvador, from Perquin to the north of San Miguel, Cerro El Tigre, Jucuapa, passing through Tres Calles, Jucuaran, etc. In all of these regions, we were continuously greeted by villagers as we passed through their communities, and people frequently came out of their houses to offer us sodas or food.

On a trip to San Luis de la Reina, we arrived tired and sweaty at a small village, and people came to greet us, as usual. A local store owner offered me a soda, but I replied that I would prefer a beer. At that moment, the rest of my comrades fell silent, focused on my person and pointing at me while the owner of the store stood in the doorway as if paralyzed.

I didn't get my beer on that occasion, but I did get a strong scolding since it was forbidden to drink alcohol of any type on our fronts. I didn't know this rule until that moment and only ordered a beer because it seemed normal, given that, as a small girl, I had watched a neighbor of my family in Meanguera drink a beer every day, saying that it was food.

In 1984, during a meeting in our strategic command center in the area of San Gerardo, north of San Miguel, with some of our most important political and military cadres present, I had another near-death experience when we were attacked by ground artillery, A-37 jet bombers and a massive number of helicopters dropping out of the sky leaving thousands of paratroopers in an attempt to encircle and annihilate our forces. This type of maneuver always generated enormous fear (sometimes panic), and this particular operation surpassed all others that I had survived over the early years of the war. Like the others, however, it generated extremely high levels of adrenaline, providing the alertness and physical stamina needed to resist and survive.

Government troops quickly had us surrounded, and everyone was in disarray, grabbing weapons and open backpacks with the contents hanging out as we scrambled to find a way of breaking through the closing enemy lines.

A comrade of mine and fellow radio operator had a personal short-wave radio that we all used for listening to music and world news, a luxury on a war front and our only contact really with the outside world, and the radio fell from her backpack as we ran together across an open field. The army had us in their sites and was firing at us with a 50-caliber machine gun, but I reacted without hesitation and ran back to retrieve the radio with bullets whizzing by my head and with my comrades shouting for me to come back. But we were able to recover our treasured radio.

In the year 1985, during the month of December, I began to perceive strange changes in my body, symptoms that I had never felt, and I realized suddenly that I was pregnant. We were camped at the time in the southeastern area of Usulutan near Jucuarán, a highly unstable zone with frequent and fierce combats with the army. It was there that I was introduced to this new and amazing experience and this miniature life that was already growing inside me.

Our troops were moving constantly between Jucuaran, Cerro El Tigre, Las Marías and the north of San Miguel, and that is how I spent practically my entire time of pregnancy, complying with the demands of my job as a radio operator, accompanying commander Chamba, Geremias or Raul Mijango.

One day during this period, we were camped in a small house on the slopes of the Cerro, El Tigre, hidden by the trees of a large coffee plantation, when government troops suddenly attacked us from several different directions. A fierce and prolonged shootout ensued, but my principal concern at the time was protecting my baby.

The eight and a half months of my pregnancy on the war fronts were, for me, the most difficult moments I experienced in the twelve years that the war lasted. We were constantly under attack by air and by land and surrounded by military checkpoints that made my transfer to a more stable and hygienic environment impossible until I was almost ready to give birth.

Nevertheless, I was finally able to leave our front to bring my first son into this turbulent world, and I remained with him in the home of collaborators for the next 15 months. When I finally returned to Morazan, planning had begun for the next guerrilla offensive at the national level, scheduled for November 1989. It would be called "Hasta el Tope" (Until we win).

I arrived in the northern area of Morazan on the Sabaneta mountain north of Perquin, an area of cool climate, given the altitude, and controlled by our guerrilla forces. We immediately began the difficult process of strengthening our communications capabilities in preparation for the offensive, given the need to ensure excellent coordination among the five guerrilla organizations of the FMLN in war zones around the country.

This required an endless chain of extensive messages that had to be copied and deciphered. Some of the more strategic messages were sent and received with double encryption. Communications quickly became the centerpiece of the planning process and the preparations for the coming offensive, and all of the radio operators busied ourselves repairing, cleaning and testing our equipment, preparing our secret codes ("claves"), both operational and strategic and organizing logistics at all levels.

I was told that I would be assigned to San Miguel during the offensive, so, when all was ready, we left from Perquin headed for this large eastern city. We walked mostly at night with hundreds of heavily armed comrades, hiding during the day so as not to be detected, and, upon arrival, hid ourselves on the outskirts of the city until the fighting began on the afternoon of November 11, 1989.

We held our positions for several weeks in San Miguel under the bombs, mortars, bullets and helicopters, as did other sister organizations of the FMLN in all of the other important urban centers around the country. The government had been surprised by our levels of coordination, force and determination and tried at all costs to dislodge us, including the indiscriminate bombing of civilian neighborhoods, but we held our ground, frequently with the support of the civilian population.

Those in charge of communications during the battle struggled to maintain our calm at all times in spite of the blood and the horror around us in order to continue transmitting and receiving communications from our troops around the city and in other parts of the country to assure the adequate coordination of attacks and rapid responses to any emergencies confronted by our troops. They were, without a doubt, the most intense days of my life.

After prolonged fighting, day and night, we withdrew when it became impossible for the other forces to hold their positions. The main objectives of the offensive, to destabilize the government of then-President Alfredo Cristiani and force the government to enter serious negotiations in search of an end to 12 years of civil war, were attained. Nevertheless, several years more of military confrontations, combined with persistent diplomatic efforts, were required before the parties came together to sign peace accords.

With the end of the war, I continued to work in communications for the demobilization and disarmament of all of our comrades who were still on the war fronts. I traveled frequently to the headquarters in El Salvador of the United Nations, ONUSAL, at the Sheraton Hotel, and, from there, helped coordinate the disarmament process of the northeastern front. As reinsertion proceeded, my life began to change dramatically from camp life to home life with a spouse and child, as well as new opportunities for self-improvement through study which I pursued, graduating with a degree in Business Administration.

In the war, I lost many dear friends and relatives, including four brothers, an uncle, seven cousins and even the love of my early school days. But I also fell in love with the father of my children, with whom we continue to share this life as a couple and as comrades who continue to struggle for El Salvador every day of our lives.

I have never regretted having participated in this revolution that, for many of us, was driven by the dream of building a better nation. I grew up in the war; I shared the experiences of the war with a large and loving family in the People's Revolutionary Army (ERP), and, together with that brotherhood, we always struggle to ensure that the historical memory of our times in the mountains will not be distorted or erased.

Ana

My name is Ana María Menjívar. I was born in 1953 in a small rural village called San Rafael La Bermuda, located about four kilometers from the town of Suchitoto and the beautiful lake, Suchitlán, in the department of Cuscatlán. Our area was in conflict since the military dictatorship of Arturo Armando Molina decided to build the "Cerron Grande" dam on the Lempa River, creating a man-made lake (the largest body of fresh water in El Salvador) that flooded entire communities along with the agricultural lands they depended upon to feed their families.

I didn't have the luxury of much formal schooling in my childhood as my time was spent accompanying my mother and siblings in the harvesting of coffee on the plantations of the oligarchy around the Guazapa volcano or cleaning the homes of the wealthier families of San Salvador for a salary of misery. As was customary in the countryside, I married young, at 18 years of age, without much awareness of the responsibilities that such a decision implied, and I gave birth to my first daughter a year later.

I didn't understand much at the time about injustice and the exploitation of workers in my country. I simply lived the reality. But I did understand that as a poverty-stricken young girl and later as a grown woman, I would have to work hard to survive. In recent times, Suchitoto and Lake Suchitlán have become attractive places for tourism in El Salvador, but during the years of my childhood, at the end of the 70s, a poor, humble and desperate peasant population risked their lives daily in a struggle for a piece of land large enough to produce and feed their families against the greed of an oligarchy blind to human suffering and allied with a corrupt military bent on keeping us down.

From a young age, I was restless and eager to learn new things. Whenever the opportunity arose, I would participate in educational programs, whether they be on health, child-rearing, agriculture, sewing, or any other relevant topic, and I shared what I learned with my neighbors in San Rafael, thus gaining the recognition, trust and affection of the people. In this way, I became a leader and a highly sought-after person in my community in times of crisis.

I enjoyed people and living together in the community, especially among women, and before long, we had developed a strong community organization in San Rafael that promoted work in collectivity. I also reached out to the Catholic Church and helped coordinate Caritas food distribution programs. Our community was united in spite of our poverty, and we lived with a true spirit of community.

We learned about the social doctrine of the Church, Liberation Theology and the preferential option for the poor. We also learned the words of archbishop Romero about our human rights, and we were pulled by Rutilio Grande's work with Christian Base Communities in Aguilares and El Paisnal. After the death of Rutilio and then Monsignor, we continued to promote the struggle of the poor through our local parish priest, Inocencio Alas, known as Chencho, promoting social awareness, commitment, love and brotherhood.

When the first grassroots popular organizations began to appear in our area, and later, when these same organizations began to link up with guerrilla organizations fighting for democracy and a halt to repression, the women and men of all ages from San Rafael, of all ages, began to discreetly and silently join their ranks. Decades of electoral fraud and state-sponsored repression finally reached appalling levels and convinced us that the only way to change our country was by means of armed struggle, and several of my relatives were among the first to join the guerrilla ranks.

I knew early on that my contribution to the struggle would not be in the military area, but I joined the guerrilla organizations all the same and dedicated myself in any way necessary to their political, diplomatic, humanitarian and logistical activities through twelve years of civil war and beyond.

Given the years of awareness-raising and organizing work that we had been promoting in San Rafael for some time, the local military authorities, the oligarchy and the death squads viewed us with suspicion and hatred, and one day, we received the news that San Rafael was on their radar at the National Guard post in Suchitoto and that a territorial map on the wall of the commanding officer displayed a large red dot on San Rafael, indicating that it was a beehive of subversive activity. It was only a short time after that before we began to see the proof of this rumor.

The death squads and the National Guard in our area began harassing any male in a leadership role, so our husbands and sons began to abandon our homes each night as darkness fell to sleep in the surrounding hills. And it was not long before women and children had to join them.

One day, the National Guard came to my house looking for my husband, who was the treasurer of our local cooperative. To protect against theft, we kept the cooperative's funds buried, and the officer in charge demanded that I tell him where the money was hidden. I was thankful that my husband was not there at the time because it probably would have meant his death, but I was also fearful for my own life and that of my children. I remained firm, however, and refused to reveal the hiding place of our cooperative's funds, so they threatened to rape me, and I began to fear that they were going to leave my young children orphaned. Nevertheless, I found the strength and courage to resist, and they finally gave up, allowing us to preserve the hard-earned savings of our cooperative

In the years that followed, the repression continued to grow in our area. The National Guard raided our community frequently, threatening everyone, while the Army and Air Force fired mortars and dropped 500-pound bombs on our houses, fields and outlying areas. The community and its outlying areas. Our husbands and sons, many of whom had moved to nearby guerrilla camps by that time, responded to government harassment by ambushing the soldiers, and life quickly became unbearable.

Death squads also came to rob us and rape women, sometimes in front of their own families. On one occasion, a leader from our community whom we called "Miquita" was murdered, and his face disfigured with acid. The cruelty was beyond our worst nightmares and so inhuman.

On another occasion, soldiers found a group of women, some of whom were pregnant, returning to our village with large bundles of firewood on their heads for use in cooking the family meals. They were all killed in cold blood and left along the roadside as a warning to anyone who might consider opposing the ruling military regime. The people who arrived later to help the women found all of them dead and reported that several of the unborn babies were still moving in their mother's womb.

Many of my contributions during those years were in the area of health and first aid, and I was frequently called upon to treat wounded combatants. I was still a born leader willing to risk my life for the revolution and serve in a wide variety of functions. On one occasion, the National Guard captured my husband's brother on the road to San Martin, and I was asked to go quickly to the site to provide witness to his innocence, insisting that he was not a guerrilla in order to avoid his being disappeared or killed. We arrived just in time to save him from certain death, but I couldn't prevent guardsmen from taking him prisoner, first to Suchitoto and then to the National Police in San Salvador.

The next day, I went to San Salvador to bring him food and to seek the support of opposition political parties and international human rights organizations to get him freed. When I arrived at the jail of the National Police, I found a long line of women also looking for relatives and loved ones who had been captured. It took almost a month before I was able to obtain the freedom of my husband's brother, and he looked like a dead man walking, pure skin and bone, when I first saw him as he left the jail. He later told me that he had been in a cell with a single rusty water faucet that provided only a few drops of water per minute and that he had survived mainly on fish bones that were thrown to him from time to time by his guards.

During all these years, death was always near, and I survived only because God is great. On March 17, 1980, days before the assassination of Monsignor Romero, a group of young guerrilla fighters, including one of my brothers, Manuel, 13 years old at the time, was sent to put up a roadblock at the turnoff for San Rafael in an effort to prevent the National Guard from coming to our community. As part of that same operation, other guerrilla units had been sent to the hacienda at La Colima in support of workers who were demanding a more just wage.

During the operation, twelve young combatants, including two women, were killed, and twenty others were captured, including my brother.

I had been assigned the task of bringing food to the combatants manning the roadblock, but at five in the morning, when I was on my way, I was intercepted by another young comrade who was also carrying food and insisted on bringing mine as well, saving me the trip.

Approximately thirty minutes after his departure, a burst of heavy gunfire was heard from the area of the barricade, and when the young comrade did not return, I went to see what was happening. I proceeded with caution until I reached the site, and I walked with great care until I reached the site, where I found the headless body of the young comrade lying among the undergrowth on the side of the road. I recognized him from his clothing but soon found his head lying nearby, with his testicles stuffed into his mouth. I continued searching and found two young females, also dead, who had participated in the roadblock and had been sexually mutilated as well by the soldiers, with their breasts sliced off.

My brother had been captured, but I was eventually able to free him by insisting on his innocence and the fact that he had simply been caught in the crossfire. The brutality and cruelty of the images I had witnessed remained with me for many years afterwards, however, along with the profound sadness I felt at the death of the young comrade who had saved my life.

We were able to retrieve a number of the corpses of the young people who had been killed, and we carried them to San Salvador, where an angry march accompanied them to the National Cathedral, where they were buried in the basement where the remains of monsignor Romero currently rest.

Following this operation, the climate of repression against San Rafael became unbearable. Death squads burned my house, leaving my family with the clothes on our backs and a small bit of food that we had hidden. Then, just before Christmas 1980, the population of San Rafael La Bermuda joined the ranks of the thousands of families across the country forced to flee from their communities of origin in the face of indiscriminate bombings and the scorched earth policies of the Armed Forces. I still remember with sadness the day that we left our homes, our lands and the memories of a lifetime.

We were accompanied by volunteers from the Green Cross led by Eliseo Franco, a brave and dedicated young man who would accompany the long years of displacement of our community until his eventual death. Under a torrent of mortars, bombs and bullets, Eliseo arrived at my door with the white and green flag of the Green Cross, shouting that we were in grave danger and that we needed to evacuate immediately. I hesitated for only a moment, hiding behind a small tree on a hillside up from my house and watched with tears as the men of the death squads broke the simple door, knocked down the walls that had not burned already, stole my few belongings, killed my breeding animals and finished burning everything that could not be stolen.

In addition to his work with the Green Cross, Eliseo was a mason who had been hired by the government to rebuild a museum on the site of the former Bermuda Hacienda, a few miles from our community, San Rafael. He offered us shelter at his construction site, but it was only a matter of days before the military found us and eventually forced us to move again.

I was pregnant with my fifth child at the time, and my husband had incorporated into the local guerrilla column of the National Resistance, one of the five-member organizations of the FMLN. We were mostly women and children in La Bermuda, and without our men to protect us, the soldiers took advantage of the opportunity to abuse the women and harass the small children and elderly. They threatened to beat us, or worse, each time we refused to provide them with information on the location of guerrilla camps and forced several of our women to serve them as cooks. On one tragic occasion, they captured and carried away a group of elderly men whom we never saw again.

The army arrived one day with several large trucks and informed us that we were being taken to the abandoned prison in the nearby town of Suchitototo, several kilometers away. The idea of moving again and to a prison generated a strong feeling of anguish, frustration and resentment among us all. Also, our men in the guerrilla camps nearby were concerned about the risk of losing the proximity to their families.

But the soldiers would not relent and began throwing people, including women, children and elderly, onto the trucks like sacks of potatoes. After they had departed with the first group, those of us who remained decided that we had to leave. When darkness came our husbands and sons arrived from their nearby camps, my husband among them, to analyze together our options. Several families made the decision to accompany their husbands and sons to their guerrilla camp, but those of us who had young children, like me, opted better to go to a Green Cross base in San Salvador.

I wanted to be with my husband, but with five small children, camp life in the middle of war was not very feasible. So, we said a tearful and painful goodbye with the sadness of knowing that it could be the last time we saw each other, and, in fact, it was. My husband died in combat a few months later in Guazapa. To this day, we do not know where his body is buried, and my children live with the anguish and regret of never having known him.

We spent the next several months in a crowded urban setting with little air and sunlight, far from the open hills and ravines of San Rafael. We later moved to a vacant lot in the center of Santa Tecla where we joined other families displaced by the war from other regions of the country and, like us, under the temporary care of the Green Cross.

Through all of this, Eliseo never abandoned us, and with the help of a North American working with the international organization, Doctors of the World, we were finally transferred to a more suitable area in the municipality of Zaragoza, which we later named Betania.

We found a setting more accommodating to the needs and customs of peasant farmers. There were open fields and hillsides where we could plant our corn and beans, as well as a small river for fishing, bathing and washing clothes. The atmosphere was similar to our previous lives but with new norms pertinent to our condition as displaced families economically dependent on international cooperation for our housing, food, healthcare and security.

We also obtained the support of the Archdiocese of San Salvador and other international NGOs. Eventually, we began to organize our lives again, insisting always on the preservation of our revolutionary principles and values, our commitment to community and our intense dedication to our loved ones struggling in the war zones to the north, from where we had come.

As a first step in rebuilding our community, we organized ourselves to work collectively in the construction of our new homes, in agricultural production, in basic health care and education. We formed a cooperative with a communal store, a clinic where I was in charge, and a small school. We planted corn and beans, raised fish and held frequent community meetings to preserve our awareness of the current situation of the country and of our right to struggle for a better future. We were a peasant community again, although the tragedy of the last several years continued to torment us, along with the concerns for our relatives who had been left fighting on the war fronts.

Over the years, many of our relatives were killed in the struggle to free our people from dictatorship and end centuries of poverty, injustice and repression. And we did not allow forgetfulness, accommodation or self-pity in the face of this reality. Everyone worked and shared the responsibility for our future, even the young children. People with a few years of school taught children without any studies and I put my accumulated knowledge in health to work to strengthen our small clinic.

Families and entire communities in other areas of the country heard of our project and began to arrive in search of refuge, and our population grew to more than a thousand people. We always kept in touch with our relatives on the war fronts. We allowed the different revolutionary organizations of the FMLN to visit our community to give political follow-up to their social base. Over the years, several young people from Betania decided to leave our community and go to the front to join their relatives and friends in the struggle. Some of them died in combat during that period, including two of my brothers, several uncles, cousins, and so many dear friends.

After several years in Zaragoza, we received a donation to purchase land in the municipality of Rosario de Mora in the department of La Paz and the lowlands of Guazapa, near San Rafael, to which many of us dreamed of returning with plans of setting up an agricultural cooperative. Given these options, our community eventually divided with a portion remaining in Zaragoza while most of us transferred to Rosario de Mora, where we started all over again, building housing, planting corn and beans and giving rise to a new settlement.

From there, a few of us eventually returned to the lowlands of

Guazapa to be closer to our beloved San Rafael and our loved ones on the war fronts. I had maintained communication with the comrades of the Guazapa front over the years and I, like my mother, wanted to return there. Despite the danger involved, my mother needed her children, now grown up and fighting with the FMLN on the slopes of the Guazapa volcano and the lowlands below.

While living in Rosario de Mora, I frequently traveled to Guazapa and entered the war fronts to help get wounded people out, to support women in the front with small children, and to stay in touch with my brothers. On one of those visits, I helped extract a woman who had been severely burned, apparently by white phosphorus.

I never considered the risks to which I was exposing myself or my family, but I eventually realized that my movements were attracting the attention of military intelligence in Rosario de Mora. Then, I received information from reliable sources that the army had me on its list of subversives in the area and that my arrest was imminent.

Since I was the president of our cooperative during my time in Rosario, I had been called on one occasion to the local army barracks to answer questions about our cooperative and my functions as its president. Then, in November 1989, in the midst of the guerrilla offensive, "Hasta el Tope" (Until the end), a frustrated and angry military went crazy bombing civilian communities under FMLN control, capturing and disappearing citizens of suspicious appearance and slaughtering six Jesuit priests in the Central American University, UCA. In the case of Rosario de Mora, they staged a large attack by paratroopers helicoptered into the area, which, according to witnesses, had among their objectives the capture of my person.

Because of the real danger of being killed or disappeared at that moment, I decided to "disappear" myself. Dressed in a costume with a blond wig and my face covered, I grabbed my six children and, with only the clothes we carried, quietly found my way through the military encirclement and took the first public transportation we could find to Guazapa. En route, I met a man who recognized me and confirmed that the soldiers were asking for me by name, so I did not stop until I reached the Guazapa lowlands in the department of Cuscatlán, near Suchitoto. I arrived that afternoon at the community of La Mora, where I live to this day.

I communicated with my brother, German, who was camped with the guerrillas nearby. He suggested that I find a way to bring my mother to this community so that she could be close. My original intention was to return to San Rafael eventually, but the guerrilla organizations of Guazapa wanted me to set up and manage a community store in La Mora to justify bringing food, tools, shoes, clothing and other items of great need to the guerrillas into the zone.

Once the offensive ended in El Salvador's principal cities, the war returned to the countryside. We were challenged to learn how to coexist with both FMLN and government or military authorities. We struggled for the right to remain in our communities in the midst of a war with two opposing forces operating on the ground.

When the army entered our area, we had to accept its authority while demanding at the same time that this authority respect our rights as a civilian population without being harassed, in accordance with the "Geneva Convention". When the army was not in our territories, the FMLN was the authority that we obeyed, made easier by the fact that most of us supported their struggle. We referred to this tactic as "poder de doble cara" ("power with two faces").

There were army checkpoints that we had to pass through to enter or leave the area, and transporting supplies for the guerrillas was a dangerous enterprise requiring great creativity. When the military was present, we suffered from constant harassment and routine searches and interrogations, although it was clear that the military was feeling the pressure of the U.S. Congress to improve levels of respect for human rights.

By 1991, as negotiations to end the war were advancing, I was working with women's organizations at the national level, such as Las Dignas, and this allowed me to strengthen my own knowledge of gender issues through their courses. For my mother, it was a time of joy given the proximity of my younger brother, German, the only son she had left who was still fighting with the guerrillas. Whenever he could briefly escape from the demands of the war, he would come down from his camp on the slopes of the volcano and visit with us in our home as long as the army was not nearby.

This situation did not last, however. In May 1991, while the government of El Salvador and the FMLN guerrillas were approaching an end to the twelve-year war, government troops of the famous Atlacatl battalion invaded the Guazapa lowlands once again, and German and his comrades went out to confront them. He died in combat very close to our house.

They say that he found himself alone and in the open at one point during the battle but that he fought heroically against enormous odds until his ammunition ran out and he was seriously wounded. They caught him alive but killed him in cold blood, then disfigured his face with a knife to remove a gold bridge that he had in his teeth. When I saw his body, I did not realize that it was him and worried only about burying whoever was lying there.

I went to the command post of the Atlacatl battalion in La Mora to inform the officer in charge that the population of La Mora requested the body of the slain guerrilla and would assume responsibility for burying it. As I was talking, however, I gazed over to a small desk in the office and suddenly recognized the military beret and other gear that had been taken from the dead comrade and realized that it belonged to my brother.

I could not reveal to the officer that I was German's sister, given that family members of guerrillas ran the same risk as guerrilla fighters themselves, so I had to convince the officer in charge that I was simply a community leader requesting a body for burial in our cemetery to avoid contamination, while tears of anguish blurred my vision and threatened to betray me.

My brother's wife was pregnant at the time with her second child, and for several days after German's death, we had to endure the constant harassment from soldiers who came to buy food in our store, accusing us each time of being guerrilla sympathizers and insisting that we tell them where the guerrilla camps were. In my anger, I would always respond, "Why don't you go look for them, if you have the nerve, up in the Guazapa volcano"?

With the signing of the Peace Accord, I became fully involved in the land transfer program for ex-combatants, coordinating with the government-appointed Land Commission and negotiating prices with landowners. Given my lack of formal education, some doubted my ability to ensure the effectiveness and fairness of this process and tried to limit women's participation in general. Still, I worked hard and became an expert on the subject, fighting at every moment against the macho positions I encountered.

In the first elections after the war, the FMLN, now a legal political party, won the mayor's office of Suchitoto, and the space for women's participation in decision-making in the municipality began to expand little by little. With the FMLN in power, I was included in the list of potential functionaries on the mayor's slate in 1994. And that's where my involvement in the struggle for women's rights in my country began in earnest. In the first municipal government of the FMLN in Suchitoto, I was appointed as an alternate to the city council. Later, I served as a syndicate and in 2000, I was appointed full-time city councilwoman.

Over the years, my knowledge, experience and commitment to women's rights have deepened as I began to understand that political parties should not continue to divide and weaken us. In recent years, I have reflected a lot on the challenges of being a woman militant in a political party in my country. I now better understand the challenges of overcoming our ideological differences to focus on our needs and strategic demands, remembering that our struggle is for all and forever.

Roberto

My name is Roberto Orlando Cortez Cruz. I joined the humanitarian emergency and rescue organization, the Comandos de Salvamento, as part of their team of lifeguards on March 15, 1977, when I was just 14 years old. From the age of 21, I have served as the executive director of this highly regarded entity, proud of the humanitarian role we have played in some of the most difficult moments of my country's history.

From my first days with the Commandos 47 years ago, I have been clear about the challenges we confront in El Salvador and determined to ensure that our role will always be one of accompaniment and service, prioritizing the most marginalized sectors of our society and the popular-based organizations that struggle for social justice and democracy.

At the same time, we have remained impartial to those who most need our services, always serving anyone in need of help regardless of ideology or class while remaining faithful to the poorest of the poor in the complex reality of our country. This characteristic has defined us at all times, even when it meant being challenged or threatened by civil and military authorities. as occurred with frequency during the decades of the 1970s and 1980s.

My first experience confronting this challenge occurred in 1977 when a large concentration of students, workers, rural peasants and other members of a broad alliance of organizations, the Ligas Populares 28 de Febrero (Popular Leagues, 28th of February), along with human rights and church activists, marched in protest in San Salvador to oppose the latest electoral fraud perpetrated by the military dictatorship in power at the time. In those days, our institution only had one ambulance (actually a converted pickup), but when government security forces began to open fire on the population gathered in Hula Hula Park, we rushed to the scene to help.

Among the protesters were large numbers of women with young children and elderly who began to flee, along with the younger, more able-bodied marchers. Many others were severely wounded or dead and quickly began dropping to the street in large pools of blood. The scene, upon our arrival, was disastrous. Those who had not been killed immediately were being rounded up by the police. We spent that entire day with our simple makeshift ambulance transporting wounded to the nearby Rosales hospital or, when injuries were less severe, to our base to be provided with first aid.

That afternoon, we continued searching for the wounded, many of whom had gone into hiding. Even during the following day, we continued to find and treat wounded marchers hiding in the vicinity of the old Emporio Market. That day, when I saw with my own eyes how the police had massacred our people, I couldn't help but wonder, along with my colleagues, if these policemen who had murdered so many unarmed and innocent people didn't have a mother and children of their own?

In those days, being young was a crime in El Salvador, and no young person was safe, not even in one's own neighborhood, workplace or school. All of us in the Commandos at that time were young and primarily from poor communities, so we were frequently victims of repression, both at work and in our homes. In those difficult years, I lost many dear friends, most of whom had no links to popular organizations or political movements.

That was the atmosphere at the time. Nevertheless, instead of despairing and following a path of violence, like so many of our compatriots, the challenges of growing up poor in El Salvador drove us to dedicate ourselves to service. We understood and supported the struggles to change our country, but we chose to contribute to that effort by providing humanitarian services and, emergency aid and hope to the most threatened and vulnerable members of our society.

In March 1980, poor people in El Salvador were dealt a horrible blow with the assassination of our beloved pastor, Monsignor Oscar Arnulfo Romero. And the protests of sorrow and anguish were not long in coming as the popular organizations of students, workers, peasants and many other sectors of our society began to mobilize.

They took over a major plaza in the center of the capital city in front of the National Cathedral for two days, transporting Monsignor's coffin. At one point, in the midst of the concentration, a propaganda bomb was detonated, and the National Police, together with the National Guard and the army, stationed around the square and on the rooftops of the buildings in front of the Cathedral, began to shoot at the defenseless marchers.

Members of the Comandos de Salvamento were already present in the plaza, and our first reaction, along with everyone else, was to seek cover from the hail of bullets raining down upon us. People began to run in all directions in disarray, some trying to get into the Cathedral with the casket of Monsignor for cover.

Again, we saw how the women, men, children and elderly began to fall all around us, dead or wounded by the bullets. Others were crushed in the massive panic. We quickly organized ourselves and started trying to assist the wounded, transporting them to hospitals once we were able to move.

With the death of Archbishop Romero, El Salvador lost the last hope of avoiding civil war, and the violence increased throughout the country. The death squads became more active, and bodies began appearing along the highways and in the ravines near poor communities. Rural villages began to suffer from the incursion of government troops or indiscriminate bombings in an effort to halt the growth of FMLN guerrilla forces in the countryside.

In May 1980, we were called to the villages around the municipality of Las Vueltas near the Sumpul River in the northern province of Chalatenango. There, we witnessed evidence of the first case of the "scorched earth" policies being promoted by U.S. military advisers and the first wave of refugees forced to abandon their villages of origin and seek refuge in neighboring Honduras.

We had never seen an area in El Salvador so alone and abandoned, with houses in ruins and the population in flight. In some of the villages, it was clear that people had been cooking, and some ovens were still hot. It was a scene of collective panic and sudden flight (called "guinda" by the people). Still, the worst scenario was along the shores of the nearby Sumpul River, where people had tried to cross into Honduras seeking refuge but had been driven back and slaughtered by the Salvadoran and Honduran militaries. Many others, especially the elderly and young children, had drowned in the forceful current of the Sumpul River. Close to 600 people were killed by the two armies on that day.

We were accompanied at that moment by a representative of the Salvadoran Human Rights Commission who was documenting the massacre and had begun to coordinate the repatriation of the population that had managed to enter Honduras. I remember that we had arrived with two vans from the transport cooperative, ACIT, and two larger trucks in which we began loading survivors to be transported to the capital city where the catholic seminary, San José de la Montaña, was receiving displaced families and providing them with humanitarian aid.

The Comandos de Salvamento, between 1980 and 1981, also suffered casualties, due primarily to our work in support of displaced communities whom the authorities clearly identified as sympathizers of the FMLN. During that period, we suffered the loss of 18 colleagues, some of whom were killed in the full exercise of providing services to people in need. In other cases, young volunteers were taken from their homes and killed by the death squads who accused us of supporting guerrillas.

In January 1981, the guerrilla organizations of the FMLN called for their first general offensive at the national level with the unrealistic hope of bringing the war to a rapid victory. Our institution once again played a key role in saving lives, providing medical care, emergency aid and transport to hospitals wherever needed. And again, we suffered our own casualties.

Early in the fighting, one of our volunteers from our base in Ciudad Delgado, the capital city, was killed by a government soldier. And, over the next 15 days, security forces and death squads pulled five more volunteers from their homes, taking them to unknown destinations where they were tortured and killed. Days later, their bodies were found on the soccer fields of Mejicanos, Cuscatancingo and Soyapango. In the following months, 11 more of our rescuers were arrested and taken to unknown destinations, where they were eventually killed in the departments of San Miguel, Usulután, La Libertad and Santa Ana.

Our response to the increase in violence directed at our institution was always to continue our focus on providing a service to the neediest, improving and strengthening our emergency response capabilities for a population that was becoming increasingly vulnerable. The courage, commitment and willingness of our volunteers to work in conditions of extreme risk, entering at times situations of intense combat in order to save wounded civilians any place and at any time, was recognized worldwide. With this fame, we were gradually able to strengthen our ties both nationally and internationally with rescue organizations from other countries, with the media and with agencies of international cooperation from countries such as Germany, Holland, Norway, Spain, Belgium and others.

We also gained fame for being the first institution to extend our services to the most conflictive regions in the country's rural areas, where bloody battles were fought almost every day. Finally, we were recognized for being the first organization to assume the longer-term responsibility of providing systematic humanitarian aid to large concentrations of families displaced by the war in coordination with the Archdiocese of San Salvador of the Catholic Church.

In mid-June 1981, in coordination again with the representative of the non-governmental Human Rights Commission, we were called upon to attend to the victims of another large massacre of unarmed civilians in the municipality of Verapaz in the department of San Vicente. It was seven in the morning when we arrived with an ACIT bus, several trucks and the few ambulances that we possessed.

As soon as we arrived, we came upon a number of half-buried corpses in the courtyards of the houses where people had been surprised by the army in the early hours of that same day. We didn't find anyone alive who could tell us what had happened until we arrived at a small village church where some of the survivors were still hiding. There, we learned that government troops had entered the village without warning and simply began shooting anything that moved, including humans and domestic animals. Over 150 people were reportedly massacred that day. Almost immediately, we began the task of transporting these traumatized people to the seminary of San José de la Montaña in San Salvador.

Another of the massacres that took place that year occurred in the town of Tecoluca in the same municipality of San Vicente, in a place later known as La Cubita. In that case, the army again massacred an entire population of about 250 middle-aged men and women, all small-scale farmers, children and the elderly. This community had been advised to evacuate their village when it was learned that the military was approaching, but sadly, they did not heed. Instead, community leaders concentrated the people in a small evangelical church, thinking that they would be safe, but it was there that they all died.

The following year, the representative from the Human Rights Commission, with whom we had been coordinating much of our work as the massacres continued in the countryside, was herself assassinated. Her body was found half-buried on the coastal highway near the detour to the San Diego beach with signs of having been brutally tortured.

In 1982, approximately 500 heavily armed guerrilla combatants from the Revolutionary People's Army (ERP in Spanish), one of the strongest member organizations of the FMLN, attacked a National Guard post in the city of Berlin in the department of Usulután. The battle lasted through the night, but by dawn, most of the Guardsmen had surrendered and were being held prisoner in their jails.

We arrived at approximately 6:30 a.m. with four ambulances and two doctors with the objective of providing medical services to injured civilians. The guerrilla commander in charge gave us permission to attend to any civilians in need and to transfer any badly injured persons to the hospitals of the municipality of Santiago de María or San Miguel for the most serious cases. He also authorized us to provide any necessary care to wounded soldiers and guardsmen.

We withdrew from Berlin at about six o'clock that evening, but the Armed Forces, shamed by their defeat at the hands of guerrilla fighters, publicly accused us of having collaborated with the FMLN by persuading government troops to surrender. This accusation was obviously untrue, but it immediately endangered all of our young volunteers working around the country. And, on our way back to San Salvador, our ambulances were stopped at several army checkpoints where they made us get down, searched our vehicles, pointed their rifles at us, accused us of collaborating with the guerrillas and threatened us with death.

After this event, we were marked by the army's high command. As the days went by, we were forced to reduce our personnel, leaving only a minimal ambulance service managed by older volunteers since the army checkpoints became danger points for our young men and women, now accused directly of being guerrillas.

Over time, we regained our role in society, and with national and international support, our contribution to the well-being of our people during war gradually resumed its previous levels.

Towards the end of 1982, we convened a national meeting of all personnel to begin to analyze ways to become more effective in our work, to expand our areas of coverage and to improve our working methods. At the same time, we knew that we had to learn how to better coordinate our work, both with the guerrilla organizations of the FMLN and with the Armed Forces, in order to allow for a more strategic and effective response in support of victims living in the country's conflictive zones. Finally, we wanted to convince all sectors of our society of the importance of having an institution like the Commandos operating in our country.

With these goals in mind, we began to train our volunteers better in operating techniques for conflictive areas. International experts, including doctors from Mexico, Colombia, the U.S., Canada, Chile, Germany, Norway, Holland, Belgium and other countries, came to train us and teach us new ways of operating in combat zones or shelters for the displaced population, the type of medicine we should carry with us and the different techniques for extracting wounded under heavy fire.

All of these new strategies and institutional approaches strengthened our vision and response capacity. They also helped us build better relations with the FMLN general command and with some Salvadoran army commanders. Through our meetings with army officers, we reached minimal agreements that allowed us to enter conflictive zones under fire to rescue not only civilians but also wounded combatants from the FMLN and the Armed Forces, especially in cases in which they would surely die without our aid.

But, for most police and security forces personnel, we continued to be perceived as subversives, terrorists or communists – the simple fact of identifying oneself as a Comando de Salvamento remained dangerous. We always had to be sure that we carried our personal as well as institutional documents, but we ran the risk of being accused, captured, tortured or killed. For those of us who worked at night, especially when there was a curfew or a state of siege in place, there was a special danger of being harassed or captured by security forces. It was very seldom that we got through a night without at least one of our volunteers being arrested.

On one occasion, while talking with the volunteers gathered at our headquarters in San Salvador, I remember asking them, "Are you willing to continue risking your security to provide services to the people in need?" They responded that they were not willing to curtail our activities. All I could do was ask them to be careful, take care of each other and always carry their documents. And that's what they did.

In the rainy season of 1982, with the country already suffering from two years of civil war and with disappearances and deaths on the rise, a natural disaster hit the country in the early hours of Sunday, September 19th, consisting of a large landslide down the slopes of the San Salvador Volcano, essentially burying the community of Montebello in Mejicanos and surrounding neighborhoods in San Mauricito, El Triunfo and the San José subdivision. More than 150 homes were destroyed, over a thousand people were killed (some statistics say 500), and 700 people were injured.

The landslide was caused by four days of incessant rain, which essentially caused a large water tank at the highest point of the volcano, El Picacho, to explode, sending approximately 300,000 metric tons of mud and rock down the slopes.

The Comandos de Salvamento reacted immediately and remained on site for an entire week until the end of the operation, digging out survivors and bodies of the dead and transferring the injured to nearby hospitals. Our staff also climbed to the top of the volcano to inspect the site of origin, determine the cause and observe the cracks it had left in the earth as it passed down over the most vulnerable communities on the volcano slopes.

In the following years, repression continued to increase throughout the country in both the urban and rural sectors, and the demand for rescue and relief services grew rapidly. In our continuing effort to improve, we summoned the heads of our local offices and bases from around the country at one point to analyze strengths and weaknesses. Through this effort, we identified several areas of urgent need.

The first was the need to grow, bring more volunteers on board, increase the number of ambulances, improve our equipment and better prepare our people. As a result of this analysis, in six months, we bought seven vehicles, which we transformed into fully equipped ambulances to attend to any emergency that called. Within the first year, we had 12 more vehicles, and in the following year, 15 more, all transformed into working ambulances.

In early 1985, we were called upon by the high command of the Armed Forces to support an urgent need to extract a number of wounded soldiers from a recent guerrilla attack on the military barracks at El Paraiso, Chalatenango. Since the barracks were located in a highly conflictive area in dispute, complying with the request would require a degree of communication and coordination with both parties to the conflict.

In the case of the FMLN, we sought out the commanders and shared with them the army's request, to which they responded the following:

1. Yes, it was OK to enter the zone and evacuate wounded soldiers, but we also had to evacuate seriously wounded FMLN combatants.
2. Our ambulances would be used to transfer FMLN combatants to hospitals in San Salvador, and they would not be captured.
3. No reprisals should be taken against wounded FMLN combatants.
4. Army checkpoints that were in the trajectory for nearby hospitals would allow our ambulances to pass without any obstacles.

With the FMLN's agreement, I met again with the colonel in charge of the Armed Forces' operation. It was confirmed that our vehicles and personnel would have free and uninhibited passage in an area that had previously required an army permit. This important and precedent-setting agreement lasted beyond the El Paraíso case, allowing us to transfer

14 wounded soldiers and officers from the army and 17 wounded guerrilla combatants.

🐦

In 1986, on October 10, our country was shaken again by another natural disaster that added significantly to the trauma of the war itself. A powerful earthquake of 7.1 points on the Richter scale left San Salvador submerged in darkness, without water or telephone service and with an infrastructure severely damaged and, in some areas, completely destroyed. Also, there were a large number of people dead or injured, burned or with nervous breakdowns and more than 1,000 people in urgent need of transfer to hospitals.

With this new and overwhelming tragedy, a temporary truce was established to allow everyone to work towards burying the dead, caring for the injured and providing shelter for the homeless. It was a unique moment in El Salvador that managed to silence the guns, even if only for a short period, while citizens responded collectively to a national emergency.

After three months, fighting resumed across the country with greater force than ever. However, the atmosphere of violence did not hinder our contributions in accompanying the return of refugees from UNHCR camps in Honduras in the second half of the decade and repopulating communities that had been abandoned by the indiscriminate bombings of the Air Force and the scorched earth of the army.

With blood flowing again, the work of the Comandos de Salvamento continued. And, of course, the accusations against our leadership of supporting the FMLN continued as well, reinforced by the fact that we were always the first to arrive at the places where a bomb had exploded, where an attack had occurred or where there had been another massacre. We were always the first to be on-site to help people who were affected.

🐦

In the second half of 1989, a powerful bomb exploded in the offices of the trade union organization, FENASTRAS, in which the much-loved and respected union leader, Febe Elizabeth Velázquez, died. And we were called again to transport the wounded. Days later, on November 11, the second nationwide guerrilla offensive called "Hasta el Tope" was mounted, and our institution, now fortified with 3500 volunteers, spent the next few weeks on the streets attending to and transferring the wounded.

At first, we didn't understand the magnitude of the situation that confronted us with the offense. On the night of the 11th, when I arrived at our headquarters in San Salvador, I met a large number of volunteers gathered there with whom I met to give urgent instructions to all. The first thing I wanted to tell them was to inform them of the seriousness of all that was happening in the urban streets around the country and that, for the first time, I did not require anybody to get into an ambulance, given the fact that the situation differed dramatically from the emergencies we were used to covering.

I was told unanimously by the 250 volunteers in front of me that no one wanted to stop working in response to the current circumstances. They told me instead that they wanted to be at the forefront of any first responder efforts to help the people at this key moment in need. My heart leaped with pride and appreciation, and I was left with the only option of wishing luck to everyone, asking that they take good care of themselves and requiring that every volunteer carry a radio to inform frequently on their location and situation.

In the capital city, especially in the vicinity of military barracks, the days were difficult and dangerous. The population suffered too much and frequently had to leave their homes in an effort to save themselves and their family from certain death. Other people took up arms alongside the guerrilla fighters.

Just outside of Soyapango, there was a large Air Force checkpoint and everyone and everything that left that sector was being thoroughly checked, including our ambulances. On one occasion, we were transporting five seriously wounded guerrilla fighters who we had dressed in civilian clothes, of course, and without their weapons in hopes of getting through the checkpoint.

Upon arriving, however, the soldiers stopped us and asked us about the wounded. We told them that they were civilians who had been caught in a crossfire, but one of the soldiers lifted the pants of one of the men and found the marks left by bootlaces. The soldiers immediately took them all prisoners as we stood there spouting the precepts of the Geneva Convention and carried them away either to arrest them or to kill them outright.

We learned of another tragic situation in the Santa Marta neighborhood, south of San Salvador, where the fighting had become intense and cruel. A number of inhabitants were suffering from severe injuries, but a government curfew prohibited them from leaving in search of an ambulance or other form of aid. The civilian population in the other cities of the country suffered from similar situations. Transportation was at a standstill, and the entire economy came to a halt as families sought places of greater safety while the hospitals filled beyond their capacity with the injured.

Twice during the offensive, guerrilla forces took over the Mariona penitentiary in the capital to free their comrades and other political prisoners. In those efforts, they provoked major clashes with the army. Each time, the Comandos de Salvamento mobilized our ambulances to penetrate the area and cover the surrounding neighborhoods in an effort to help the injured civilian population. At that time, we also supported the common prisoners who remained in the penitentiary, our ambulances being the only entities with permission to circulate in those areas under fire.

Institutional data for the days of the offensive indicate that we transferred 1,715 people to the country's hospitals with gunshot or shrapnel wounds. Another 1,005 people were transferred with a variety of other diagnoses, along with 275 deceased. Over 125 people were treated for dehydration due to being trapped without drinking water in neighborhoods where heavy fighting had occurred, twelve shelters were set up to relocate people who had nowhere to turn, and 85,200 people were evacuated.

After the FMLN offensive in 1989, the war continued to fluctuate, becoming more intense at moments when the process of dialogue became stymied. The logic was that the results on the battlefield would define the progress at the negotiating table. Meanwhile, the blood of the people continued to flow, and the Comandos de Salvamento continued with our commitment to reduce the suffering of a population that had now endured more than a decade of war.

Throughout the country, there was not a day without heavy fighting in some areas, and the Commandos would respond. We were recognized by our bright yellow uniforms with the large green cross, our flag waving from a cut-off stick held by one of our skinny young volunteers as he or she readied to go into battle, like any solder or guerrilla combatant, armed with a stretcher and medicine chest crawling under the bullets.

This long and cruel war finally ended with an impressive array of Peace Accords that dismantled the structures of repression in the country, established a series of institutional reforms that gave promise to an incipient democracy and gave hope for a better future in our country.

In the same way that we had accompanied the people in the darkest days of the war, we accompanied them in the celebrations for peace, constantly mobilizing our ambulances and our volunteers should any need arise. In this new reality, the Comandos de Salvamento's commitment has always remained firm in the face of the persistent needs of a suffering people facing new challenges and threats.

In the 12 years of civil war, the Comandos de Salvamento provided a limitless service that included:

- 7349 people transferred with gunshot wounds
- 1234 people transferred with stab wounds
- 34,478 people were provided temporary shelter
- 66,071 people transferred to hospitals for other diseases
- 3893 people transferred due to psychological trauma

When I look back on all the events and great challenges of the 1980s, I am deeply saddened by so many brothers and sisters who died in the armed conflict. At the same time, I feel enormous gratitude for all of our foreign friends who came to help us when the institution needed them most and for the friendly governments that supported us.

Most of all, I thank from the depths of my heart every one of the Comandos de Salvamento who struggled together for so many years to respond to the most urgent needs of a people immersed in a war that frequently seemed eternal. I also thank so many dear friends who have always supported me in the process, with special mention for Efraín Solís, David Martínez, Francisco Campos, and Armando Castillo and a very special thanks to Mr. Edgar Cornejo Díaz. May he rest in peace.

Chamba

Driven by a utopian dream for my beloved country, El Salvador, I found myself in 1984 en route to the war front in the northern mountainous department of Chalatenango. My childhood and adolescence were marked by poverty and a gradual political awakening during my years of militancy in the student organization UR-19, as well as the lessons I learned from four years in exile. My decision to join the armed struggle arose from a profound conviction, confirmed countless times over the previous decades, that this was the only viable option for change in my country.

In May that year, I finally received details about the date, time, and place where my contact would pick me up for departure to Chalatenango. I was also given instructions on what to carry in my backpack. A few days later, we met again at a designated location in San Salvador and took a city bus to Apopa, where we got off at the edge of town.

From there, we started to walk and, after several hours, reached a small, well-hidden guerrilla camp near a place called Joyas Galana. Here, I spent several days getting to know the young guerrilla comrades in the camp and learning about the special security measures required for a location so close to an urban center. I also immediately began sharing the responsibility of standing guard at night. During the day, we maintained strict vigilance over the movements of the civilian inhabitants of the area, who moved back and forth from Apopa, where they shopped or worked.

At the end of the first week, I was instructed to prepare my backpack for departure that night to Chalatenango. Just after 11 p.m., I joined a group of young comrades and several older civilians who were carrying bundles on their shoulders, heading towards the camps in the north.

We walked through the darkness among endless fields of sugarcane, then crossed the Acelhuate River. At dawn, we approached the dangerous northern highway, Troncal del Norte, where ambushes by government soldiers were frequent. We maintained total silence as we ensured there were no soldiers present that night, then quickly crossed the highway. I felt tense, and my survival instincts were on full alert, but we passed without a problem and continued toward the Guazapa volcano, arriving at our destination at approximately 6 a.m.

In the first community we reached, the houses were almost completely destroyed by aerial bombing. In one of those houses, an elderly woman, who was busy making tortillas at the moment of our arrival, was suddenly distracted by a jet bomber that flew overhead and dropped a bomb a short distance away. Welcome to Guazapa!

We left the village and continued walking and quickly arrived at the site where the bomb had fallen, and, in a nearby ravine, found the body of a dead comrade who had been hit by shrapnel. People of the village explained to us that the bomb that had killed the comrade was a "squeegee", as local people referred to it, explicitly designed to explode in all directions just before making contact, sending millions of razor-sharp pieces of metal flying through the air destroying anything in their path. Several of these pieces of shrapnel had cut off the arm and penetrated the thorax of the dead comrade.

We were informed that we were in the community of Mirandía on the slopes of the Guazapa volcano. Knowing that we were new, comrades from the area came to greet us warmly and provided us with our first instructions on measures to protect ourselves in the event of a bombing. They explained that the subzone of Guazapa was one of the most heavily bombed areas of the country, and, as if to prove their point, we spent the rest of the day running for the trenches at the approach of government aircraft.

That first night was spent in the nearby community of El Zapote with a family of combatants from the local guerrilla column. I couldn't rest, however, given the discomfort and my lack of experience with sleeping on the ground over a thin piece of plastic for a bed.

The next day, we moved on to the community of El Corozal, on the shores of Lake Suchitlán, and, in the afternoon, government helicopters arrived, flying low over the village with their machine guns roaring as we again ran for cover.

From there, we traveled in a small rowboat to the village of Copapayo, bailing water constantly to keep the boat afloat. I hadn't slept the previous two nights, and, sitting on the wet bottom of this boat, I was thoroughly soaked by the time of our arrival. From Copapayo, we walked to the abandoned community of Cinquera, where there was a small guerrilla camp hidden on a wooded hillside and, once there, I began to feel more at ease until the comrades in the camp began to tell us about the frequent incursions of government infantry.

We left in the darkness that same day to cross Lake Suchitlán for the northern department of Chalatenango and reached the other side without incident. There, we were met by several comrades from that zone whose first warning after a warm greeting was to be careful where we walked because "the whole area was mined." We were now in territory controlled by the FMLN guerrillas.

It took us almost a month, stopping for weeks at a time in the villages along the way, to finally reach our destination, Las Vueltas. There, I was assigned my first responsibility: administering the FMLN's monthly budget in the Apolinario Serrano Front of Chalatenango.

I was not on the war fronts to participate in armed combat, but during my time in the front, I frequently found myself in areas under continued attack by aviation and scorched-earth military operations by the infantry. On several occasions, we were also dangerously close to battle sites between our guerrilla forces and government troops, generating enormous stress, especially during my early days. Nevertheless, as time went by, I gradually adapted to the conditions of a heavily contested warzone, and the stress returned only when I was in imminent danger of death.

During those moments, I was aware of a strange sense of heat disseminating through my body (probably from adrenaline), followed by a profound calm and almost a spiritual sense of acceptance of whatever was going to happen, including death. Once the danger had passed and the adrenaline gradually left my system, I would be unable to keep my eyes open and frequently fell asleep wherever I happened to be at the moment.

In the mid-1980s, the FMLN guerrilla forces controlled almost a third of the countryside in El Salvador. In the northeast of Chalatenango, the FPL, the largest of the five organizations of the FMLN, to which I belonged, organized the civilian population in Local Popular Powers (PPL), taking the place of traditional municipal governments, but assuring broad democratic participation and responding to the special needs of a people at war.

A subregional governing board (JGS) of the Local Popular Powers was also elected, made up of a presidency and several secretariats with responsibilities for the conduct of the different aspects of local governance, such as education, health, economy and production, legal affairs and conflict resolution. In December 1984, I was assigned to work with this entity.

The territory governed by the JGS consisted of three subregions. The first included the original municipalities of Arcatao, Nueva Trinidad and part of San Antonio de La Cruz. The second subregion included San Isidro Labrador and San Antonio de Los Ranchos, and the third included San José Las Flores and Las Vueltas.

The JGS had a technical team where I participated, providing support in the area of good governance. In addition, we organized talks on human rights and attended important visits to our front, such as the visit of the mayor of Berkely, California, in 1985 and the pastoral visit of Monsignor Arturo Rivera Damas at the beginning of 1986, as well as visits by solidarity delegations that arrived with an interest in establishing "twin cities" between communities from the United States and El Salvador.

Part of my tasks was to promote collective production in support of female heads of households, the elderly and comrades wounded in combat. This included managing communal stores and supporting the distribution of production inputs and goods. I also ensured transparency and accountability in each area of government and emphasized training for the different secretariats.

In the midst of a war where the civilian population had been declared a military target by the government, we had to be on the lookout at all times for a possible bombing, strafing or military operation requiring a rapid withdrawal of the civilian population (referred to by the people as "guinda"). It implied being careful about where one hung clothes to dry or when the smoke from a cookfire might alert the enemy to our location. When government troops entered our controlled zone, those responsible for security would warn the population to get ready for guinda. If the troops were headed in our direction, we tried to mobilize in the darkness of night to avoid being detected.

The bombings were almost daily, and large ground incursions by government troops were carried out with an average frequency of once a month. In August 1985, we suffered one such incursion with thousands of government soldiers headed towards us with the intention of annihilating the civilian population, destroying their houses and agricultural production, killing their domestic animals and anything else that moved.

As always, we waited for nightfall before mobilizing the civilian population with women, children, the elderly and middle-aged. On this occasion, we did so under a pouring rain. I noticed during the guinda that Don Rumaldo, one of our elderly, about 75 years old, was having a particularly difficult time and that he kept removing his worn leather sandals in order to walk through the mud and the rain. The next day, when the army had left the area and we began to return to the communities, a comrade of the PPL proposed to Don Rumaldo that he leave our front and transfer to the Mesa Grande refugee camp in Honduras, where he could avoid so much suffering. But he quickly replied in the negative, assuring that, "here, even if it is with my small cornfield, I am contributing something to our struggle and to our comrades."

The incursions by the armed forces were part of a strategy designed to force the population to leave their home communities, cutting off a key source of support for guerrilla forces. Whenever an incursion was in process, the military passed through our front, killing anything that moved, burning the terrain and destroying houses, makeshift schools, agricultural production and anything else of use to the population.

If they discovered an underground tunnel where we hid food and medicines, they destroyed it. If they located the population, they would massacre the people, as happened in the massacre of the Gualsinga River, where the Salvadoran army opened fire on a column of women, children and elderly who were trying to reach the border with Honduras where the Gualsinga River joins the Sumpul River.

For many days after the massacre, human skeletons, scattered clothes, children's shoes and other belongings that people carried in Guinda were found along the river banks, evidence of a grave violation of the Geneva Convention protecting the right of civilians to remain in their villages without being harmed, even in war zones.

In defense of the Geneva Convention, we designed and implemented a persistent campaign beginning in the mid-1980s and lasting until peace was finally signed in 1992. Our Local Popular Powers, in coordination with the Christian Committee for the Displaced of El Salvador (CRIPDES) and with international solidarity organizations, such as CISPES, the Monsignor Romero Solidarity Committees and innumerable organisms of international cooperation in the United States, Canada, Europe, Australia and Latin America constantly focused on assuring this right.

🐦

One of our most important strategies in this effort was a program of establishing "Sister Cities" between communities in the battered areas of El Salvador under FMLN control and cities in the United States to provide humanitarian assistance and to pressure their government to curtail all weapons sales to the Salvadoran army.

In February 1985, the United Nations Special Rapporteur for Human Rights in El Salvador, Mr. José Antonio Pastor Ridruejo, presented his report on the country's observance of human rights. His conclusions supported our struggle against the forced eviction of civilian communities in conflictive areas.

That same year, we received a visit from the mayor of Berkeley, California, who came to express the solidarity of the people of Berkeley with its new Sister City, San Antonio de Los Ranchos, and to receive testimony from the civilian population about the violation of their rights by the Armed Forces. During his visit, he came under fire on several occasions but continued to exhibit an attitude of staunch solidarity with our struggle.

On the first day, the army launched an artillery attack with a 120-millimeter cannon, and mortars fell close to the site where we were meeting.

The mayor was a large man, even for a North American, and tensions rose further when we discovered that he didn't fit into a nearby trench that would hopefully provide us with cover.

The next day, the people of San Antonio de Los Ranchos prepared a horse with a saddle to take the mayor on a tour of the surrounding villages, but the horse could not carry his weight. Then, halfway to the first village, we were attacked by a Cessna "Push and Pull" aircraft launching its rockets nearby.

The mayor had to get down from his horse and throw himself to the ground to avoid being hit by shrapnel. Despite the difficulties and hair-raising close calls, he experienced during his visit, however, he left satisfied, assuring us that our struggle was his struggle. The warm and supportive relationships established during his days in our controlled zones remained strong throughout the remaining years of the war.

At the end of 1985, the PPLs of Chalatenango asked the archbishop of San Salvador, Monsignor Arturo Rivera y Damas, to visit the front to meet with the communities, and a pastoral visit was arranged for the first days of January of the coming year. On January 5, 1986, the inhabitants from all of the communities in the Apolinario Serrano front of Chalatenango traveled to the town of San José las Flores, a small urban center now in ruins due to the war with most of the houses collapsed and abandoned.

There was no civilian population at the time, so each of the visiting communities set up its small camp around the center of the town. The camp had a kitchen for cooking and disciplined security measures, including a plan for rapid evacuation in case of a surprise army attack.

In the early morning of the 6th, the day of the visit, the sun was just beginning to rise when we heard the A-37 jet bombers come streaking over the area, dropping several bombs on the slopes of the nearby hillsides, about eight kilometers east of Las Flores. Another bombardment occurred in the Montañona, about seven kilometers northwest of Las Flores. The general analysis was that it was intended to frighten us, so we took precautions but remained where we were, waiting for the arrival of our visitors.

Around nine in the morning, the PPL comrades arrived with the archbishop and his entourage. Immediately, the men, women and children who had come from the surrounding villages approached the delegation. True popular power was showing its face as the people greeted each other with hugs, children ran up and down with glee, and people crowded in to greet the archbishop and those who accompanied him.

The day's events began with personal testimonies and presentations to the archbishop on the systematic violations of human rights committed every time the army came into the area. At one o'clock in the afternoon, the archbishop and his entourage took a break to have lunch and to assimilate all that they had heard. They also began preparing the mass that would be celebrated in the afternoon. In that space, a small plane flew overhead, dropping flyers urging the population to evacuate the area. At the same time, loudspeakers attached to the aircraft tried to convince any guerrillas who might be present that their commanders were in Managua, living in luxury hotels and eating sumptuously while they suffered in the war zones of El Salvador.

The mass began at around three pm in the atrium of the church, with people overflowing into the park in front. It was broadcast by the guerrilla radio, Farabundo Martí, which established a link with Radio Venceremos in the eastern part of the country. The homily focused on the denunciations of massacres and other human rights violations described earlier by the people, followed by demands that government and military officials recognize and respect the rights of civilian inhabitants in the conflictive areas of the country.

Early in the morning on the seventh, the archbishop officiated a second mass, blessed the population gathered in San José de Las Flores, and, following breakfast, set off for Arcatao, 16 kilometers away. Upon arriving at the Sumpul River, now famous for the massacre of 1981, the archbishop and his entourage stopped to bathe. From that day on, the site became known as "the bishop's pool."

Arriving in Arcatao, near the border with Honduras, people from the town and surrounding area were waiting to welcome us. It was late in the day, so after a warm welcome for the archbishop, we proceeded to the center of the town where the church was located and entered the convent where the archbishop and his entourage would spend the night.

The next morning, the archbishop once again met with the crowds and listened to their testimonies, as he had done in San Jose Las Flores.

In the afternoon, he officiated mass, again with a sermon denouncing the human rights violations committed by the government against the inhabitants of the area. As we had done the day before, the mass and homily were broadcast by the guerrilla radios.

The following day, the archbishop officiated a second farewell mass before leaving for Guarjila, 24 kilometers away, fulfilling his promise made months earlier to visit the people in the conflictive zones of El Salvador. By visiting the area and witnessing firsthand the living conditions and the systematic violation of basic human rights, the archbishop could speak with greater authority each time he denounced the government and the military. He even forced the Minister of Defense at the time, General Carlos Eugenio Vides Casanova, to recognize the presence of the civilian population in the area, an important step towards achieving the right of the population to live in their places of origin without harassment from military authorities.

The archbishop's support encouraged our team working on this issue from within the controlled zones to redouble our efforts to collect information from each community, document abuses and send these reports abroad through the networks of comrades responsible for international relations with the citizens and governments of other countries.

On March 5, 1986, just two months after the visit of archbishop Rivera y Damas, we were told that army patrols had been sighted in our area, passing through Guarjila and headed in our direction, marking the initiation of another large-scale scorched earth campaign that was given the name, "Chávez Carreño". At that time of year, it rains little. Hence, the greenery where the populations usually hid during guindas was sparse, rendering it more difficult for the civilian population to evade the army and Air Force.

Within a few days, the infantry had advanced towards our camps, combining air strikes with paratrooper drops from helicopters into our territories, setting fire to everything in their path. They captured the first civilians they found (varying from their normal routine of slaughtering civilians) and transported them out of the area towards the outskirts of the city of Chalatenango.

It was a new tactic in the military's strategy of "low-intensity warfare" in which civilians were no longer massacred but instead placed forcefully under government control where they were fed, entertained (sometimes by clowns when there were children) and offered alternative places to live in an effort to win hearts and minds and remove the water from the fish.

In response, a special group of our PPL leaders was organized to promote a communal march from San Jose Las Flores to Dulce Nombre de María in order to take over the church and denounce this new form of aggression. Immediately, the participants in the march were captured by soldiers based in Chalatenango and transferred to the local military barracks in that city, where they were roughly interrogated and accused of being guerrillas.

They were saved by officials of the International Committee of the Red Cross (ICRC), who visited the barracks to protect the captured villagers. Journalists from national as well as international media were also present, as well as solidarity groups, trade unions and human rights organizations who managed to negotiate the release of those captured and transfer them to the Calle Real shelter for displaced families managed by the Catholic Church. From there, in coordination with CRIPDES, the population continued its struggle for the right to live in their communities of origin. Clearly, a new phase had begun in the war in El Salvador.

Operation Chávez Carreño continued its course and, on April 8th, the Air Force bombed the town of Arcatao then, again, dropped paratroopers from helicopters throughout the surrounding countryside. The army again captured any civilians who had not been able to flee the town and concentrated them at gunpoint in the town church. But this time, they returned to their old, repressive practice of taking them into the nearby hillsides where the people were tortured and finally killed.

The operation continued for more than a month, sweeping the entire territory of northeastern Chalatenango, capturing civilian families and forcing many of them to flee the area in search of the refugee camps of Mesa Grande in Honduras. With this latest operation, the civilian population of northeastern Chalatenango was decimated, and the Local Popular Powers lost much of their dynamism and relevance.

In May 1986, the villagers who remained joined together to analyze and plan our next activities in an effort to reorganize and re-establish some basic conditions for subsistence. Meanwhile, in San Salvador, CRIPDES and the group of villagers who were captured in the church of Dulce Nombre de María were developing plans to return and to repopulate San José Las Flores in Chalatenango and El Barrillo in the Guazapa area of Cuscatlan province. It was the beginning of a new phase in our struggle for civilian rights focused on repopulation.

CRIPDES and the PPLs of Chalatenango initially proposed to the government a return to San Jose Las Flores and El Barillo. Still, the proposal was rejected because it involved resettlement in areas controlled by the FMLN. So, our leaders and CRIPDES opted to return without government approval and sought out international solidarity groups to accompany them.

El Barrillo was repopulated with little publicity on June 15. A few days later, on June 22, with highly publicized support from national as well as international NGOs, churches, solidarity groups and well-known personalities, a contingent of displaced families in the Calle Real shelter on the outskirts of San Salvador left to repopulate San José Las Flores. With massive accompaniment, these two communities set an example for others. They became a new symbol of the conquest of the right of the civilian population to live in their places of origin.

The Local Popular Powers of Chalatenango were transformed into a movement for repopulation, a process that was taking shape in all of the conflictive zones of the country. The process did not take place in a calm or peaceful environment. The war was still raging, and the army, security forces and death squads continued to harass civilians with selective arrests and massacres. However, the efforts to return to villages of origin and to repopulate other areas with the refugees returning from Honduras increased little by little.

In October 1987, the first repatriation from the UN camps at Mesa Grande, Honduras, took place. Four thousand refugees returned to Guiarjila and Las Vueltas in Chalatenango, Copapayo and Santa Marta in Cabañas and San Antonio de Los Ranchos and Teosinte in Chalatenango on August 13, 1988.

Our team dedicated to repopulation continued to be a military target for the army, so with each incursion of government troops, we were still forced to leave whatever community we were in at the time and join up with local guerrilla columns to evade death. On Sunday, March 8, 1987, five of our comrades (two women and three men) were ambushed by government troops on the stretch of road that leads from the village of Zapotal to the town of Ojos de Agua and cut to pieces with bayonets.

I was in Arcatao at the time and heard bombs exploding in the distance. Then I heard the helicopters flying in to pick up the troops that had carried out the ambush. I left Arcatao and walked the sixteen kilometers to San José Las Flores, arriving at four that afternoon and upon reaching the first houses in San Jose, people began to share the horrible details of the incident. I was overwhelmed with sadness at the loss of close friends, such as those with whom I had been living and working for the past several years. But experience in the war zones had taught me that life goes on and the challenges of our struggle give no truce for mourning.

On the 24th of that same month, the anniversary date of the assassination of Archbishop Romero, we were warned that the army was entering our controlled zone again, this time through the Montañona. We were also advised that the soldiers were advancing in our direction, so we moved from San Jose Las Flores to Arcatao, closer to Honduras.

Two days later, while in Aracatao, we were informed that the army was already gathering along the Sumpul River, on the Chichilco hill and at the heights of Carasque in Nueva Trinidad. So, we were told to move to Patamera, towards Nombre Jesús, and to join a supply unit made up of comrades of the National Resistance (RN), another member organization of the FMLN who was camped in that area. We passed through the village of Los Guardado and established contact with the comrades of the RN. Then, together, we traveled down from the Los Planes village, passed through Los Dubones and continued down into the Guayabo ravine, where we took refuge in the forest as night fell. The plan was to follow a complicated route that would allow us to evade the approaching army and eventually return to San Jose Las Flores, but it was strange that we had heard no combat during our long march. We discussed this among ourselves while we ate our last remaining food. Then we waited for the darkness of night, formed our column with a scout out front and placed the members of our repopulation support unit in the rear.

At night, the pace is always slower, and we had advanced little when our scouts suddenly made contact with the lead of an army patrol that had camped on Pacha Hill. The bullets began to fly, along with shotgun blasts, hand grenades, a 50-mm machine gun and a 90-millimeter cannon launching mortars. Tracer bullets lit up the night like noisy fireflies as the red projectiles flew over our heads like angry bees on fire.

At that moment, I was sure I was spending the last minutes of my life. Our column was disorganized. Those in front managed to continue towards Santa Anita, those in the middle jumped into a nearby ravine to avoid being hit, and those of us in the rear left turned around and ran for our lives.

We were most afraid of the projectiles of the 50-caliber machine gun, which aimed its shots directly at the path we had to follow to escape. We had no alternative but to cross that path, and miraculously, the machine gun stopped firing at the exact moment we were passing, allowing us to get away.

In all the disorder and confusion, we had no information about where the army was headed, so at approximately 3:30 that morning, we decided to divide ourselves into three groups. Each group found cover to hide themselves on the banks of the river, leaving about seventy-five meters between us.

My group was made up of three comrades. We filled our canteens with water and shared our remaining toasted cornflour (the standard food reserve for guindas), a small bag of sugar and some candies. Then it dawned on me suddenly that whenever I was in this kind of situation, I always felt the hungriest, recalling my favorite foods and promising myself that, if I survived, I would eat a whole chicken. Still, the truth is that once you remove yourself from fasting, your stomach can't tolerate large quantities of food and you have to start always with small portions and work your way up gradually.

On the third day, we decided to attempt our departure from the area, so we formed a single file with approximately ten meters between each of us and headed upstream towards Arcatao, observing the hillsides as we walked along to see if people were working their plots in a normal fashion preparing for the rainy season and planting. We approached a villager at one point and asked if the army was nearby. We were informed that they had recently departed from the area, so we continued to Arcatao and eventually to our base in San Jose Las Flores. The next day, the first of April, news arrived that our combatants had overrun for a second time the Fourth Brigade at El Paraiso in Chalatenango.

Shortly after returning to San José Las Flores, as the sun was just about to set, a barrage of helicopters poured out of the basin of the Lempa River, soared over the mountainous terrain of San Jose and, in seconds, began to circle the town strafing and shooting their rockets. In contrast, an O2 ("Push and Pull") and a C-130 Hercules shot more rockets and riddled the area with machinegun fire. Moments later, another barrage of helicopters began dropping paratroopers around the outlying regions of the town, in essence, surrounding us.

We met quickly in the church of San José and decided that there was no escape and that we needed to blend in with the townspeople to avoid capture or death. We decided to take refuge in a nearby convent together with two nuns (one Spanish and one Salvadoran) who lived and worked in San José, accompanying the community. We stripped ourselves of everything that could identify us as guerrilla supporters. We assumed the role of religious brothers and sisters as the troops began to occupy the town, moving from house to house.

Minutes later, they arrived at the convent and asked to speak with the nuns. The officer in charge indicated that they had come because someone had reported the presence of guerrillas, but the nuns insisted that the guerrillas pass through all the time and that, precisely at midday, they had seen them in the park.

By the time the soldiers finally noticed us, we were well prepared with our alibis concerning our roles in the convent. I had previously written down my real name on a piece of paper and given it to one of the nuns in case I was captured and disappeared or murdered so that they could inform my family.

The next day, April 2, we got up early and began working on our invented tasks. I recall that I took an axe and started splitting some logs to make firewood. Then we had breakfast, and I took a Bible, grabbed a chair and sat down in the corridor to read.

At around 10 a.m., we began to organize our departure. We had been warned that several guerrilla fighters were in the town who had been unable to break through the encirclement the day before. Without attracting attention, we asked them to lend us several horses, some axes and some lassos. We then disguised ourselves as peasants and went out one by one, some on horseback, others with axes on their backs, and others with lassos, as if we were heading off to work our fields.

The women with us also dressed as peasants, wearing aprons and carrying large baskets on their heads. By one o'clock that afternoon, we were out of danger and approaching the Sumpul River. Many months later, when I returned to San Jose Las Flores, I passed by the convent and told one of the nuns there, who hadn't been present in April, about our ordeal. She replied, "You are like the Maccabees, a mighty little army protected by God."

One day at the beginning of May, while I was in San José Las Flores, the commander of our elite battalions of the Vanguard Units of the FPL, Dimas Rodríguez, informed me without warning that I would be leaving the front the next day to take on new responsibilities in "the metro" (San Salvador). "Copied and understood, comrade," I replied, assuming the discipline of a militant of the FPL (as a militant, one must be willing always to follow orders and assume the mission assigned to him at any given time).

I was overcome with sadness and nostalgia, however, at the thought of leaving Chalatenango, where I had suffered so much but enjoyed such incredible people and experiences during the previous four years of my life. From the people of Chalatenango, I had come to know the meaning of love, commitment and revolution, and I knew that leaving would not be easy. On the other hand, I must admit to being thrilled at the thought of seeing my family again, especially my mother, whom I had not communicated with within four years.

That night, I couldn't sleep, thinking about so many things at once. We departed early the next morning, along with three other comrades, carrying correspondence for our guerrilla camps in other zones. During the day, we passed through several villages, finally arriving at our destination that night at around 7 p.m., from where we would depart for the capital city.

Shortly after our arrival, intensive combat began nearby, forcing us to move again to a safer location. Just before dawn on the following day, we heard more fighting close to where we had camped, so the order was given for the non-combatants among us to move out once again headed toward the Sumpul River. Upon our arrival, scouts detected the presence of a column of soldiers from the infamous Atalacatl battalion on the other side of Sumpul, in Honduras, in an apparent attempt to encircle us. So, we began moving again.

The soldiers had set fire to the dried brush all around us, and it felt like an inferno. The aircraft also arrived and began bombing and strafing the area while our combatants confronted an unknown number of infantry troops in several different lines of fire. The only element favoring our small group of non-combatants was the fact that our comrades were keeping the military busy, creating an opportunity for our escape.

After several days of endless walking, we finally arrived at a "safe house" on the edge of our controlled zone, where a family of collaborators lived. There, we spent the night. Early the next morning, a peasant farmer picked me up in a small truck loaded with potatoes and took me to the market in the capital city.

We hit our first army checkpoint just outside of the tourist city of La Palma. The Atonal battalion was stationed there at the time, but they did not stop us, nor was there a search of our vehicle. The next checkpoint was located on the bridge of the Acelhuate River, at the junction with the Lempa River. Still, they didn't stop us either, and, from there to San Salvador, our route was clear, allowing us to arrive at the busy Tiendona market by six in the afternoon.

I said goodbye and thanked the old man driving the truck. Then, I took a taxi to the house of my cousin, whom I had also not seen for four years. From there, we called my mother and father, who rushed over to see me, and tears fell like rain.

I established communication with my contact in San Salvador, who instructed me to travel to Mexico City for a meeting with the FPL's international team based there. So, I left by land for Guatemala City and, there, purchased a ticket to travel to Costa Rica, where I updated my Costa Rican identity (at that time, it was safer to travel with my Costa Rican identity than with my Salvadoran identity) and bought the ticket to Mexico City. It was the month of July 1988.

The day after my arrival, I was guided to the small office of the FPL International Task Force. There, they informed me that I had been assigned to assume the direction of a new entity being created to work openly in El Salvador in coordination with CRIPDES and the Coordinator of Repopulated Communities of Chalatenango (CCR in Spanish) to support the ongoing program of returns of refugees and displaced families to their communities of origin. The new entity would be called the Foundation for Community Cooperation and Development of El Salvador (CORDES in Spanish).

It was a beautiful idea, a great challenge, a big responsibility and a new life that I took on with joy, enthusiasm and gratitude.

Lorena

I was born into a poor family in the countryside of El Salvador. My childhood years, alongside my mother, father, siblings and grandmother, were years of scarcity and constant search for the necessary means for our survival. My parents were farmers, and we lived off the land with the crops that we produced each year. We spent the days of the coffee harvest on the large haciendas of the oligarchy, where we picked the mature coffee beans on the steep hillsides of the volcanos alongside hundreds of other poor families, rising before sunrise each day in an effort to earn a few cents.

The foremen in charge of the harvest kept us under the yoke, driving us each day from sunup to sundown until every ounce of energy had been drained from our bodies in order to obtain maximum earnings for the owners. When it came time to weigh the bags of coffee and pay the workers for their labor, however, the scales were manipulated in order to pay less than what we had rightfully earned.

We didn't understand much about politics in those years, about the exploitation of the poor by the rich, about repression and structural injustice, but our life experience was our best teacher, enlightening our awareness day by day.

I was a "cipota", a young girl, at that time accompanying my parents and working long hours with poor food and bad treatment from the foremen, observing how we were systematically robbed. We sometimes left our village at four in the morning with the rest of the young people, boys and girls, to travel to the coffee farms in Santiago de María. Sometimes, we accompanied my father on the slopes of the San Salvador volcano, enduring cold, hunger, bad treatment and the attempts of the national guardsmen who patrolled the farms to take advantage of the more attractive young girls among us.

When there was no work on the coffee farms, we worked harvesting cotton, collected in large sacks with the same maneuvers of the owners to exploit our labor, but it was the only way to have a few cents in our pockets for Christmas and New Year's or to buy notebooks and shoes for school. I did the math, taking into consideration the cost of transportation, the cold and insufficient food that we ate, our hours worked and how much we had left in the end. And so, little by little, I began to understand the reality of the life of peasants in our country and the reasons for the struggles for land to provide a minimum diet for peasant families that we were beginning to hear about.

We began at first to organize ourselves in Christian Base Communities through the Catholic Church, where one of my cousins was a Delegate of the Word. Later, we joined more political organizations with a clear agenda for change. And, finally, we found the more radical political/military guerrilla organizations promoting armed struggle.

We found support in the words of Archbishop Oscar Arnulfo Romero, whose sermons, filled with love for the peasants and criticism of structural injustice and repression in El Salvador, were fundamental to the hopes of the poor, especially those residing and resisting in the country's rural areas.

They gave us encouragement, strength and the assurance that our struggle was genuine and just, that the country was not lost and that we had to fight to change the system at its roots. The death of our martyr, now a Saint, had a strong and significant impact on the young people already participating in the popular organizations and on those considering joining. It impelled us to defend ourselves and to be what he told us in his homilies: "Christians worthy of living that commitment of solidarity with the poor."[1]

The situation of poverty, abuse and oppression of the poor in El Salvador, of which I was a part, drove me toward the struggle. But it

1 Archbishop Romero, Homily, July 22, 1979

was my brother, Rafael, who became my greatest motivation, encouraging me to join other young women and men of my age committed to change. At that time, I was studying, along with my brothers and sisters, at the school in our village, El Aceituno, in Usulután. The school was actually located in the courtyard of my great-grandfather's house, and it was there that I finished fourth grade. I then accompanied Rafael to the village of San Antonio, where the school had higher grades, and we continued studying together. I always followed him.

San Antonio had already witnessed the slaying of several of its youth who were commuting each day to the high school in Santiago de María when they were found murdered along the Pan-American highway. Those students had been acquaintances and friends of ours, and they were killed for no reason other than the fact of being young. That was enough of a threat to the authorities in power.

In my family, we were six siblings, four girls and two boys. My brother, Rigoberto, was the third, but he was the first to join a revolutionary group. He was 18 years old at the time and no one in the house knew that he was organized, that he was part of the revolutionary struggle. I was the first to discover it one day when I found under his mattress propaganda in the form of posters and banners calling on the people to unite to defend the rights that had been taken away from us and to join the resistance through popular struggle.

Rafael was my brother's "Nombre de guerra" (war name), but in our house, where he continued to reside, he was still Rigoberto. He had been recruited by several friends, including Rodolfo, the leader of his organization at the local level, who, years later, would be someone very special in my life. In the beginning, his responsibilities included the production and dissemination of propaganda supporting the struggle, which he distributed among the population of nearby villages in an effort to motivate people to organize and participate in the efforts for change. Later, his responsibilities included military actions, and he eventually traveled to Cuba and Vietnam where he received training for the Special Forces (FES) units of the incipient guerrilla army being built in El Salvador.

By the early 1980s, we young people were highly aware of the situation in our country, determined and ready to fight. We lost our fear of organizing and our initial reluctance to take up arms against the dictatorship, in spite of knowing the consequences. Doing nothing provoked more fear in us than doing something to stop the oppression, and even when there was fear, we knew we had to take action in order to defend ourselves. Hence, we began to prepare ourselves for the battle to come. There were no other options.

By 1980, the National Guard and the death squads had our village on their radar, frequently visiting to search for and capture or disappear "subversives", that is, anyone suspected of being a guerrilla sympathizer. My brother was captured twice, and it was only through my mother's rapid action that he was released on both occasions.

So, in 1981, at the age of 16, I left my village, following the path of my 18-year-old brother. I left family, studies (which hurt me the most), friends and community life. I was sent to participate in the formation of the first guerrilla camps in the north of San Miguel. I was initially trained in health to work as a "sanitarium" (nurse) in charge of providing first aid and other health services.

I joined the guerrilla organization, the Popular Liberation Forces (FPL), one of the five organizations of the Farabundo Martí National Liberation Front (FMLN). And the comrades of this organization became my new family. I was not a combatant, but I learned the use of weapons and was usually armed, although I was never in combat.

My role within the revolutionary movement continued for many years to be in health, providing first aid to comrades wounded in battle. At the same time, I worked as a "correo" (messenger), carrying communications from one guerrilla camp to another in the department of Usulutan or to the camps in San Miguel. Finally, I was assigned tasks to help strengthen the levels of political and social awareness among the civilian population of our front, teaching that our struggle was just, that we were not the evil ones, that we were defending basic human rights and that the organization and mobilization of the people was the only way out of oppression.

At the beginning of January 1981, I was transferred to a clandestine hospital of the FPL. It was there that I spent the days of our guerrilla offensive at the national level in a rustic, dark, underground bunker ("tatu") along with another sanitarium and a severely wounded comrade, as heavily armed and angry government troops invaded the area with the intention of annihilating every human being they found.

When the January offensive failed, massive incursions of government troops, with the support of artillery and the indiscriminate bombing of civilian communities, became more frequent in an attempt to halt the advance of a guerrilla insurgency that would soon come to control almost a third of the countryside of El Salvador. The immediate objective of the government and its military was to displace the civilian population from their communities of origin in order to eliminate growing support for the FMLN. It was in this context that I learned of the death of my mother and other relatives who had remained in our village.

The news reached us at the camp where I was stationed along with my brother Rafael, although at that time, he was on a mission outside the country. I was the first in the family to learn of this tragic incident. According to my informants, the Third Infantry Brigade had arrived in our village, slaughtering entire families who had been accused by "orejas" (local spies) of collaborating with the guerrillas. They came with lists in hand, looking particularly for families with the surnames Rodríguez, Araujo and Martínez (our family). This massacre came to be known as the Massacre of Aceituna, and it took place on September 9, 1981. At that time, my mother was 48 years old and was best known locally for selling cheese.

They say that my mother was taken out of the house along with my uncle and murdered along the roadside that leads from El Triunfo to Sesori. My brother and I did not have the opportunity to bury her because the village remained occupied for some time by the military. We later learned, however, that it was my grandmother, 70-year-old Ignacia Araujo, who retrieved the mangled body, cleaned it and took care of burying it. The remains of my mother, my uncle and about 20 other people who were murdered that day were buried in the courtyard of our house. This massacre of defenseless and innocent people became the daily bread of our country.

My brother Rafael and I were always close, and living together in the same guerrilla camp in Usulutan united us even more until the tragic news of his death shook my soul to the roots, marking my life again with a wound that would never heal. He was killed in battle in a mission in Chalatenango against the barracks of the Fourth Infantry Brigade and buried in a mass grave.

The war and my decision to participate deprived me of being an adequate mother to my firstborn daughter, whom I had to leave in the hands of a sister who cared for her over the years, with an enormous cost in terms of bonding between mother and daughter. But the only other option would have meant risking my daughter's life on a war front.

I had witnessed enough of the cruelty and terror of war. I had seen soldiers take the lives of innocents, even newborns, along with older children and the elderly. So, with this unbearable pain in my heart, I protected my daughter and kept her as far from the battlefield as possible. Many other women combatants made the same decision.

Early in the war, the FPL formed the Association of Women of El Salvador (AMES) in Chalatenango with the mission of incorporating women into the struggle and making their role visible. At one point, I was assigned the task of strengthening this effort.

Life in the camps was made more bearable through the friendship and support of my comrades. There were always difficulties and differences among us, but a cause united us, and the determination to build a fairer, more democratic country and to recover our freedoms and rights. My life within the organization has given me the greatest satisfaction because I have been able to help others, women, men, and children when they have needed it most. It has also marked me and caused me deep pain for the murder of my mother, my brother Rafael, the disappearance of my sister, Vilma, the murder of Rodolfo, the father of my children, and the death and disappearance of thousands of friends, brothers in struggle who now only exist in my mind and my heart.

Two years had passed since the birth of my first daughter when I found out again that I was pregnant, this time with twins Juan Jose and Juan Alberto. With their arrival, the FPL helped me get installed in a small house where we could be together, and I was able to recover my daughter, Carolina. But I was alone and unemployed and now in charge of three small children, so I was forced to look for work forty days after the birth of my twins. My sister helped me set up a shop and I survived on the income provided by sales, the paradox being that my biggest customers were the soldiers and national guardsmen who patrolled the area. I was 22 years old at the time.

When the twins were one year old, the local guerrilla commanders called me back to the front with new responsibilities. I was frightened that my children would die in my absence, so I initially refused to go. Our discipline demanded that we always put the mission first, however, so refusing to return to the mountains took work. In search of a solution, the organization assigned me a task that would allow me to spend time with my children while fulfilling an urgent need of the revolution.

I was assigned to work with an organization built in 1984 in defense of the hundreds of communities displaced by the cruel, scorched earth strategies executed by the army. The indiscriminate bombing of civilian populations and the large-scale incursions of infantry troops, killing everything that moved while destroying houses and agricultural production, had uprooted so many communities residing on the war fronts in an effort to separate the guerrillas from the civilian population that supported them. The organization to which I had been assigned to direct at the national level was called the Christian Committee for Displaced People of El Salvador, CRIPDES. At the time, I didn't know much about it or how important this organization would become in my life.

Many displaced families ended up leaving the country and taking refuge in Honduras, Nicaragua, Costa Rica, Panama, Australia, Canada and the United States. In the case of Honduras, they were grouped in large camps managed by the United Nations, such as Mesa Grande, Colomoncagua and San Antonio. Many of this population had also been victims of the largest massacres of the war, such as Sumpul, Rio Lempa, El Mozote, Las Hojas, Copapayo, San Nicolás, La Quesera and others. CRIPDES and the National Coordinator for Repopulation CNR) emerged as their organized voice in defense of the right to return and live in their communities of origin.

The process of organizing the repopulation of abandoned communities was a complicated and dangerous challenge requiring coordination with the central government, with the Ministry of the Interior, as it was called at the time, and with other authorities who consistently tried to block the return of the people to areas under FMLN control, like Las Vueltas, Guarjila, Nueva Trinidad, Arcatao, Copapayo, Santa Marta, Rutilio Grande, Huisisilapa, Itamaura, Ignacio Ellacuria, Los Ranchos, Teosinte and El Temedal in the departments of Chalatenango, Cuscatlan and Cabañas.

The settlement process also required identifying places where refugees from the UN camps in Honduras could settle when returning to their original community was not possible. All of these locations had to be negotiated with the government.

After the return and resettlement, the process of survival in these emerging communities began. Because the people were organized, they easily adapted to their new homes, beginning with the construction of simple housing, roads, agricultural production, education and health. With the eventual signing of the Peace Accord, many were able to return to school and, in some cases, the university to graduate as professionals, including teachers and doctors, with the aim of returning to serve their own communities.

My life during the war was not easy, and there were several occasions when I seriously considered that I would never see my children again, but I was always miraculously spared. The first time I was arrested for my work with CRIPDES, I was accompanied by my daughter, Carolina and both of us were blindfolded, handcuffed and beaten in the face, head and back with rifle butts in an effort to break our will. We eventually gained our freedom due to the intervention of the International Red Cross.

In October 1989, I was captured again, this time on the border between El Salvador and Honduras, known as El Poy, in the midst of repopulating thousands of families from the UN camp, Mesa Grande, in Honduras. Before we realized what was happening, the Salvadoran and Honduran militaries had us surrounded and were arresting our leaders. They captured five of us in all and transferred us to the army base in Chalatenango, where we were interrogated by a "gringo" soldier. From the Chalatenango barracks, we were sent to San Salvador, where hooded national guardsmen beat and tortured us, accusing us of "stirring up the people."

In 1991, I gave birth to my fourth and last daughter, Lorena, but continued my work with CRIPDES, forced again to leave my youngest child in the hands of friends. That's the way it was for my poor children.

Although I served as director and president of the CRIPDES board for a period, my role has always been one of an organizer, promoting human rights and advocating for democracy. If CRIPDES had not existed, displaced people perhaps would have wandered from place to place without the recognition of their rights or respect for their lives, becoming victims of repression, disappearing or being assassinated. For this, I am proud and thankful to have been involved with this organization and its struggles.

When recounting the years, the losses weigh upon me, but I find enormous satisfaction in the achievements that we have attained. It was difficult to live the long years of civil war, but it taught me that I am a survivor, an agent for change and a defender of people's rights. I am uncertain if I would do it all again, but I am filled with pride with the knowledge that I never surrendered during the darkest moments of our struggle.

The war has left its mark on me, and I am a different person for having lived it. It was not easy, and I only ask that you remember that I did it all for love.

Orlando

I have been a revolutionary since my youth. I must accept that my years at the National University of El Salvador (UES in Spanish) greatly influenced my social awareness and political formation. In my later years, it influenced my decisions and the direction of my life.

Art was the medium for my first steps towards political organization in the Popular Culture Movement. In 1982, I learned to sing a thousand and one songs steeped in social content and protest, and I took my first steps towards joining the struggle for change in my country. But at that time, I still had one foot outside and the other inside the Salvadoran revolution.

Thousands of thoughts were going through my head in relation to my options. The decision to join the revolutionary process that was brewing in my country was not an easy one. I was recovering from mumps and suffering from lingering fevers, which kept me prostrated in bed in Managua, where I had been running a photographic darkroom and learning about the technicalities of photography.

"Do not go back to El Salvador, I beg you with all my heart," my poor dear mother, who had come to Nicaragua in response to my deteriorating health, told me. "You saw how they are murdering people in our village. Your mama Aurelia (my great-aunt) left her home and had to emigrate to the town of Nejapa in order to find safety," my mother exclaimed. "You know that you are my only son." And, as she said it, tears rolled down her aging face.

She looked me straight in the eye as if imploring the heavens. I couldn't stand it and I hugged her forcefully as we cried together. I had left El Salvador with my great-aunt Aurelia and my mother, Tránsito, who will always be in my mind and heart, after the night of madness when the death squads arrived at the house of my cousins in Nejapa, threw them to the ground and murdered them all. They were five very dear people, and it is still an open wound that will never heal.

But my decision to return to my country was firm. I had always been enthusiastic about cameras, and I put a lot of love into my work of almost a year in Managua with responsibility for the photo laboratory of the Popular Liberation Forces (FPL), a member organization of the FMLN, imagining, during those days developing negative and positive images of life in the war zones. The photos we developed in Managua gave me an idea of life in the midst of armed conflict and, in that darkroom, learning and practicing the art of magic, my mind had become clear about what I wanted to do.

I had an archive of more than 800 black-and-white photographs showing various themes of life on the fronts, such as the production of basic grains, fishing, religious rites, literacy initiatives, recreational activities, theater, dances, health training, the operation of field hospitals and the flagrant violations of human rights by the military. These photographs also included guerrilla attacks on military garrisons, which ultimately influenced my decision to become a war correspondent in the guerrilla ranks.

In one of those photos, I met Father Rutilio Sánchez while he was giving a mass in the church of La Laguna Seca in the northern front of Chalatenango. He raised his hands, holding the Eucharist, in front of a large group of villagers among houses destroyed by bombings. It was a surreal image that broke the barriers in my mind and finally placed my two feet inside the revolution of El Salvador, where they belonged.

Through photography, I met many exemplary and heroic comrades in Managua. Many of them later died in combat, while others bear the scars of war. I remember José Roberto, Jesús Rojas, and Susana (la Chana), among others, with great affection. In Managua, I received weekly bags with rolls of film that came from the fronts.

I waited for them anxiously in order to continue weaving the stories of the struggle in the darkness, accompanied, as always, by a red spotlight (safety spotlight so as not to affect the photographic paper). There,

I carried out my struggle, looking for the tonalities and contrasts that each image required. Afterward, large packages were put together with photographs that were sent to the solidarity committees with El Salvador in the United States, Europe and other countries of the world.

I remember one period in that developing room when I spent several months without seeing the sun at the time of my departure, observing only the stars as I ran to the waiting vehicle that would take me to my sleeping quarters. During those lonely and dark days, I trained two colleagues, Miguel and Pancho, who later joined the FPL's film structure.

When the events of April 1983 occurred in Managua, with the assassination of Mélida Anaya Montes (Commander Ana María) and the suicide of Salvador Cayetano Carpio (Commander Marcial), I had been part of the Revolutionary Film Institute of El Salvador, the propaganda organ of the FPL, for a year and a few months. It was a blow to the organization that greatly affected our work at the international level but had little impact on the fronts. Nor did these events affect my decision to enter the front as a correspondent.

In the second week of June 1984, I traveled to El Salvador carrying a legal press credential from a foreign media outlet. After the usual procedures at the Comalapa airport, I stayed in a hotel in the capital until my contact, Lillian, contacted me.

The place of our meeting was a Pollo Campero (a popular chicken restaurant) in Mejicanos. Among the instructions she gave me was to leave for the northern front in two days. A young woman dressed in a pink skirt with an off-white headband would be waiting for me at noon at the El Rosario church in front of the Plaza Libertad, and they gave me a password to make sure I was in contact with the right person.

My instructions were to board a bus bound for the city of Apopa, sitting behind my contact without speaking but never losing sight of her. When we arrived in Apopa, she told me hurriedly, "Follow the comrade," indicating a second contact who proceeded to board a bus to the village of Joya Grande. When we got down, we entered a dirt road with several other people and soon began our journey on foot, following the train tracks.

At that moment, I heard a strange sound that I could not identify and suddenly saw that it was the motor car known as "the bullet" that was still used for transport by some in El Salvador. In this case, it was being used by several national guardsmen en route to some unknown destination.

The comrades traveling with me reacted immediately, throwing themselves into the underbrush to hide. Still, I didn't have time to react and remained motionless next to the old and rusting tracks while the bullet passed by carrying the soldiers who did not close their pupils nor stop pointing their G-3 rifles at me. It was my first experience with stark fear in many years.

We arrived at a small guerrilla camp on the outskirts of Apopa in the guerrilla subzone of Chapín, where there were approximately 25 well-armed guerrillas. There, I spent the next six days waiting for the army to dismantle several ambushes that our comrades had detected at various points along the northern highway (Troncal del Norte). We could not avoid this area on our trip north to the camps in Guazapa.

Our intelligence informed us finally that it was safe to travel, so we departed and walked through the night, passing through several small villages with names like Mirandilla, Palo Grande, Platanares and Consolación. With daylight, I observed people of the civilian population working and playing, with small children running up and down, setting up make-believe ambushes and mimicking the actions of their fathers and older brothers in the real war.

At one point, I observed several children playing in a nearby underground tunnel ("tatu") pretending to be protecting themselves from government aviation, and I thought how tragic it was to see this new generation deprived of a safe and healthy childhood, mimicking the war as if it were a natural part of life's routine.

At the end of June, I was in the village of El Ceretal on the lower slopes of the Guazapa volcano, where I shared the remains of a bombed-out shelter for several nights with an elderly couple about 70 years of age. The days were filled with fear and anxiety due to the intense bombardment by the Air Force, forcing us to spend long hours in the darkness of a small underground tunnel nearby. The lack of light took me back to my days in the darkroom in Managua observing photos with images that I was now experiencing in real life. When I departed from the old couple, we exchanged goodbyes and a prolonged hug, and I suddenly realized that I didn't know their real names, nor did I ever find out if they had survived the war.

Several days later, I discovered a small guerrilla field hospital where I met a young Mexican doctor named Julia, who was responsible for several injured comrades from a recent attack against soldiers guarding the Cerrón Grande dam. I would learn years later that Julia died heroically in Chalatenango defending another field hospital and several wounded comrades who could not be moved. They were all shot in cold blood.

At the time of our meeting, Julia was coordinating the transfer to Chalatenango of more than twenty wounded comrades. She was waiting for several small boats to cross Suchitlán Lake, so I was assigned to travel with her in order to reach my final destination in that department.

We left several days later from the village of Copapayo with a beautiful sunset and waves of white egrets dipping and soaring over the peaceful waters of the lake, leaving us all dazed by the stunning beauty of this highly contested war zone. We had only been traveling for about fifteen minutes, however, when the skies opened up with a powerful and persistent downpour that soaked us all, including the wounded. The rain finally stopped, however, and by the grace of God, we arrived safely in Chalatenango several hours later.

I had little previous experience with sleeplessness and endless walking, but my trip from Chapin to Guazapa gave me a small taste of life in the controlled zones. This was reinforced by the all-night walk to the guerrilla hospital at San Antonio de Los Ranchos, where we arrived in the early morning of the following day. We were given a delicious meal of rice and beans, and I was then guided to the propaganda camp, where the rest of my film crew was waiting.

What a joy it was to meet again after having shared the experience of Managua together. It was a triumph for all of us to have made it this far. That night, we celebrated among myself, Julito, Alfredo Zamora, Toñito Cañenguez (Francisco Lemus) and Miguel (Milton Portillo) with a cup of hot coffee. Our cameras had not yet arrived, however, so we still felt "unarmed."

Our camp in those early days was located in the village of Honduritas in the municipality of San José Las Flores. Thankfully, we were able to spend our first two months there without military incursions or bombings. With the only camera available to us, I traveled throughout the municipality, photographing agricultural production and other activities of the civilian population organized in Local Popular Powers (PPLs in Spanish).

The rains had been abundant, and I could tell that the production had been good as I gazed over the open fields of corn and beans. Later, I visited Los Amates, where the people fished in the Sumpul River and saw abundance again. August came in relative peace, but we still did not know when our photographic equipment would arrive.

Upon finishing breakfast one morning, we heard several explosions in the nearby hillsides. Minutes later, several projectiles whistled over our heads and crashed into the Anonal hill. Augusto, the leader of our camp, shouted to take refuge and started running with his newborn son in his arms in search of cover.

The army was shelling much of our controlled zone that day with heavy artillery from their barracks in the city of Chalatenango. We knew that they had a range of approximately fifteen kilometers, so we were within easy reach and ran to take shelter by a large rock formation nearby. Only Julito and Miguel from our photography team were present in the camp at that moment, and we continued to be under fire for the next two hours. At one point, a message arrived informing us that the mortars had killed a newborn child in the nearby village of Tamarindo, and I was ordered to travel to the village to document what had happened.

It took me almost an hour to get to Tamarindo. Just before my arrival, I ran into a local guerrilla platoon whose leader advised me to take great care because a radio message had been intercepted from soldiers of the Atlacatl battalion ordering their troops to occupy the high points in the zone in preparation for an attack against Las Flores, from where I had just come. At that moment, I was at a crossroads, uncertain about what to do, but I decided to take a gamble and continue to Tamarindo in order to complete my mission.

When I arrived, there was no one on the street, so I started searching until I found the small house where a dead child lay covered with flowers. The mother was crying by her side while several women from the village tried to comfort her. The rest of the inhabitants of Tamarindo had fled and were in hiding from the approaching soldiers.

I took several photos and left as quickly as I could, trying to determine the best way back to our camp, but as I approached the site, I heard heavy gunfire nearby. Arriving at our campsite, where I had hoped to find my comrades, I found it empty. I suddenly realized with growing trepidation that I was alone in unfamiliar terrain with no communication. At that moment, however, another comrade appeared and informed me that he had been sent to look for me and guide me to the site nearby where the others were now waiting, along with María Chichilco.

By this time, the soldiers had occupied Las Flores and Tamarindo, and all of the civilians were now in "guinda" or hiding. We waited until dark to begin our exodus, harassed by constant rain and the slippery muddy mountain paths. I protected my camera with a small plastic bag, and we set off in a single file in a column of more than a hundred unarmed civilians from the surrounding villages of Honduritas, El Conacaste and others, accompanied by several armed combatants. We were heading in the direction of the Sumpul River with the hopes of crossing a small suspension bridge that would allow us to escape into neighboring Honduras.

There were many women, children and elderly among our ranks, and people were constantly slipping and falling as we slowly advanced through the night. In the darkness, only the voices of small children could be heard, with their mothers and our guides urging them to keep silent, keep walking and not get lost.

I felt helpless and regretful that I could not do more to assist those who had problems walking or to mitigate their hunger and their fear. We arrived at the hanging bridge at four in the morning, but it was in ruins, and many of the old people and young children were unable or too afraid to cross through the turbulent waters below. We had no alternative but to take out our flashlights to light our trail in order to avoid falling into the river, and this increased the risk of being detected by the soldiers as we continued along the river banks.

At that moment, I ran into Goyo, an old friend and comrade who worked in Europe, strengthening international alliances with the FMLN in that part of the world. He explained that he was at the front to learn more about the Local Popular Powers, a form of local government in the FMLN's controlled zones, and about life in the midst of war. We greeted each other warmly and walked together without much communication for a while as the column slowly moved through the darkness.

Eventually, the people became too exhausted to walk anymore. A few had managed to cross the river on the old and rickety hanging bridge, but others had stayed behind. I was in a small group with María Chichilco and my other two companions from the photographic team, Julio and Miguel.

At 6:00 in the morning, a Cessna 02 plane appeared overhead, armed with rockets and machine guns. A few minutes later, we heard the first bursts of gunfire and realized that Atlacatl had the entire civilian population surrounded and were firing at the people at close range. Our small group, with Maria, managed to sneak through the encirclement of the army under heavy gunfire and reach the Chichilco mountain. At the same time, helicopters fired indiscriminately on the civilian population gathered below and cornered near the Gualsinga River that flows into the Sumpul.

When the attack ended and the army had evacuated the area, we counted more than eighty deaths among the women, elderly and children. It was my first experience in heavy combat, and I had come close to getting shot.

We spent the next three days without eating with the exception of half of a tortilla that we managed to find near the village of Los Pozos. In the afternoon of the fourth day, my legs felt weak, and my body could give no more, so Maria sent several of us across the Sumpul River to purchase food in the Honduran village of Talquinte. Sigfredo, a combatant, and I would make the purchases in the store while two women comrades would look for ground corn to make tortillas. The only complication was that Honduran soldiers patrolled the village every day.

Upon arriving at a store, we found it closed. The owners, with fear in their eyes, opened the door slightly when we started knocking and informed us that several soldiers had passed by about an hour earlier, "accompanied by several gringos," so I stood guard. At the same time, Sigfredo shopped, filling several sacks with food.

The next day, after eating part of our newly purchased supplies, we began to feel energized and decided to return to our camp in Honduritas. I still had a roll of film left, so I took several photos of the massacre the day before. Many of the corpses were of small children, leaving me indignant at the theft of an entire lifetime in a matter of minutes, and, as the "zopilotes" (buzzards) flew over our heads, I wondered, "Why so much madness?" It was August 1984, and this massacre became known as "the Gualsinga massacre."

Days later, we were in the "Montañona", as they referred to the site where zonal commanders were generally based and where the guerrilla radio, Radio Farabundo Martí, was located. There, we learned of an underground tunnel nearby where film and camera equipment had been buried since 1982.

Without thinking twice, we headed off to the area where the tunnel was said to exist, along with Miguel, Toñito and Luisón, pulling a mule in case we were lucky and unable to manage the weight of our newfound treasure. When Luisón opened the tatu entrance, however, it was immediately apparent that the humidity and rain had damaged almost all of the cameras, lenses, rolls, film and other materials. We were only able to save two cameras, an 8-millimeter cinema projector and a film, "El Salvador, the armed people will win."

Juan Carlos, one of the technicians for our clandestine radio, Radio Farabundo Martí, disassembled and cleaned the projector, and we were optimistic that it might still be operable. Upon returning to the Montañona, we learned that the projector and the film worked well, so we organized a mobile cinema trip to the nearby villages with a portable source of energy, gasoline and an improvised screen made of wood and blankets. In the first village, the documentary was shown for the first time to people who had never seen cinema, and all were fascinated. Wherever we traveled after that, people crowded together to watch the film.

At the end of October 1984, our photography team was ordered to travel to Cinquera in the department of Cabañas, known by the comrades as the Radiola subzone. We took the camera that we had rescued in the tunnel and arrived in Cinquera after two days of hard walking. After resting, we presented ourselves to the commander of Radiola, Ramon Torres, a young but experienced warrior with many years in the front. From him, we learned that we would be accompanying a special mission, although the details remained secret until the following morning.

We awoke the next day before dawn and joined Ramon and his troops. As we walked, Ramón informed us that we would be filming an ambush that the FMLN was planning with a large fleet of government helicopters used to transport paratroopers deep into our controlled territories to attack our camps and the civilian population residing there. Under Ramon's command were several well-armed guerrilla columns carrying a 50-caliber machine gun and a large quantity of ammunition. Later in the afternoon, I tried to get several photographs, but no matter how much I raised the ASA or the ISO of my analog camera, I could achieve little or nothing with a roll of 100 ASA.

After passing the Quezalapa bridge, we stopped to rest. During that brief interlude, I suddenly saw a young couple embracing each other among one of the guerrilla columns as a beautiful sunset lit the distant horizon. Given the nature of our mission, this scene was moving and strange, but I took several pictures just before the couple noticed me and started laughing, still holding tightly to each other in an attempt to halt the movement of time.

When the order to move out came, we all quickly stood up. The young couple took their place in the column, still holding hands, as they disappeared among the trees. I never saw them again, but the scene remained planted in my heart and mind, and I have always wondered if they survived the war.

When we reached our destination on top of a high mountain, allowing us to view the countryside for many miles around us, Ramon gave the order to begin "digging in" to construct a series of trenches and foxholes on this sparsely wooded hilltop in order to provide some minimal protection from the aviation that would soon be incoming. In the words of Ramón, "This would be the only possibility of surviving the horrors that were approaching."

At 1 a.m. the next morning, guerrilla units hidden around the town of Suchitoto began attacking the Treasury Police installations in the center of town. The fighting continued all night, and two observation planes arrived before the first light of dawn, firing their rockets at our position. They were not very accurate in the darkness, but they filled the sky with flares, trying to detect any movements on the ground. Meanwhile, our photographic team remained in our trenches, listening to the heavy fighting inside and around Suchitoto.

As the sun was coming up, A-37 jet bombers appeared overhead and began to saturate the area with 500-pound bombs, at which point I entrusted myself to my God with growing uncertainty about getting out of this in one piece. The bombs exploded around us, too close for comfort, as the earth shook like an earthquake and the air filled with deadly shrapnel, but we were ordered to remain in our positions and resist. Suddenly, I heard the roar of what sounded like a thousand helicopters heading in our direction and realized that I was observing my first landing of paratroopers bringing visions of the movie thriller *Apocalypse Now* although, in truth, this was much more terrifying.

With the helicopters directly over our heads and, it seemed, only a few meters away, Ramón gave the order to "fire," and I immediately heard the roar of our 50-caliber machine gun. The comrade next to me then stood up with an M-60 machine gun and began firing while the rest of our combatants followed suit with their M-16 rifles. Several of the helicopters started to fall out of the sky, with smoke pouring out of their tails. It was pure Hollywood.

There was not a second to waste, so I began photographing with my camera as the helicopters began to circle like a swarm of angry hornets. Our combatants began to scream with euphoria each time they saw them fall out of the sky. After several aircraft were downed, the A-37s returned to resume their bombing, and government paratroopers dropped from the helicopters and joined the combat on the ground.

In the madness of the moment, human beings ceased to be human, transforming themselves into wild animals. In the face of such horror, several comrades broke from the line of fire in search of a better place to protect themselves.

I lost contact with Ramón at one point and, along with another comrade, also fled down the hillside to a nearby ravine, with the bombs and bullets close behind. Years later, during a return visit to Cinquera, I found the place where several of these bombs had fallen, including one on the street leading into the town that had left a small school in rubble with a crater as big as the moon's.

We slept that night in our camp in Cinquera and awoke the following morning without bombs falling on us. Hence, we prepared to leave for a festival to celebrate our victory in the nearby town of Tejutepeque.

Government soldiers who had occupied the town for years had finally been driven out by a series of guerrilla attacks in 1982, and we danced that night without worries with girls from the town and in the company of several guerrilla columns assigned to defend the subzone.

In December 1984, our photographic team was ordered to travel to the town of La Palma in the department of Chalatenango to cover the first dialogue between the government and FMLN guerrillas. That morning, I had been pleasantly surprised to receive several new rolls of film for our camera; and, in preparation for our trip, several of us went to bathe in a small stream that ran past our camp.

Just as we were dressing, however, we were attacked by an angry swarm of hornets, and most of us were stung in several places on our bodies. I was stung several times on my right foot, and when the time came to leave, I saw that my foot had swollen to the extent that I could not fit it into my boot. And it was painful to walk. The trip to La Palma would be long and arduous, and I wasn't certain that I could make it, so I handed the camera to Toñito Cañenguez and watched in profound disappointment as my comrades filed out of our camp to make history. I was depressed for days at being unable to cover such a memorable event, but we couldn't risk detaining the whole column for one hornet sting.

On December 24 that year, we celebrated Christmas in the village of Zapotal. For security reasons, we gathered just outside the village in abandoned houses that remained standing after years of incessant bombardment. With pork rinds, beans, tortillas, a few drinks of "chaparro" (a strong alcoholic drink made by the peasants) and the jokes of Toñito Cañenguez, we had a uniquely sensational time.

In 1985, I started working full-time with Radio Farabundo Martí (RFM). One of my areas of responsibility was producing the news gathered by monitoring news broadcasts from around the country and the world. I also learned to operate the equipment in the booth and worked with the mixers every day for transmission.

On one occasion, we were broadcasting on Mount Chichilco, called La Siberia, not because of the cold but because of the incessant sunshine that burned us daily. At about 5:30 in the afternoon, A-37 jets appeared overhead, but since we were on the air at that moment, it was impossible to halt the broadcast and run for cover, as that would have signaled our position to the aircraft. So, we had to continue transmitting, hoping that the bombs would not fall on top of us. After dropping several bombs in the vicinity without affecting the radio, the planes finally flew off and left us in peace.

La Siberia was valued as a location for the radio because it was well hidden and difficult for the army to reach without being detected. To protect the site, we applied various measures, like removing our boots upon entering the camp to avoid leaving footprints, making sure that we did not damage the tall elephant grass that surrounded the area, speaking softly at all times, listening to the news with the radio close to our ear, cooking on a Vietnam stove to avoid smoke and never revealing the location of the radio to other comrades or visitors to the front. We also managed to install a large diesel engine underground in an attempt to reduce the noise of this key source of power.

Of the five different sites used for the radio over the years, all had their own underground tunnel where the transmission equipment was kept and where our team worked. When army incursions were detected in close proximity, we quickly evacuated and moved to another site where we maintained adequate conditions for continuing transmissions. The goal was to never go off the air.

In October 1985, one of our commanders, Ricardo Gutiérrez, gave me orders to travel again to Cinquera with my camera, and I knew in my mind that something big was going to happen. Like our last journey, it was a long and difficult walk that left us exhausted and sweating profusely, especially with camera equipment.

We arrived in Copapayo where other comrades helped me with the cargo, and there I was informed of the purpose of our trip. We were going to film a prisoner exchange involving the daughter of President José Napoleón Duarte, who had been kidnapped months earlier on the sidewalks of San Salvador by a small squad of urban commandos and held in our controlled zones while the terms of an exchange were negotiated. The event would take place in the town of Tenancingo.

I had not slept or eaten for several days in order to arrive on time, but I realized immediately that the exchange had already been executed a few minutes before I got there. Nevertheless, my journey was not in vain as I arrived in time to film the freeing of FMLN political prisoners by the government along with the official act in which the ambassadors of several countries participated together with Jesuit priest Ignacio Ellacuría, Dean of the UCA, and Monsignor Rivera y Damas of the Catholic Church, among others. I gave all of the material that we produced that day to the commander, Facundo Guardado, although I never knew what happened to it or how it was used.

I returned to Chalatenango and continued my duties with Radio Farabundo Martí during the remaining months of that year. During that period, we also established a plan for filming the destruction of villages by the Air Force with testimonies from the affected population. I spent several months on this task, accompanied by comrade Erick (Salvador Orellana), who was experienced and highly knowledgeable about the work of the Local Popular Powers and was very close to the civilians who inhabited the controlled zones in those difficult years. I learned later that the video materials that we developed on this theme reached solidarity groups in Mexico and the United States and served to document the abuses to the civilian population perpetrated by the Armed Forces.

Several months later, I was ordered to accompany the guerrilla columns that attacked the army barracks at El Paraíso in Chalatenango for the second time. I carried with me a video 8 movie camera that was almost useless at night when the lighting was insufficient. But the audio was great, and I was able to cover sound during the attack.

I was about 400 meters from the front gates of the barracks, not very promising for recording either images or sound without a zoom. At 4:30 in the morning, which was the hour for the withdrawal of our troops, I was able to record the happy and optimistic shouts of our combatants as they evacuated the demolished fort. The wounded were loaded into hammocks, and the images I captured came out quite well with the help of the flares launched by the AC-47 plane flying overhead, illuminating the entire sky and the remains of the barracks.

It was almost 6 a.m. when our last combatants were leaving, and I noticed all of a sudden that only I was left, recording the immense fire that was now consuming what remained of the barracks. Comrade Justiniano saw me and began yelling for me to hurry my departure because replacement troops were on the way. I ran in his direction, and as I caught up with him, we passed a number of our combatants, some of them with the new rifles and uniforms they had taken from the warehouse of El Paraíso.

I could hear the sound of the helicopters approaching and knew that they would soon be unloading hundreds of paratroopers in an attempt to encircle us, so we looked for a suitable place to hide as I continued to film. Soldiers now on the ground began firing at us, but several of our combatants heard the shooting and returned to where we were hiding and fired an RPG-7 rocket at the soldiers so that we could all escape.

Once we had put sufficient distance between ourselves and the government troops that continued to arrive in and around El Paraíso, we stopped at a small country store and consumed several soft drinks with sweet bread, which gave us the needed energy to catch up with our other comrades in Ocotal later that night.

I remained with the radio between 1987 and 1988, always alert to the dangers of Long-Range Reconnaissance Patrols (PRAL), small and agile units that penetrated our fronts in search of our camps and command posts in order to guide government aviation and ground troops bent on our annihilation.

I was informed at the beginning of October that a professional video camera would arrive soon in Chalatenango, and I thought to myself. "My God! After how many years?" They brought it to me several days later, just in time for our national offensive, "Hasta El Tope!" in November 1989.

In preparation for the offensive, our commander, Dimas Rodriguez, was already stationed with other commanders on the slopes of the San Salvador Volcano, overlooking the capital city. In his absence, Commander Milton was in charge and called me with instructions to prepare everything we would need for the radio and for photography and to bring it to Talzate on November 11 to join Tino's column of combatants.

We arrived in Las Vueltas a few days before the offensive and were able to film the military formation of several of the guerrilla columns, with approximately eighty heavily armed comrades, preparing to head off for the city of Chalatenango, where we had been assigned. From Las Vueltas, we traveled together to La Antena, a high mountainous area from where we could see the first houses of the city of Chalatenango and the lights of the city itself in the distance.

We settled behind a large stone wall for protection. I was accompanied by Jaime Cáceres, a legendary correspondent and announcer for Radio Farabundo Martí. He was equipped with his tape recorder, cassettes, microphones and his radio transmitter to make links with guerrilla communication signals and keep track of what was happening in the attack, minute by minute.

Early in the evening, Tino finally gave the order to open fire on enemy trenches just below us, and the comrades launched an RPG-7 with minimal response from the government troops, most of whom had evacuated the area, not knowing that a massive, well-coordinated offensive intended to change the course of the war was about to be launched against them.

Soon after revealing our position, we were attacked with M-79 mortars, wounding one of our comrades. We could hear heavy combat in the distance as several guerrilla columns attacked government positions near the Chalatenango soccer stadium.

We could also see the military barracks in the city of Chalatenango as fighting spread throughout the city. On the morning of November 12, I was filming this scene from a nearby hillside when, from one moment to the next, we were attacked with a 50-caliber machine gun and heavy artillery, forcing us to retreat in search of better cover. Minutes later, two A-37s appeared overhead and began to bomb our positions as we began to move again.

As the bombs fell and the bullets from the aircraft whistled over our heads, Tino yelled for us to move to a larger rock formation close by. So, without halting my filming, I got up and started running just seconds before one of the bombs fell directly on our position. By this time, my nerves were a frazzle, and I was certain that we were all going to die, but I was able to maintain enough control to film the final seconds of the A-37 diving on top of us, ready to drop its bombs. I couldn't compete with the nerves of steel of Tino and his men, however, who never wavered in battle, never stopped fighting, and never demonstrated the least bit of fear in the face of death.

After several days of intensive combat, without sleep and without eating much, several of us went to bathe in the Tamulasco River nearby, and I took several images of the heroic comrades in Tino's column bathing, washing clothes and joking with their fearless leader until my batteries ran out.

As always, I gave the material recorded that day to Commander Ricardo from the radio and was able to verify later that it had arrived in Mexico to support our international work. Months after the signing of Peace Accords, I was visiting comrades in one of the San Salvador offices of the FMLN, now a legal political party planning to participate in the next elections, and a comrade named Rina, well-remembered for her dedication to the struggle and who died soon after the war, told me to search through a storage area on the second floor where there were some "video cassettes that we brought from Mexico that might be of interest to you."

With my hands trembling and my heart full of hope, I climbed the stairs and found several old boxes sitting on the floor. When I looked at their contents, reviewing them slowly with expectant eyes, much to my joy, I found several videos and packets of still shots with notes written in my handwriting and the following titles:

Fighting on the hill, La Antena, near the outskirts of Chalate,
Images of the hill overlooking the barracks,
A-37 aircraft in the moment of attack,
Lake Suchitlán and
City of Chalate.

Best of all, among the pile of images thrown together in the boxes, there was Tino, bathing in the Tamulasco River together with his platoon.

Janeth

The idea of writing this short story came to me on a cold, snowy night in Norway where, after almost 40 years, a group of old and unforgettable friends from different countries had gathered in a snug mountain cabin in front of a large fire to exchange stories of a distant past in the civil war of El Salvador. This is the story that I told.

In my early childhood, I was a girl with many dreams, but I was the youngest daughter of a poor family of seven children without a father. My mother worked as a cook, caring for other people's children or cleaning other people's houses, and I was usually at her side. I went with her wherever she went, making it difficult at times for her to find work because they had to accept me as well.

My childhood was not easy. We moved frequently, and I had few friends. My only escape was my studies, which I adored and dedicated myself to completely, always aspiring to get the best grades and hoping to eventually get a university degree.

I was at the height of my basic education when my mother suddenly informed me that we were moving to the countryside to take care of one of her sisters, who had fallen gravely ill. I took advantage of that time to get to know my aunt and my cousins better, but the area where we lived was filled with danger from death squads and a military that was harassing the civilian population, accusing us all of being guerrilla sympathizers.

Almost every day, soldiers patrolled our streets and searched our homes until it finally became impossible to remain in our houses at night, so we snuck off each afternoon as darkness fell to sleep under the stars or the rain in the nearby hillsides along with most of our neighbors to protect ourselves from being arrested, tortured and killed.

Being victimized in this way pushed us little by little into the hands of the revolutionary organizations in our area of Usulutan, and the day finally came when we joined the struggle for justice and democracy and against the repression in our country. Given her experience as a cook, my mother was assigned to run the kitchen of the guerrilla camp where the local command structure was located. People quickly fell in love with her and affectionately called her "Abuelita" (grandma). The people brought her fruits and delicious things to eat because she was everyone's grandmother!

I don't know how much political awareness I had at that early age, but life itself and the struggle for survival were my best teachers. In the war, everyone had a special role to play. My mother, with her skills in the kitchen, prepared the food for the comrades. I spent most of my time on military drills and exercises at our training school set up for the younger recruits. But I was soon assigned the role of radio operator and this task often took me to places quite distant from my mother, to the point where I would rarely see her.

For a while, I was assigned to a combat squad but later became responsible for developing and protecting our system of encrypted codes for radio communications between commanders and guerrilla camps throughout the front. This was highly delicate and strategic work in order to ensure that the enemy could not intercept and decipher our radio communications during operations, and I am pleased to say that, during the course of my years in the guerrilla fronts of Morazan, the army never managed to break our codes.

My comrades in radio communications were all young women working together on a daily basis to carry out this important task. We were camped in the more remote mountainous areas of our front with few people knowledgeable of our whereabouts. In essence, we were clandestine. When the army attacked our front, and we had to "guindiar" (flee), we hid most of our equipment and other materials and carried the rest on our backs, along with our weapons and knapsacks.

On one frightening occasion, I was seriously wounded in an army ambush. I am not sure of the day because all days were basically the same for us. There were no Mondays, Sundays or holidays. They were all the same, except for Christmas, which we made a special effort to celebrate by having a small party with lots of food and dancing when circumstances allowed. We would party until dawn, with rifles constantly hanging from our shoulders. What a way to dance!!

On this particular occasion, I remember that there was a bright full moon and that we were somewhere in Usulután. I was accompanying a small reconnaissance squad gathering information in preparation for a future attack against government troops stationed in the town of Berlin. Our squad consisted of approximately twenty combatants under the command of a comrade named Jeronimo.

We had departed from our base in Morazan and walked for three nights consecutively to reach our target destination, arriving tired and hungry. We passed by a small house of peasants, supposedly collaborators, who we hoped could provide us with a few tortillas and information about recent movements of the army that we knew to be close.

After a brief rest, we thanked the people for their help, said goodbye and continued on our way. But we had walked less than a hundred meters when we were fired upon by soldiers hiding behind the little house that we had just left. We immediately began to run in an effort to distance ourselves and search for cover, but I was one of the last in the group and highly exposed. As shots rang out, zinging past our heads, a powerful G-3 bullet pierced my left lung and sent me flying to the ground face down.

It all happened so fast! I had been carrying my backpack with my belongings, which consisted of a small blanket, a towel, a pair of pants and underwear. The bullet went through all of this and entered my left lung five millimeters from my spinal column, as I was later informed. Everyone else kept running as I lay there alone on the ground.

Minutes later, I began to hear someone screaming and felt a pair of arms around me, lifting me to their shoulder in an attempt to carry me. But another voice was shouting, "Leave her, maybe she's already dead! We cannot sacrifice the life of another comrade," as the shooting continued without stop.

Blood was running profusely out of my ears, mouth, nose and the wound itself, and I was certain that I was in the process of bleeding to death. The bullet had not come out on the other side of my body, so it was still someplace inside, risking further damage to vital organs and my spinal cord. I don't remember feeling pain or anything at that moment other than something hot running through my body. Then I lost consciousness, and everything went black.

The comrades of my group, certain that we would all be killed if they continued to carry me, threw me to the ground and left me hidden in a shallow ravine. According to my calculations, that was about three o'clock in the afternoon.

At around six in the afternoon, I awoke totally soaked and shivering from the cold. Parts of me were purple and others were white as paper. There had been a tremendous rainstorm while I was lying there in the ravine, and I was immersed in water, unable to move. The water had washed away most of the blood that had been covering my body, and it was getting colder.

My mind finally began to work, but all I could think about was my mother and how I wanted to hug her at that moment, and I am quite certain that my spirit actually did depart for some time, bidding her a final goodbye. At the same time, however, I couldn't believe that my life was ending here, like this, like an abandoned dog.

I lost consciousness or slept for a time but suddenly awoke to find a man in a hat carrying a large machete standing over me, and I realized immediately that his intentions were not good. He began to examine me to see if I was still alive, but I was totally paralyzed and did everything I could to breathe without him noticing.

He took everything of value that I had been carrying, including my weapon, my ammunition belt and water. What was worse, he took my communications radio and code book (something of great value to the military). I realized at that moment that this man had probably been sent by the military because they knew that someone had been left behind, perhaps dead. He then took my belongings and left.

Hours later, a younger man appeared. I was by this time freezing to death and in tremendous pain, but he spoke to me softly, saying that his name was Daniel and that he had come to see if he could help me. He said he was happy to find me alive but that I could not remain here, so he began to lift my body in an attempt to get me on my feet. I had no strength, however, and could barely walk, and the pain was *UNBEARABLE*.

We stumbled along for a little while and when we could go no further, he left me buried under a pile of leaves and branches of the nearby coffee trees, instructing me to remain hidden and still until he returned. I remained that way, buried under a volcano of dried leaves all day long, without eating, without drinking anything and without being able to move.

When it began to get dark, Daniel reappeared with water, food and a blanket. I was in such great pain that I was neither hungry nor had the strength for anything, but he made me eat and drink a little as best I could. He then told me that we needed to wait until I could walk a little and promised to return the next day to try to move me to a small house nearby.

It was nightfall on the following day before he returned. My pain was getting worse by the minute, and I still had no strength, but he told me that we had to move, that it was dangerous here. With great care and effort, he helped me on my feet again and I took a few steps while holding on to him. We walked slowly through the darkness until we finally reached the house of an old man that he knew.

The old man was afraid because the military was still nearby, but he finally allowed me to lie down for a while in a very hard bed. My pain was unbearable, and I hadn't received any medicine, so my body was fighting this battle on its own and enduring. When I finally managed to find a slightly comfortable position and felt myself falling asleep, the young man woke me abruptly to tell me that the military was on its way and that we had to leave at that very moment. I don't know how I managed, but we got out and away as quickly as possible.

Somehow, my comrades were informed that I was still alive, and that same night, they came looking for us in a small group of heavily armed combatants. When they finally found us, they were prepared with medicine and a hammock to carry me to one of our camps, where a doctor was waiting to treat my wound. The camp was a long distance, so we stopped at midnight to rest until the first light of dawn. They carried me in the hammock and for periods on their backs, under a torrential rain, slipping and falling frequently on the wet, muddy foot trails for what seemed an eternity, but we finally arrived.

The guerrilla hospital was headed by Dr. Fidel, who was going to treat me. By this time, I had a high fever and a huge loss of blood. I was also having trouble breathing since my lung was saturated with blood, rendering it almost useless. They began to take blood samples immediately from all of the comrades in the camp but found no one who was compatible with my blood type, O Rh negative, somewhat uncommon. I have no idea how many samples they tested, but finally, after much searching, they found a suitable match with the blood of my best friend, Emma. And that saved my life.

I needed emergency surgery, but our Dr. Fidel was actually only a medical student who had dropped out of school to join the guerrillas years earlier. He had learned much over the years, but he had never done this type of surgery, so he had to perform the operation consulting step by step by radio with our more experienced doctors in the camps to the north. We were also without access to blood serum, so coconut water was used for this purpose. Luckily, I was not allergic to this liquid.

I don't know at what point they put me under anesthesia. I just fell asleep. I remember, however, that I had a horrible nightmare in which I felt like I had been put in a plastic bag without air to breathe. Then, I felt a pricking sensation, like with a needle, all over my body and awoke to realize that my operation was still going on and that someone was sewing up the wound under my arm where they had removed large quantities of coagulated blood from several days without medical treatment.

In spite of this frightening moment and our circumstances in general, all went well with my surgery, a bit of a miracle given the lack of hygiene and standard medical supplies. Nor do I recall any problems with infections afterward. But scarcely five days after the operation, while recovering on a hard bed of bamboo and half asleep, two warplanes suddenly flew over our position, and I had to leap from my bed and throw myself to the ground, opening my wound again. Nevertheless, I was able to receive treatment immediately and resume the process of healing.

A month passed, and the conditions in Morazan were becoming unstable with frequent military incursions and bombings, so the military commanders decided that it would be better for me to transfer to a hospital in San Salvador where I could receive higher quality and more professional attention.

Getting me out of the front required a journey of several days through the mountains, partly on foot and partly on horseback, until I could reach a paved road where collaborators were waiting with a vehicle to take me to the capital city. They also provided me with more appropriate clothing in order to blend into the urban population, and I began my new adventure as a guerrilla fighter hiding out in civilization under the enemy's nose.

For security reasons, I had to develop a "leyenda" (alibi) to explain who I was and how I had been so gravely injured and memorize it well so that it never varied. I also had to prepare myself in order to be able to respond to people's questions without hesitation. That included the questions of medical personnel and military authorities. It was not an easy challenge. My case was far from routine, and I knew that I would be in the crosshairs of military intelligence, given the nature of my wounds.

My alibi was that I had been traveling with a group of young people in a jeep after a party when, out of nowhere, we were caught in a cross-fire (not uncommon in the context of the war) with bullets coming at us from all directions. Our driver speeded up, trying to get us out of danger, and it was at that moment that a bullet pierced my lung. I was the only one in the group who was wounded.

The problem with all of this remained the lack of medical records covering my surgery and initial care. My operation was not registered in any hospital or health center, nor was there any record of who had done the original surgery, which was highly unusual given that this type of surgery would normally be performed by a specialist.

The first time I had to use my alibi was during our trip to San Salvador when I was questioned at a military checkpoint. We were able to pass that and other checkpoints without delay, however, and I arrived safely to our destination, where I was admitted to Rosales Hospital. Once there, I would have to use my alibi frequently during my month-long stay.

A variety of doctors ran an infinity of tests on me. I had to be careful with the doctors and hospital staff as most of them I could not trust, knowing that the military would instruct them to try to get information from me on the true origins of my wounds. They constantly asked me questions about how my injuries had occurred and where I was operated on, but I gave my simple, made-up version of an answer without variation.

I awoke one night to find myself surrounded by soldiers, and they questioned me incessantly about my "accident", although I had been slightly reassured by the knowledge that the International Red Cross had taken up my case, providing me with a certain level of assurance that I would not be killed outright or disappeared. During my stay in the hospital, I completed my 15th birthday, although, for me, it was a date like any other.

After my release, I stayed for several months with a family of collaborators in San Salvador until it was time to return to the front. My only dream at that time was to see my mother again, who knew nothing about my ambush, my injury or my time in San Salvador, and I longed to see her upon my return to the controlled zones of Morazan.

I rejoined the war and spent the next eight years developing radio codes with my beloved comrades in clandestine camps in the mountains, where we awoke each morning and went to sleep each evening, wondering if we would survive another day. The dangers were limitless, from being torn to pieces by government aviation, being shot or mortared by ground troops bent on our annihilation, stepping on a land mine, getting lost alone to snakebite or any number of other possible circumstances.

At the end of my first year back, I started to feel something strange in my body, something that I could feel with my fingers and almost grab onto near my collarbone. We later discovered that it was the bullet, or rather, the remains of the bullet, that had penetrated my lung without coming out the other side. One of our doctors cut it out, and I gave thanks again for not having been paralyzed by a projectile that entered so close to my spine. Over time, my lung also returned to normal, and I have not been bothered with problems breathing.

Eight eternal years passed with the full gamut of emotions: fear, stress, exhaustion, joy and a profound love for my comrades. We were like a family, sharing everything, the good along with the bad, and supporting each other always during difficult moments. It was the only explanation for our ability to survive and carry on in the midst of so much suffering.

I currently live in Sweden, where I managed to study and finally earn my much-dreamed-of university degree. With my degree, I was able to find a good job and start my family again, now with three children and two grandchildren. The children and grandchildren are pure Swedes and know little about their mother's previous life.

One day, I will have to find a way to explain all of this to them. But I know that it will not be easy in the civilized ambiance of Scandinavia to explain a country so different on the other side of the planet where a blind and greedy oligarchy, the lack of democracy and the violence of a repressive military drove its youth to war.

Rogelio

Perhaps I should begin by explaining what brought me to El Salvador. At that time (the late 1960s), there was a priest in Belgium, where I was born, named José Carden, who later became a cardinal and founded the organization of Young Christian Workers (JOC in Belgian), a movement to which my parents strongly subscribed. So, in our family, there was always much discussion about social structural injustice and the struggle of workers. It was a heavily politicized environment in favor of the working class.

My bishop in the diocese of Bruges at the time had participated in the Second Vatican Council and played a key role in the elaboration of the final document on religious freedom. Upon his return from Rome, he explained to us priests his view that not only was he the bishop of our rather small diocese but also of the Universal Church and that the priests under his care should consider opting for positions outside of Belgium, in Africa, Latin America, Asia or any other part of the world where there was need, assuring us that we had a "green light" from him.

Of course, at that time, there were quite a few priests in Belgium, so with this generous mentality on the part of our bishop, we felt encouraged to consider working abroad, with a special emphasis on Latin America.

Apparently, while in Rome, my bishop had met and conversed with monsignor Chávez y González, archbishop of El Salvador at the time, and perhaps they had talked about the need for more priests to cover the work that was going on in that small country. Parallel to this was the cultural movement within the Church of Latin America and the Latin American Conference of Bishops (CELAM) promoting a new theology of liberation with a preferential option for the poor, which I found highly attractive.

No one in Belgium was surprised when I opted to work in Latin America, and I felt confident that this was my path. My family also supported me, as usual, and continued to do so throughout the difficult years in El Salvador, including the moment in which I made the decision to join the armed struggle (without touching a weapon, of course, but being present in this struggle). So, I left my country of birth, traveling fifteen glorious days by ship across the Atlantic (a trip I would recommend to everyone) and arriving in Panama.

It was my first experience in Central America and I found the heat almost unbearable, leading me to wonder if I could survive in this region of the world. At breakfast, I was surprised again when the waiter put a large glass of water on my table, something you would never see in Belgium; maybe a beer, but never water, which I drank with great enthusiasm in an effort to quench an enormous thirst caused by the heat.

There were several North American priests in Panama at that time who were working with communities applying the methods of Ecclesiastical Base Communities (CEB in Spanish), and I was highly grateful for the days that I spent with them learning about their work and the techniques that I would later apply for the rest of my days in El Salvador.

I finally arrived in El Salvador in 1970 and was sent to work in the parish of Zacamil in San Salvador along with another Belgian priest and close friend, Pedro Declerc. Together, we agreed to apply the methods that we had learned in Panama, forming Ecclesiastical Base Communities in an effort to offer options to communities in our parish confronting a difficult social, economic and political reality in search of social justice and a life with dignity.

We continued working in Zacamil for the next ten years while parishioners became more socially and politically aware, applying the message of Jesus related to love for thy neighbor, especially with the poor. People began to better understand and analyze the reality in which they lived and to search for concrete solutions to the problems of poverty, exploitation, dictatorship and repression through organization and struggle. At that time, popular-based political organizations were beginning to form and unite for political action, and many Christians began to join them.

One day, towards the end of the 1970s, there was a march in San Salvador called by the Popular Leagues 28th of February (LP-28). It was a march primarily of peasants demanding land in order to produce food for their families. The march was attacked violently by security forces, and about thirty people were killed.

I had been invited to participate in the march by some of my parishioners who were members of the LP-28. I was also friendly at the time with a number of leaders of other popular movements, so following the massacre, I was invited to celebrate a mass in the Church of El Rosario.

It was a mass that I will never forget, surrounded by the corpses of the slain, with peasants weeping at the loss of their comrades. In my years in El Salvador, I had celebrated mass with urban populations, including university students and workers, who didn't know much about liturgy. But this mass was celebrated with peasant farmers who had been attending mass all of their lives in small towns and villages.

They understood the liturgy and read it with tears in their eyes and followed up with political slogans promising victory in their struggle. It would stay with me forever, strengthening my conviction to accompany the people, even if they chose the path of violence through armed struggle.

For us Christians, the issue of violence is a difficult one to resolve, especially when considered in the abstract. It was an issue that we frequently discussed in the community. However, I finally became convinced that the issue of violence must be resolved in practice rather than theory, especially when it is perceived as the only viable alternative.

Widespread poverty throughout the country and barbaric repression, along with decades of failed attempts to change the situation through nonviolent means, led many to armed struggle and led me to the simple conclusion that my path lay in accompanying those people always.

The time arrived when I became a target of the military and the death squads and had to leave Zacamil. The authorities had become aware of our organizing efforts through the CEBs which led gradually to the people's participation in more political and, later, more militant organizations promoting the overthrow of the dictatorship.

So, when the offer was made for me to travel to northern Morazan and incorporate into the revolutionary movement there, I accepted. I was not linked to any member organization of the FMLN at that time, nor did I feel obliged to follow orders from anyone but my bishop. I could as easily have gone to Chalatenango or to Belgium, but the offer came from Morazan.

In 1980, after the assassination of archbishop Oscar Arnulfo Romero, my friend, Pedro de Clerk, with whom I had been coordinating my efforts for the past decade in Zacamil, joined me on our clandestine route into the war fronts and a new world filled with challenges for both of us.

Our welcome was warm and friendly among the guerrillas of that area under FMLN control. Most of whom we met were combatants armed to the teeth. Years later, they reminded me of my first words to them upon my arrival, arguing that the rifle does not have to be seen only as an instrument to kill but rather as an instrument with which to struggle for a new, more fraternal and sustainable, society where everyone can live with dignity. A bit romantic, perhaps, but that's how we began our relationship of trust and mutual respect.

At first, I wasn't sure exactly what my role would be on the war fronts. There were frequent military incursions into northern Morazan, and we spent much of our time in "guinda" or recuperating. There was little time left for pastoral work, so I spent my hours with the comrades grinding corn, washing dishes, or building shelters.

Later, we found more time to develop a pastoral plan, but even that consisted mainly of celebrating masses. Mass with the civilian population who remained in the area, and with the guerrilla comrades when they had the time, was a highly rewarding experience, often accompanied by recreational activities and the excellent music of the local group, Torogozes, a highly popular band of combatants who wrote and performed songs of the victories and challenges of the revolution in Morazan.

Europeans who visited the front sometimes had a difficult time understanding our version of religion mixed with revolution, bringing armed guerrillas into a church for mass. But people generally liked it and I always failed to see the contradiction. With the arrival of Father Miguel Ventura and a number of lay people in solidarity with the struggle, we were finally able to develop a broader and more sustainable pastoral team with a more systematic work plan. My friend, Pedro, from Zacamil, participated for periods, but he was frequently ill and had difficulties withstanding the hardships of life in the countryside.

In our pastoral work, we visited all of the civilian communities in the front, accompanied comrades with any difficulties in their lives and, of course, celebrated mass on Sundays or special days of worship, including the anniversary each year of the assassination of monsignor Romero, Rutilio Grande and other martyrs. We also promoted groups for collective reflection on Salvadoran reality in an effort to help comrades understand the value of their personal role within the revolution and the fact that their commitment was not contradictory to their Christian faith.

I was always amazed at the spirit of sacrifice and solidarity among the comrades, whether it be for combat or other more mundane tasks related to the war. There was almost a sense of joy each time they picked up their weapons to go off together to confront the enemy, in spite of the knowledge that they very possibly would not be coming back.

I have to admit that there were moments when I experienced uncontrollable fear myself, caused at times by the far-off sounds of the helicopters coming to attack us or the knowledge that the infantry was headed in our direction. At such moments, my knees would tremble, and my heart would pound, but I would always think of the bravery and enthusiasm of our comrades going into battle, and I would ask myself how it was possible that a helicopter could cause so much fear.

The line of fire during combat is a horrible place to be, with bullets flying everywhere and grenades and bombs exploding nearby, and I experienced it on several occasions. I also remember the story of a German doctor who one day insisted on having that experience, so they gave him a weapon and allowed him to go. An hour later, I found him hiding and trembling in a nearby ravine, and he confessed to me, "It was hell!!"

Fighting was a serious thing, and it is for that reason that the comrades, always ready to put their lives at risk to confront the enemy, deserve so much admiration and respect. And this helped me greatly to control my own fears, at least a little.

Among so many difficult moments here in Morazán, my participation as a priest accompanying the people and their struggles has been the most beautiful experience of my life. It taught me to be Christian and to serve others, and I thank God that I am still here to share its many stories.

Lito

My name is Rafael, but for most of my life, I have been known as Lito. I was born in the neighborhood of Montserrat in San Salvador to a working mother who spent most of her days cooking and cleaning the homes of the middle class. I never knew my father, although I saw him once briefly during my childhood.

I was the oldest of three brothers, and my first memories of my early years in poverty begin with the day in 1971 when, together with my mother, my siblings, my maternal grandparents, my mother's sister with her husband and their two children, we moved to our new home on an abandoned lot in an area known as El Ángel (the Angel) due to its proximity to a sugar mill with the same name.

I don't remember who took us there, but I do recall arriving with only the clothes on our back, a few well-used pots and pans and a machete to begin our new adventure. I also carried with me my school materials since, at 12 years old, I was preparing to enter sixth grade. It was one of the saddest days of my life.

There was no house on our lot at the time, just the recently leveled embankment which, according to my grandmother, belonged to us. I learned later that the brother of my grandmother had purchased it with money he had inherited when their father died.

With no house, we were left to defend ourselves from the elements as best we could in the open, with nothing but the sky as our roof. The only place to sleep was on the ground on top of the recent tire tracks left by the tractor that had leveled the muddy earth just prior to our arrival, so we spread out several old pieces of discarded cardboard to serve as our beds.

The first evening began well, but shortly after dark, the stars all of a sudden disappeared and the lightning, thunder and wind began, followed by a heavy and persistent rain. We covered ourselves as best we could with the cardboard that remained, but it was impossible to avoid getting totally soaked.

With time, we finally managed to gather enough discarded materials to build a small tin hut where we could sleep without having to wake up wet. Since I was the oldest, most of the responsibility for domestic tasks fell on my shoulders, including searching for dry firewood, preparing some of our food and bringing water from a natural well nearby.

With the arrival of October, the weather turned cold, and we began to wake up most mornings with frost on our sheets. My aunt suggested that we sign on to harvest coffee in a nearby plantation in order to earn a little money; so, one morning, we awoke in the darkness of the pre-dawn to begin our journey of several hours along narrow and muddy mountain paths to reach the farm.

We didn't have adequate baskets to pick coffee, but on the farm, the foreman gave us some sacks to use. Our first week was difficult since we were from the city and had no experience harvesting coffee, but with a few weeks of practice, we became more proficient and were able to keep up with the more experienced workers under constant pressure from the foreman and by our own sense of urgency, given our economic situation. It was a life of extreme poverty that gave rise to an incipient social conscience that would later define my revolutionary path.

Eventually, with the meager earnings obtained over the years, we were able to improve our small house, building walls of adobe and "bajareque" (bamboo and mud), although we still had neither electricity nor water.

As the years went by, I began to earn a degree of recognition as a blossoming artist, and the teachers of our school encouraged me to arrive early each day to practice my art on the blackboard, usually depicting what we would be studying that day. This often involved drawing pictures of the respiratory system, the digestive system, plants and maps. It also brought me a few enemies among some of my fellow students who envied my ability to draw and the attention I received from some of the teachers.

As a teenager, I became more self-conscious and aware of our dire poverty. I had attended school for three years in the same clothes and with the same shoes; and when they were completely worn out, with holes in my shoes, I attended my ninth year of studies barefoot. By the age of 14, I was living in misery with an absence of dreams or hope for anything better, and this strengthened my resolve to dedicate my life to assuring that no other child would be forced to live this way or to be so vulnerable.

I took refuge during those years in music, falling in love with singer-songwriters like Bob Dylan, Joan Baez, Joni Michell, The Band, Emerson, Ike and Tina Turner, Pink Floyd and one of my favorites, Jim Croce. As I was an artist with a taste for strange music, the girls my age were attracted to me, seeking me out to talk or help them with their homework, which I exchanged for kisses and food.

By the time I had turned 15, my grandmother had recognized my artistic skills and, with the financial aid of members of her family, enrolled me in the National Center of Arts, where I formally began my life as an aspiring artist. My knowledge of American rock and pop music continued to grow, and I began to relate to other students who shared my tastes.

We exchanged records and photos and talked about books, revolutionary movements, just wars, art, as well as music and love. It was at the age of seventeen that I first tried marijuana and alcohol, but these things were expensive, so I only accepted what was offered freely without ever buying drugs or becoming addicted. I was still rather oblivious to the political situation in my country at that time, but I understood that the atmosphere of the country was tense, that we were governed by a military dictatorship and that every day there were arrests and disappearances.

A fellow student who was studying painting and engraving with me began to talk to me about the revolution and the urgency of fighting against the military dictatorship that oppressed us in order to build a true democracy. That comrade was the son of workers and our conversations gave rise to new feelings and ideas that began taking seed in my heart and mind. I learned later that my friend was a leader of the student organization, the Association of High School Students (AES), belonging to the Communist Party of El Salvador.

He started taking me to clandestine meetings and I began, in my spare time, to design and print flyers with anti-government propaganda and with calls for student organization. Later, we began painting "graffiti" on the walls of the city's buildings, held rallies in different schools and mounted unarmed operations of protest.

Little by little, I became aware of other organizations forming to struggle against the dictatorship with names like BRES, FAPU, LP28, BPR, and AES, and that many of them had their centers of operation in the National Center for the Arts. The People's Revolutionary Army (ERP), one of the first guerrilla organizations in the country, had kidnapped Roberto Poma at that time in one of the most sophisticated urban guerrilla operations of that period, which left my young teenage mind more disquieted and dazzled than ever.

One day, at the end of February 1977, a comrade from AES suggested that we go to a march in protest against the electoral fraud that had just been consolidated in the recent presidential election. I made the decision to accompany AES in this activity and was assigned the task of constructing barricades in the area of the National Cathedral.

We were waiting there while the leaders of the Christian Democrats, the main opposition party in El Salvador at the time, sent out their calls to all Salvadorans to come to the square to defend the electoral results, which had given a clear victory to the opposition. As darkness approached, the army, together with the National Guard and the National Police, began to surround us and, within minutes, began shooting. I don't remember how I managed to escape that night, but I eventually made it home.

The next day, I learned that there had been a massacre of students, of members of the Christian Democrat party and of an untold number of activists from several different popular organizations in the Plaza Libertad the night before. The comrades from AES asked me to accompany them to the square to investigate, and when we arrived, we saw the tanks and soldiers on every corner of the square. There were also several tanker trucks throwing water onto the asphalt, and the water that accumulated there was red. It was obvious that something horrific had occurred that night, and I got goosebumps thinking about my narrow escape from that hell just before it happened.

Seven years later, in 1984, I found myself in the war zones of northern Morazan, completely immersed in the revolutionary struggle of my country and applying my skills as an artist in the design, production and dissemination of propaganda and communications in favor of our struggle.

I was also sleeping again under the open sky, with the earth as my bed, frequently with rain, mud and memories of a cruel childhood on an abandoned lot in a subdivision called El Angel, with my mother, grandmother and siblings in what seemed like a different lifetime.

The 1989 Offensive

During the months of August and September 1989, guerrilla units were in permanent meetings in the northeastern front of Morazan, as they were in other parts of the country, planning a military offensive at the national level that would hopefully change the course and the balance of forces of the war and force the Salvadoran military and the Cristiani government to negotiate a just peace.

In late November, a fellow artist, Rubén, and I had been called to join a meeting in the town of Jocoaitique of our field commanders together with the heads of service areas, including hospitals, communications, propaganda and others. The purpose was to receive information, orientation and assignments in preparation for our upcoming departure from the controlled zone to join guerrilla fighters from war fronts around the country in the largest and most important military initiative since the war began.

The top commander of northeastern El Salvador for the People's Revolutionary Army (ERP), Jonás (Jorge Meléndez), conducted the meeting and provided us with some of the details of the offensive.

As we met, the Arce battalion of the Salvadoran army remained camped close by in the town of Perquin, trying to convince the population of Morazan that they had total control over the northern area of the department of Morazan. We, of course, knew otherwise that the Arce Battalion, trained by the United States, had suffered severe casualties over the past few days in combat with our troops and was currently surrounded by our guerrilla units. They had no idea regarding the seriousness of our current planning or what it would mean for the Armed Forces and government in the coming days.

Without knowing all of the details, we all understood that the coming initiative would be a venture of enormous dimensions. We were also informed that each one of us would participate, applying the skills and accumulated knowledge of the areas in which we had been working over the previous years and that we must be ready to sacrifice our lives if need be.

That was the last time I saw my dear friend, Rubén, with whom I had worked closely and intensively for so many years developing and disseminating propaganda throughout our front. I was horribly saddened to be separating from this bohemian artist and friend, crazy like me, dreamer, stargazer and lover of nature. As we parted, I also said goodbye to many other friends and teammates whom I knew it was unlikely that I would ever see again, although I would cross paths with several of them during the course of the offensive.

As the column that I was assigned to was leaving the meeting and beginning to cross the main highway of Morazan, we were suddenly attacked by a Hughes 500 helicopter that people called the "abispa" (wasp). This aggressive and agile aircraft had been specially adapted for aerial combat against guerrilla forces and was mounted with a pair of powerful machine guns capable of filling a soccer field with bullets in a few seconds. As it passed over our heads, we all threw ourselves to the ground and tried to escape into the ravines nearby, leaving Jocoaitique behind.

Two A-37 jet bombers then took the place of the helicopters, dropping 500-pound bombs and machine gunning our positions as we lay scattered on the ground throughout the foothills and nearby ravines, miraculously without suffering a single loss. The explosions were tremendous, however, and the entire surface of the earth trembled as I hid among dried tree branches, many of which had been torn from tree trunks by shrapnel with which the exploding bombs filled the air around us.

When the planes finally disappeared, we were told to form our column again to begin our march. In each camp that we passed our column became smaller as comrades assigned to other units separated and said goodbye.

Our column continued, headed for the edge of the controlled zone of northern Morazan, close to the municipality of Joateca, where other guerrilla columns were concentrated. As we rested, Commander Jonas explained to me that my principal task leading up to the offensive would be the preparation of a number of personal identity documents so that our comrades, including myself, could move freely around the city of San Miguel, making preparations for the coming attack. For this task, I was provided with a Polaroid camera, a stapler, IDs and a rubber stamp and, still in Joatica, we immediately began our work. The days passed quickly, and I often reflected on the delicacy of this responsibility, recognizing that a mistake on our part could result in the capture or death of our comrades.

The time finally came for me to make my own document and prepare for my departure from our front. I would be traveling by motorcycle, and at the moment of our departure, my heart was thumping a thousand beats per second as someone shouted to me, "We will win, Lito"!

We set off in the darkness, and I could see the dust rising off the dirt road in the flickering light of the motorcycle, but a short time later, we turned onto a well-illuminated and paved street, telling me that we were entering "civilization".

We arrived at a small and humble house where people were resting in hammocks and a woman was cooking and I realized that we were in the small town of Guatajiagua, still in the department of Morazán. We ate and rested and, the next day made the trip to the city of San Miguel, where I had been assigned the task of preparing propaganda for the offensive. As we entered the city, I could see soldiers everywhere, and my comrade driving the motorcycle commented, "Look at these bastards (referring to the soldiers and police), they don't know what is coming at them, poor assholes."

We arrived at the park in the center of San Miguel and walked down a bustling street of vendors and buyers with people selling everything. After seven years in the mountains of Morazan, it felt hot as hell.

We arrived at the doorway of a simple house that I assumed belonged to a family of collaborators with our organization. It had a sign saying "soup kitchen," and a man sat at the entrance selling fruit. The dining area of the house was to be our logistical base, and the comrade on the motorcycle told him, "Here, I bring you Lito so that you can give him a place to sleep and eat. He will be coming and going frequently because he has many things to do."

The next day, I was taken to a fancy urbanization on the outskirts of San Miguel, where we parked in front of a luxurious home, also of collaborators, that would be another of our work areas for the production of propaganda.

The owner explained to us that he was a university professor and that we would be working together to develop manuals on the use of different kinds of weapons and explosives as well as measures to protect oneself from bombings, all for distribution among the civilian population in case people opted to join the offensive once the fighting began. In the meantime, I continued to receive new information about the offensive and was finally informed of the final date and hour, information I was sworn to protect with my life.

The day of the offensive finally came, and more comrades began to arrive at the house where I was staying. One of them brought specific details on where we would be stationed once the fighting started. We were told that two hours before the first battles began, we should clean the weapons that had been arriving at the house during the previous days.

We were also told to expect the arrival of several special forces guerrilla units who would be coming down from the Chaparrastique volcano to occupy positions along Roosevelt Avenue and at the strategic entrances of the colony where we were housed. We also knew that a special commando force would be grouping in houses strategically located near police headquarters in the center of the city.

Given the indications of our comrades, I decided to go for a last walk around the city, bought some new clothes and had my last good meal. I even went to the movies. By nine pm, I was back in our house, where I received a new AK-47 rifle with ammunition and two hand grenades, which I cleaned and made ready for combat.

Once we were armed, we left the house with several other comrades while the rest of our combatants went off in search of their own designated locations where there were weapons that had arrived days before and were waiting to be cleaned.

We eventually arrived at a crossroads where we could see the lights of San Miguel as well as the road leading down from the San Miguel volcano, where the shadows of heavily armed comrades began to appear. I found among them many of my companions from Morazan and we hugged as they began occupying their positions. At exactly 10 pm, explosions began to be heard throughout the center of the city, telling us that the offensive had begun.

After four days of uninterrupted combat, our situation was dramatic, with dead and wounded comrades being attended in our field hospitals along with civilians who had been the victims of indiscriminate bombing by the Salvadoran Air Force. In this context, I witnessed the death of an entire family when a bomb fell directly on their home.

My shoulder was bruised purple from constant firing, and I reflected on how infrequently I had found myself in combat during the previous years of the war. My principal mission at that moment of the offensive was to accompany our military units with a megaphone in hand, trying to urge government soldiers to surrender with the assurance that their lives would be spared, as was our policy always. The din of the fighting was of such magnitude that the megaphone was only effective during the minutes and seconds of sudden silence in the midst of the almost permanent battles.

It was about eight o'clock at night when I was sent, along with another comrade, in search of more ammunition and explosives in a safe house on the other side of the city. I had hardly slept since the offensive began and was exhausted, but I said yes to the mission, as was our custom.

We got into an all-terrain pickup truck that we had confiscated and made it without problems to the indicated house. Upon arrival, we gave the password and the door was opened by a comrade that I knew and greeted with a big hug. We were informed, however, that the weapons in their possession were still buried under the floor of the house and needed cleaning and that we should return later to pick them up.

As we were leaving, the comrade driving the truck stepped into the cab, and I climbed into the bed just as the silence of the evening was broken by the explosion of rifle and machine gun fire, as well as hand grenades. My comrade accelerated without warning, and I fell off the back of the truck but regained my footing immediately and began firing my AK-47 in anger at the truck as it fled off into the darkness.

A storm of bullets followed, and the night became illuminated by the flames leaping from the barrels of M-16 rifles and high-caliber machine guns. Then, I suddenly lost all of my strength and fell to the ground. I tried again to stand, but I couldn't. My body felt hot, and I was sweating profusely, and the thought occurred to me that I was already dead because I couldn't hear anything anymore.

I took off my military harness with my remaining magazines of ammunition and hand grenades, slipped a new magazine into my rifle and started shooting again while the soldiers, hidden in the darkness, returned my fire.

I lay in the middle of the dusty street covered with volcanic ash that quickly began irritating my skin as I moved my hands over my body in search of wounds. I quickly found that one of my legs had been seriously injured, almost completely destroyed, by machine gun fire, and, by that time, I was lying in a lake of my own blood, but I still felt no pain.

In an effort to stop the bleeding, I took the shoelace out of one of my boots and made a tourniquet on my leg just above the knee. I think by then that the army had gone as it became deathly silent, and when I looked up, I was shocked to see a large white disk of great intensity in the dark sky above me, quickly realizing that it was a beautiful full moon that had slipped from behind a cloud to light the surroundings with its brilliance. It had never seemed so macabre to me as that night.

I began to crawl on my belly, looking for a place to hide, leaving my rifle behind and carrying only a hand grenade with the idea of exploding it if the army appeared, putting an end to my life but taking a few of the enemy with me.

I came to a small open area with a poorly built zinc hut on it with a door made from sticks and I shouted to the people inside to open. They shouted back that I should leave, that they were afraid of the army, so I warned them to either open or I would blow their door down with my grenade.

Immediately, a man opened the door and gave me some water, then, noticing my situation, he brought me a pillow and a blanket to give me some comfort against the cold. My body was shivering, and the pain was now quickly becoming unbearable. It hurt to breathe, but I still had my grenade pinned to my chest. The people closed the door again, and, in that instant, I lost control of my bowels and bladder, urinating and defecating all at once, producing some slight relief from the pain for a few seconds. Then I lost consciousness.

It was about five in the morning when I awoke, thinking again that I was dead. I wanted to find out. Someone or something in my subconscious appeared in my mind, and I asked him out loud who he was. I was told then that I already knew.

It was a warm and serene voice, a voice for a peaceful ending. I boldly asked him if I was dead and told him that I needed to know, and he replied that I had only a few minutes left. I asked him about my companion who had stayed in Morazán, if she was still alive, and he answered yes. Then I asked him my last question, if my wound had been in the spine, and if I would be able to walk and to make love, to which he replied that of course, I would, that I would walk again with technical help, and if I made love I would do it perfectly, like before. He then added, "But you won't be able to do either anymore because you are dying." Angered by this contradiction, I screamed as loud as I could, saying to the voice, "You are wrong! My life cannot end here in this way. This end cannot be for Lito."

The family inside the hut, upon hearing my screams, opened the door again and told me that they would carry me to the main street where perhaps my comrades would come and find me. At that point, I felt like I was losing my sight. Everything was blurry, but I could hear perfectly sporadic gunfire in the distance and the sound of helicopters. When the couple tried to pick me up, I screamed like a lion on the verge of death. The pain was unbearable, so they quickly wrapped me in blankets and left me.

I remained motionless for a long while until I suddenly felt the presence of someone by my side. According to the voice, it was a young boy who had gone out with his bicycle, and I wondered what a boy could be doing with a bicycle on a battlefield. He spoke to me and told me that a column of men was coming, but he didn't know if they were guerrillas or soldiers. They were all dressed the same, he said, and it was impossible to know which side they were on.

A few minutes later, the boy left, and I removed the safety from my grenade while I waited and watched to see if those who were approaching were friend or foe. I then heard someone scream, "Hey! Don't move!" And I responded, "If you come closer, you bastards, we'll all die!" And, at that moment, I suddenly heard my name, "Lito! Lito! Don't worry, I'm Paquito, the singer. Don't worry, we've come to get you out of here."

In a matter of seconds, I was surrounded by comrades, and everyone was murmuring about my physical condition, saying to each other, "Poor Lito." I then heard them communicating on the radio, informing them that they had found me, and I heard the voice of the great Sabino, the head of our regular forces, giving orders to look for some sticks and boards to improvise a stretcher. One of the comrades found my AK-47 and handed it to Sabino, and they took the grenade that I was still holding and returned the safety to its position.

When they picked me up to carry me, I screamed again because of the unbearable pain. I still don't understand why I didn't faint. They started walking, and I recall that it was the longest journey of my life, fighting off the agony while battling to hold onto life and not give way to that serene voice inside me, still saying that all was already lost.

We arrived at our field hospital where a young woman doctor, whom I had seen a few days earlier in the heat of battle, began crying immediately and informing those in charge that there was nothing left to do, that she could not amputate the leg and if she did, I would most likely not survive the surgery. Our commanders began to consider our options in the midst of heavy fighting nearby that was becoming louder by the minute. Warplanes were flying constantly overhead, dropping their bombs, while helicopters strafed and launched their rockets. I heard an order given to the doctor to clean me up and get me ready for evacuation.

A pick-up truck driven by a priest accompanied by a young woman arrived and placed me in the bed while the woman gave me mouth-to-mouth resuscitation and told me that we would soon arrive at the hospital. I just kept looking up at the sky where those terrifying aircraft kept flying overhead, causing so much death, and I felt the intense smell of gunpowder. This was my evacuation in the midst of heavy fighting and constant bombardments.

I woke up in a hospital bed in a small room with several others who had recently been operated on. I noted that we were surrounded by men in olive green uniforms with a red bandana tied around their heads. They all smelled of gunpowder, and one soldier, maybe about eighteen years old, said to me, "How are you? Are you a guerrilla?" He asked me which guerrilla unit I belonged to and who my commanders were. "Were you with Raúl?" asked another. "Where did you leave Jonas?"

I was confused and asked them, "Have we won? Is it all over yet?" A young soldier asked me who I was referring to and told me that the Salvadoran army had won the offensive. There were several murmurs among the soldiers because they were not sure about who I was, a guerrilla or a soldier. They then asked me if I knew who they were, and I answered, "No."

At that instant, one of the soldiers pushed his way through the others and put his rifle to my stomach, shouting, "We are from the Arce battalion, you son of a bitch! And you're sure to be a damn terengo (derogatory name for the guerrillas)! You won't get through this night, asshole!", he shouted at me with so much hatred. Another soldier came over and took off my white sheet, and yelled at me, "Look, you son of a bitch. You have no leg, and you can see the bones of your elbows. You've probably just crawled out of combat." Then they warned me that I better start talking or else.

Eventually, a doctor and a nurse arrived to transfer me up to the sixth floor, where I found more injured comrades. One of the soldiers stationed on that floor shouted at us, "Look, sons of bitches, here I bring you another terengo. You screwed up. You didn't achieve anything, and now the terengos have withdrawn and abandoned you!"

It was about eleven o'clock in the morning when heavy fighting began again nearby, breaking the windows of our room, but I no longer cared about anything. I didn't feel the slightest fear. I was in their hands, and it was only a matter of time before we would all be killed. As if to confirm this notion, one of the Salvadoran officers arrived and left orders to assassinate us all if things got out of hand. This put me on permanent alert, and I began to formulate a plan for pouncing on one of the soldiers in order to die fighting instead of being killed like a dog.

I spent a few more days in that room recovering from my surgery while a different nurse came in to treat my wounds each day. Some were humble women with fear in their eyes. Others were full of hate and treated us badly. Sometimes, officers came to interrogate the other comrades, but they rarely said anything to me.

One day a young doctor came in and brought with him several X-rays. He was nervous in the presence of the soldiers and told me that he had done his best to save my leg, but I had arrived in a coma, and my wound was untreatable.

That same day, more soldiers arrived with a nurse and told me that they were transferring me somewhere else. The doctor opposed that idea, given that I was not yet fully recovered, but the soldiers replied, "These sons of bitches don't deserve pity, they need to be exterminated."

I was carried out by two soldiers supporting me and thrown face down on the bed of a military pickup, burning hot in the midday sun. I felt certain that I would then be taken off and shot, but I was handcuffed and transported to the police station in downtown San Miguel.

The walls of the police station were full of bullet holes from our attacks during the past several days. A group of vendors passing by with their merchandise saw me lying handcuffed in the truck and said loudly, "That's what you terrorist sons of bitches deserve. Kill them all!"

I was so hurt by this cruel and cold expression of hatred by people for whom we were fighting and dying, but I knew, at the same time, that people were afraid to demonstrate their true sentiments in front of the police or the army.

I was then carried from the pickup and led to a cell that could only be described as an earthen dungeon, with a hole in the floor for relieving myself and a jug of water for drinking. It was pitch black, and I was alone in my underpants and a t-shirt torn and covered in blood.

I soon began to suffer from contradictory thoughts, wanting, on the one hand, for all of this horrible experience to end quickly, permitting me to die fighting, while, on the other hand, I thought about my beloved partner in Morazan, my dear friend and fellow artist, Rubén, and my brothers and sisters in combat, and that made me want to live.

The police told me that it was about ten o'clock at night as I lay on the floor in a fetal position with hordes of cockroaches climbing over my body and rats coming out of the toilet hole in search of food as I concentrated on protecting my wounds that had not yet healed.

The following day, several more comrades were brought into my cell, and we were now a group of approximately twenty, all young, all wounded and all in deplorable conditions. One comrade was brought in on a stretcher with a spinal cord injury that had left him paraplegic. We spent that night together, eating the small portions of parboiled beans that were given to each of us on disgusting plastic plates, many dropping crumbs that brought an army of cockroaches again and rats determined to eat the leftovers.

The next day, they took us all out to the courtyard of the police station, where they sat us on the cement floor in front of several tables with typewriters. Some of the police officers had instruments to conduct paraffin testing on each of us, looking for signs of gunpowder on our hands.

We were then sent, one by one, to the tables where the officers tried to force us into declaring ourselves as guerrillas and accepting that our leaders had deceived and abandoned us. In that group of comrades, I didn't know anyone, nor did I think anyone knew me. That provided me with some relief when my turn finally came to pass in front of a policeman with harsh features and a look of hatred, with weathered hands and a gun at his waist.

He began my interrogation by asking my name, and I told him the truth by instinct, although the real truth was that I simply didn't care anymore. If they killed me, they would find that I had given them my legal name so they could inform my family of my death.

When they asked about my occupation, I returned in my mind to my youth and told them that I was an art student. They didn't believe me, but it didn't matter. They asked me about Joaquín Villalobos, Jorge Meléndez and Radio Venceremos. They brought me maps so that I could point out the location of our hospitals and guerrilla camps, to which I replied that I didn't know anything about those people or places.

The policeman only wrote that he did not pressure me on anything, and that's how the interrogation ended. They sat me down again on the cement floor where a soldier who looked like an officer passed by, kicked me in the ribs and told me, "Look, son of a bitch, you're going to live to tell the others that we gave them dick." I didn't feel the kick, and I wasn't in a good position to snatch the policeman's gun and try to end everything there and then. After the interrogation, they sat us all together and took photos of us, one of which ended up in several local newspapers.

That night, they took me out of that disgusting cell and, to my horrible shock, placed me face to face with Commander Sabino, one of our best and most loved field commanders, a magnificent leader and friend.

Like me, he had been seriously wounded and captured and looked like he had a metal plate in his head and the loss of one eye. They asked him if he knew me, and he said no, so I followed suit and said that I did not know him. Then they handcuffed us together and tied us to the wall at the entrance of the jail, telling us, "If the terengos come to attack us tonight, they will kill you bastards first!" Then they kicked us several times and left.

We didn't sleep that night, and neither of us spoke. We just looked at each other in silence, each one yearning to say something to the other, and I longed to tell him how much it saddened me to see the great Sabino imprisoned, the daring guerrilla fighter of a thousand battles, the hard, humble, simple man with a heart of lion committed to the revolution.

The next day, we were all given a medical check-up by a doctor who was completely drunk and trembling with fear. The fear of that doctor gave me hope because, in his eyes, I could read that the guerrillas were still strong and that, at any moment, they would attack again. That was the perception I could read in all of them.

A few minutes later, a tall blond white man appeared along with a tall blond woman, and they identified themselves as representatives of the International Committee of the Red Cross. They asked us for our names, looked at our wounds, and told us that if we were guerrillas, then we were prisoners of war and that we had the right to be treated well.

It seemed to me like a joke at the time, given everything that had already been done to us. The woman, who I later realized was Swiss, went out for a moment and then came back with a pair of crutches and handed them to me.

The next day, several policemen took me out of the cell again and put me in a pick-up. I thought again that they were taking me to kill me, so I confessed to them that I was from the FMLN, that I didn't want to die like a dog and that they should bring me one of our flags and kill me wrapped in it.

They all laughed and told me, "We won't kill you. Others will step on you and kill you." It was mid-day and hellishly hot. I think it was already the end of December, although I had completely lost track of time. The truth is that I didn't think about anything anymore, only about my partner in Morazan and Rubén.

We arrived at a large building with shacks all around it, part of the San Miguel prison. There, we were led to a circular area with bars, much like a cage, where I was told to sit in a chair and wait. When the soldiers came to hand over the papers they were carrying, the other prisoners gathered around the bars and began to stare at me, yelling insults and threatening to "skin me alive."

The Prison

The soldiers returned from the administrative offices of the prison and began shouting at the other prisoners, "Here, we bring you a terrorist." "Terengos, come and receive your comrade." I was no longer afraid of anything. Instead, I felt strong and eager to win this battle that I found myself in.

As my wounds from the amputation of my leg began to heal, my overall physical condition improved, but I was frequently bothered by a sensation of head and, at night, I frequently wept silently, traumatized by the loss of my leg. On frequent occasions, I thought that it would have been better to die and not have to face the world in this condition.

At the steel-barred door of the prison, a light-skinned Latino male arrived and helped me with the bag of clothes I was carrying, leading me through a corridor of small workshops where several prisoners sat, most of them working on a variety of handicrafts. The man then took me to a small cell with a small gas stove, where several other prisoners slept amongst their personal belongings.

I sat on one of the beds with the man who had brought me to the cell, and he told me that his name was William and that he belonged to the

Central American Revolutionary Workers' Party (PRTC in Spanish). I replied that my name was Lito and that I belonged to the ERP (People's Revolutionary Army).

William asked me how I had been treated since my capture, if I had been tortured in the police station and if I had lost my leg in combat, to all of which I replied in the affirmative. I didn't really know who this William was, but under the circumstances, I felt the need to trust someone and for that reason, I had revealed to him my true identity.

Other prisoners came over and also introduced themselves. One of them was an old man, and I don't remember his name, but he had also been with the PRTC. We talked about the current situation in the prison, and I was informed that more wounded comrades were arriving each day and that I was not alone.

Later, William told me that I should stay with them in that cell, making us seven in a space of about three meters by four, with four people sleeping on canvas cots while three slept on the floor. Although I was new, I was given one of the cots due to the severity of my wound, which had not yet completely healed.

I hadn't eaten anything all day, and I was anticipating another sleepless night, but I wasn't prepared for the levels of pain that I began to suffer from the stump of my amputated leg. My comrades were able to get hold of some pills that were called "mejórales", but they didn't work for me. Thus, the routine of life in prison began.

William advised me to always be vigilant due to the potential for violence and the numerous deaths suffered daily and nightly in the prison from fights between rival groups of prisoners.

One day, shortly after my arrival, William took me on a tour of the prison, although I felt insecure without my rifle and my leg. It looked like a market where everything was sold. There was a dining area and a kitchen with a table and two rickety chairs, occupied at the moment by several homosexuals, but William and I found a space to sit for a while to share a coffee and have our first serious conversation.

He told me that he and the other comrades that he had introduced to me had belonged to a PRTC commando unit that had carried out an attack against U.S. Marines in the "Zona Rosa" of San Salvador during the offensive, so they had little chance of ever being freed. The gringos wouldn't allow it. It was an interesting and informative conversation that deepened our trust in each other and marked the beginning of a gradual transformation in which William became my key source of information on everything. He also became my bodyguard.

He explained to me how the prison system worked and all the shenanigans that occurred there. Many things that happened outside were decided there on the inside, from land disputes, purchases and sales of everything that had an economic value as well as acts of revenge between people, including murders.

I learned that the capacity of the prison was about 300 inmates, although there were about two thousand people incarcerated there at that time. FMLN members made up a small part of the population but continued to arrive during my stay, eventually reaching a population of approximately 120.

There were several "capos" (bosses) who dominated prison life, and all of them had bought off the warden and all of his guards. Many things happened in that microcosm, and one day, when William accompanied me to bathe, we passed by a cell the same size as ours but with only one man in it who greeted William and invited us in. His cell had a television, furniture, a good bed, a stove, a radio and boxes filled with exotic foods. He had a name that sounded like Figueredo, appeared to be about fifty years old, wore a suit, and, without a doubt, was one of the prison bosses.

When we sat down in his cell, he asked me my name and I replied that they called me Lito. "Are you a commander?" he asked me, to which I replied no, that I was an artist and painter. "Of course," he replied as if he didn't believe me. "And where did they wound you?" I told him in La Colonia Milagro de La Paz. "Puta! I have a lot of friends there!" he told me.

The man was anxious to know what the battles had been like in the offensive, but I told him that I did not want to talk about that subject. "Well, no problem", he told me. "I live here and am at your service for anything you need, so do not hesitate to ask me." With this, we got up, I shook his hand and went to take a bath. Later that night, William and I began to draw up a plan to meet the needs of all the political prisoners in the prison, especially with medicines, clothes, shoes and food.

As the days went by, the prison routine became clearer. On the weekends, the prison was filled with visitors, including mothers, wives, lovers, lawyers and hitmen who moved through that small perverse universe.

We were inside our cell one Saturday, and a lady I knew well from Morazan suddenly appeared before me and we greeted each other with trust and joy, although she couldn't hide her sadness at seeing me in those circumstances.

I asked my comrades for a few moments alone with her, and once the others had gone, she told me that she had been sent from Perquín by our guerrilla commanders to find out if there were comrades imprisoned here. I shared the information that I had on this subject and asked her to carry several messages back to the comrades in Morazan. One was for Jonas explaining our situation here, and another was directed at my beloved partner, alone and pregnant with our first child in the controlled zones of Morazan.

As if to confirm the warnings that William had given me several days earlier regarding the dangers of prison life, the guards came with the warden one morning, pulled us out of our cells and took roll call. One of the prisoners did not respond when his name was called, and they found him lying dead from stab wounds on the floor of his cell. After that, this ritual was performed more frequently, in the morning and, at times, at night, although it was generally in the mornings that the murders were reported.

That same day, at about eleven a.m., a beautiful and very tall blond woman dressed in white came to the prison, and I recognized her as the same nurse from the International Red Cross that I had seen at the police station. She met with us in our cell and asked about the wounded, how we were doing, if we needed special medicines or if we needed to have our wounds treated.

She looked to me like an angel in this atmosphere of misery and decadence, and I told her about the horrible pains in my leg that were depriving me of sleep. She then took out a syringe and several vials of morphine from her briefcase and asked if any of us knew how to inject. William said that he could learn, so he assumed the responsibility for injecting me whenever the pain became unmanageable.

I could sense that the nurse was sympathetic and supportive of our cause, even though she worked for a politically neutral organization. Her visits became more frequent, and I gradually began to develop sufficient trust to ask her if she would be willing to travel to Perquin to meet with our political leadership, and she agreed. I was unsure about how such a thing would work out, but we had to be willing to take risks to advance our struggle.

That night, we got hold of a small radio and listened to the broadcast of Radio Venceremos at low volume, something I had not done for some time, and it was an enormous boost to my morale. We could finally learn what had happened in the offensive and get information on the current situation in the war. During the broadcast, there was a strong denouncement of the horrible conditions of our wounded combatants in the prison of San Miguel, telling me that my messages sent with the woman from Perquin had been delivered. The radio called upon international organizations to defend the human rights of our captured comrades and demanded respect for our rights as prisoners of war. That night, we ate well and celebrated with coffee after the radio signed off.

That following weekend, my "angel", as I began to call the Red Cross nurse, returned from Perquin and came to the prison to bring me close to a thousand dollars sent by Jonas, the commander of Morazan. It was a lot of money, and I assumed the responsibility for hiding it and managing it well, knowing that any prisoner would quickly kill any of us in order to steal it.

I also received several messages, one of them from Jonas. In the first message, I was informed that my partner was pregnant, doing well and living in the community of Segundo Montes with the civilian population who had returned to El Salvador from the United Nations camps in Honduras. My heart and my guerrilla soul leaped with joy as I read the news, and I shed more than a few tears of happiness. The other message from Jonas simply instructed me to use the money for food, clothing and medicine.

In his message, Jonas also asked about the number of comrades in the prison, the seriousness of their wounds, if we needed help to move, etc. He also suggested that I try to send him a map of the facility, and I suddenly understood where his guerrilla mind was leading, so I sent a message back telling him not to even think of attacking the prison and trying to rescue us, that they would kill us all.

Later that day, an elderly man from Perquin visited with the horrifying news that my beloved friend and comrade, Rubén, had been killed in an ambush during the offensive. The enormous joy of knowing that my partner was well and that I was to become a father came crumbling to the ground.

My body began to tremble with sadness. I wanted death to take me too so that I could follow Rubén always. I couldn't hold back the bitter tears and the feeling that part of my being had been ripped from my body. I asked my comrades to leave me once again, and I cried bitterly for almost an hour while my heart and mind battled with the challenge of living the rest of my life someplace between the joy and the tragedy that I had been dealt that day.

The loss of Rubén left me with wounds that will never heal, and I carry his memory and the pain of his death wherever I go. They are with me to this day, accompanying the joy and satisfaction that I have now found as a working artist in Europe. They remain embedded in the depths of my conscience torturing me and reminding me of the rarity and special beauty of such love between men (more common among women) who join their lives together in the path of struggle for a better world for all.

We continued to denounce on Radio Venceremos the cruel situation of our comrades in the prison, and international organizations began to visit us, along with the office of archbishop Rivera y Damas. We hired lawyers to help free our comrades, except for those of the PRTC on whose shoulders remained the horrible weight of the attack on US marines in the Zona Rosa.

I remember the three of them with tenderness. I saw one of them almost every day as he slowly built me a prosthesis from a beautiful piece of conacaste wood brought by his relatives from Usulután. It was a work of art and did much for my morale on the first day that I looked at myself in the mirror, standing on two legs again. That wooden prosthesis still hangs in a small prosthetic museum in the town of Västeras in Sweden.

One afternoon, at midday, I heard my name called and found myself standing in front of a man in a black suit. He turned out to be a lawyer in charge of my case and he had come with the news that my purgatory was finally over and that I should get ready to depart.

I was, of course, overjoyed at the idea of leaving this hellhole, but I was also saddened to leave my comrades, especially my friends from the PRTC who had been so helpful during the darkest hours of my captivity and who now hugged me and wept with me as I readied my departure. I gave William the money that remained for aiding our imprisoned comrades with instructions to continue the struggle for their freedom, and shared my contacts with whom I had been coordinating this effort.

As I stepped outside the prison, the sunlight blinded me, so we had to stop and wait while my eyes adjusted. But I was finally able to locate the white vehicle of the International Red Cross waiting across the street along with that beautiful Swiss nurse. My nervousness gradually began to vanish as the fragrances of the nearby market and the hot Salvadoran afternoon penetrated my body and mind, assuring me that I was free. I had spent six months in prison, including Christmas and New Year's Eve, and I spent that night at the Salvadoran Red Cross headquarters, still unable to sleep due to the detonations of bombs and bursts of gunfire nearby.

The lawyer explained that they had paid off one of the judges to get me released, even though there were no accusations or evidence against me, and I left without charges. All I had to worry about now was being killed by the police or the army, who were unhappy with my release and still convinced that I was a guerrilla, although I probably no longer seemed so dangerous to them in the condition I was in.

I was taken to the house of a friend in Usulutan without a clear plan for my future, but several days later, there was a knock on the door, and I opened it to find my partner standing there, fat, pregnant and happy. My emotions soared out of control, and my body trembled as we hugged, cried and laughed at the same time in the midst of an encounter that we had both longed for but feared.

My head and my heart were in a whirlpool of contradictions, filled with joy on the one hand but filled with fear on the other, not knowing if my partner could truly love me in my new condition of an emaciated amputee. But I was a fool. With the passing days, we talked through our shared traumas and fears and found again the love that had flowered in the mountains of Morazan in what seemed like a lifetime ago.

As peace negotiations proceeded, giving promise of ending this horrible war, we found our way to Europe, where our first daughter, Constanza, was born, filling our lives with wonder and hope. Years later, now separated from my partner, I was blessed again, this time with a son, Mauro, a bold and adventurous young man, like his father, to whom I have bequeathed the happiness and well-being of a life that I never knew. Life is good now as I dedicate myself to my new family and to my art, returning on occasion to my country of birth where the memories of so many beloved friends lost still haunt my soul.

Mirna

I have lived most of my life in an environment of danger and fear, but thanks to the miracles, I am still here to tell my story, the story of the Salvadoran people.

I was born into a family of limited resources but an abundance of human qualities. My father was a self-taught born leader with only four years of formal schooling, but he was always ready to solve the problems of others, especially the poor.

He had a great knowledge of the law and was consistently helping neighbors and friends in the resolution of conflicts over land tenure, property rights and other concerns. I can't remember from my earliest years ever hearing him turn down a request for help, always motivated by a profound respect for the rights and needs of others and the challenges to building a life with dignity for all.

My mother was a strong and courageous woman with tenacity and a strong Catholic faith, in charge of a household overrun by five rambunctious children, trying always to instill in us a sense of ethics, Christian values and solidarity with the poor. She always dreamed of her daughters becoming professionals and sacrificed everything in order that we complete our university studies.

I was finally able to achieve that goal, obtaining a degree in Legal Sciences, thanks to a scholarship from the public University of El Salvador (UES). But my studies were delayed by the occupation of the university by the dictatorship of Arturo Armando Molina on July 19, 1972, accusing the institution of being a boiling pot of subversion and full of "communists." It remained closed for almost two years, during which time it was looted by soldiers, national guardsmen and police in flagrant violation of its status as an autonomous institution enshrined in our Constitution.

The university scholarship system survived the military intervention, but with many deficiencies, forcing us to organize ourselves and demand respect for our rights as university students and scholarship holders. That is how the Society of Salvadoran University Scholarship Students (SEBUS) was founded, where I met Herbert Anaya Sanabria for the first time.

Herbert was born in San Salvador and grew up in the city of Chalchuapa. Along with his three siblings, he combined his academic studies during his youth with hard manual labor, cutting coffee during the harvest season like so many children and adolescents of his time and, from that experience, developed a strong social conscience that would guide him for the rest of his days.

He stood out as a sensitive person in a world of machismo and violence and was known always, much like my father, for his spirit of service to others. Like me, he obtained a degree in Legal Sciences at the University of El Salvador, standing out as an excellent student while at the same time understanding the difficult problems of his country.

Herbert was an activist in the University Front of Revolutionary Students, Salvador Allende (FUERSA), where I was also a member, so we spent long hours together in lengthy discussions about national reality. As our paths continued to cross and our struggles brought us into constant contact, our lives began to interweave, inevitably producing a loving relationship that would last until his death.

In the early years of our university studies, our efforts were divided between academics and the struggle to transform the National University into an institution at the service of the nation, maintaining its traditional role in democratizing and transforming our country. My first confrontation with death in this struggle was on July 30th, 1975, when government security forces attacked one of our marches in San Salvador with some 2,000 university students from the UES and the Francisco Morazán National Institute (INFRAMEN), accompanied by professors and university workers in protest of the military occupation of the Santa Ana branch of our Alma Mater.

On the day of the march, we left the university campus at about three in the afternoon and from the moment we entered North 25th Avenue, Air Force spotter planes began flying overhead, trying to calculate our numbers, our route and the most effective moment to attack us. We knew that our march would be repressed, but we had assumed that the violence would be ameliorated by the presence of so many eyewitnesses on the streets. Peasants of La Cayetana in San Vicente had been attacked and massacred in November of the previous year, and that was followed by the massacres of Tres Calles and Chinamequita by combined forces of the police, the army and local paramilitary patrols. But in downtown San Salvador, in plain daylight, we were anticipating more restraint.

We were wrong! For the dictatorship of Arturo Armando Molina, there were no holds barred. Our march was attacked by the army, the Air Force, the Treasury Police, the National Police and the National Guard, leaving twenty-five dead and bodies riddled with bullets to be run over by tanks, then thrown into military trucks and subsequently disappeared without a trace and without an accurate body count of the missing.

I suffered serious injuries while trying to get off the overpass in front of the Social Security Hospital, where the brunt of the attack occurred. I was trapped initially between the police with tear gas, the gunfire of the security forces and the advance of the army tanks. Dizzy from the tear gas and affected by my anguish to save myself, I threw myself blindly from the overpass at a height that I had not calculated well (it was like jumping off a high cliff) and fell with all of my weight onto the concrete below, losing consciousness.

When I woke up, I tried without success to get up and run, but a multiple fracture of my knee prevented me from putting weight on my right leg. Two comrades from the student organization UR-19 de Julio picked me up and carried me in their arms to a mechanic's workshop nearby, essentially saving my life, until I could be transported to a hospital from where I could contact my family to inform them of my whereabouts.

During the confusion of the moment, I had seen Herbert Anaya, along with several other comrades, being detained at gunpoint by plain-clothes police who had infiltrated the march, but they bravely resisted and were able to escape and finally reach La Libertad Park, where we had all agreed to meet at the end of the march. There, they were interviewed by local as well as international media and denounced the massacre. The news quickly spread throughout Central America and to allies in the countries of the north.

A year later, on April 30, 1976, I was illegally detained and held by paramilitary members of ORDEN in San Antonio Abad; but, thanks to the rapid intervention of my family, making it impossible to disappear me, I was handed over to the National Guard and finally released, after several hours of torture.

Then, in October 1979, upon my return from an official meeting representing the National University, police detained me at the airport, accusing me of being a subversive because of correspondence they had found on my person.

At the end of the 1970s, a group of valiant and committed citizens, many of whom were from the National University, founded the Human Rights Commission of El Salvador (CDHES) with the purpose of disseminating International Human Rights Law and defending victims of human rights violations in El Salvador. This urgent resource became a reality thanks to the visionary action of professionals and students and, from its first day, was pursued and attacked by the government, the oligarchy and right-wing ideologues, forcing its first two presidents to flee into exile.

The institutional crisis afflicting El Salvador demanded the existence of organizations such as the CDHES, which clearly and courageously questioned the repressive policies, programs and practices of the government. In September 1980 , Herbert Anaya Sanabria joined the CDHES as a member of its legal team.

At that time, the CDHES was practically clandestine, with a small and humble office located on Avenida España near the San Miguelito Market. Marianella García Villas, who had been a congresswoman for the Christian Democratic Party and had training as a jurist and philosopher, was among the leaders, working in defense of political prisoners, doing research and documenting murders, illegal detentions, torture and forced disappearances carried out by the so-called security forces and death squads formed by the security forces and acting under the protection of the authorities. (In the mid-1980s, Marianella Garcia was ambushed by government troops on the war fronts near the town of Suchitoto while gathering evidence of the indiscriminate bombing and massacre of civilian villages by the military, including the use of white phosphorous).

Herbert was aware upon joining the CDHES of the great risk he was running. The attacks on people and groups opposed to the dictatorship were also directed at people working with the Commission. It was a time in El Salvador of growing repression against peasants, union activists, members of opposition parties, the Catholic Church, teachers, university students and other sectors of society who were being systematically pursued, arrested, tortured and disappeared or killed.

The defenders of human rights were also among those on the radar of a government bent on eliminating all opposition. For that reason, entering or leaving the premises of the CDHES was dangerous, and there were multiple cases in which visitors and employees were detained and sometimes disappeared or killed with evidence of having been cruelly tortured.

Herbert managed in the first years to maintain a low profile, attempting to avoid showing his face publicly and using pseudonyms rather than his legal name. A few days after he began, one of his co-workers, Magdalena Henríquez, was kidnapped near her home and murdered. Days later, her body was exhumed from a clandestine grave in the port city of La Libertad. This was a litmus test for Herbert, but he made the difficult decision to continue in his job, accepting, as he said, the possibility of being killed, kidnapped, tortured and disappeared.

Herbert's work on the Commission in the early 1980s was carried out in the context of a country that had suffered decades of military dictatorship and was currently governed by a civilian-military junta promoting minimum reforms but prioritizing repression, leading archbishop Romero to make his famous assertion, "Reforms are useless if they are stained with so much blood."

In practice, the job brought with it the horrifying routine of daily images of mutilated, headless, burned corpses with fingernails torn out and facial skin peeled down over their eyes. It also meant investigating the massacres of student marches, the slaughter of rural communities, the slaying of union leaders, the assassination of activists occupying embassies in an attempt to call the world's attention and the blood-curdling attacks on citizens on the steps of the capital city's churches and cathedrals, documenting all of these events with written testimony, videos, and photographs.

The aim was to help the victims' relatives identify friends and family members in an endless chain of disappearances. In addition, periodic reports were developed for the organizations of the United Nations, international human rights organizations, democratic governments and groups around the world in solidarity with El Salvador.

On the afternoon of May 26, 1986, as Herbert and I, along with our three children, three-year-old Edith, four-year-old Rafael, and five-year-old Gloria Maria, were making a purchase in a store near our home, a group of five men in civilian clothes carrying machine guns pointed their weapons at Herbert, violently grabbed him by both arms, threw him into a blue pickup truck with tinted windows and no license plates and took him away.

This brutal act was committed with total impunity in front of many people in broad daylight, and it was only because of the quick and bold action of organizations of the disappeared, like COMADRES and COMAFAC, that Herbert was not murdered or disappeared himself, as was the modus operandi of that time.

A broad and loud denunciation was made both nationally and internationally, and popular organizations took over the National Cathedral to demand respect for his physical and psychological integrity.

Herbert, along with three other comrades from the CDHES, were held and tortured in the prisons of the Treasury Police, applying a recent government decree empowering the security forces to keep those accused of subversion incommunicado while they tortured them in an attempt to force them to renounce their work in defense of human rights.

In order to halt the torture and save his life, Herbert was forced to accept publicly that the crimes that he had been denouncing were all lies forming part of a "guerrilla plan to destabilize the democratic regime of Napoleón Duarte." They warned him that if he did not accept this offer, he would be killed. Despite his forced admission of guilt and the threats that followed, he never gave up on his unwavering decision to defend the victims of abuses by the state.

Fifteen days after his capture and torture by Hacienda Police, he was taken to the "La Esperanza" prison in Mariona. When we finally saw each other and talked, I could see how affected Herbert was by the horrible experience he had gone through, but when I explained to him the struggles of the social movements in support of him and his work, his resolve returned.

While still in prison, he and his team began documenting conditions and violations among the 1100 political prisoners (with approximately 100 women) inside Mariona. The prison during that time became the equivalent of a "liberated territory," and some referred to it as the "fifth front."

Political prisoners had organized themselves into the Committee of Salvadoran Political Prisoners (COPPES) and developed a program of care for those who had been severely tortured. They also taught literacy and held workshops for political, ideological and disciplinary training. Finally, they produced some of their own food to complement the meager portions provided by the prison and set up a small shop to facilitate access to basic necessities.

The CDHES team, five in number, carried out investigations to document the systematic torture applied by security forces or prison guards. They received 433 testimonies of tortured political prisoners and identified 40 different forms of physical or psychological torture being used by prison guards, a study that was delivered to the Interamerican Commission on Human Rights and the United Nations Special Rapporteur for El Salvador, José Antonio Pastor Ridruejo.

Along with this, 300 habeas corpus petitions were filed, and multiple interviews were held with delegations from international organizations that visited Mariona, confirming the arbitrary conditions under which more than a thousand people had been detained without having committed any crime.

In February 1987, the CDHES prisoners were finally released through an act called "Goodwill Gesture," in which political prisoners were exchanged for hostages being held by the FMLN. When he regained his freedom, Herbert, despite death threats against him and his family, continued his work with greater intensity than ever until the threats to his life by members of the security forces of El Salvador were finally carried out in October 1987.

Today, as members of the Herbert Anaya Sanabria Human Rights Collective, we continue my husband's efforts to promote respect for human rights, end impunity, provide access to the truth, and seek justice and moral and material reparation for the crimes of the past and present victims.

"The agony of not working for justice is stronger than the possibility of my death... the latter is only an instant, the other constitutes the totality of my life..." – Herbert Anaya Sanabria (1954-1987), President of the Human Rights Commission of El Salvador

Paco (for his ex-wife, Paty)

Forty-one years after the fatal and tragic events that changed the course of our lives, my family and I continue to suffer from the emptiness left by the disappearance of Paty and Don Mauricio.

On July 28, 1982, between 3 pm and 4 pm, in the midst of the civil war in El Salvador, a combined group of army and other security agents of the Salvadoran State illegally detained my ex-wife, Patricia Emilie Cuéllar Sandoval (Paty), the mother of our three children, Maite María, Javier Ernesto and Ana Gabriela Álvarez Cuéllar. The exact site of her kidnapping is not known with certainty, but there is a high probability that it occurred while leaving the home of her aunt, María Consuelo Cuéllar, located on Constitution Boulevard and East 3rd Street in San Salvador. Patricia had dual U.S. and Salvadoran citizenship.

That same day, between 10 and 11 pm, another group of military and security forces raided the home of Paty's father, Mauricio Cuéllar, located at Pasaje Caribe and South 65th Street in San Salvador, and after searching his house and confiscating documents and other belongings, they proceeded to take him and his domestic worker, Julia Orbelina Pérez, to an unknown destination.

Simultaneously, or shortly after the arrests of Paty's father and Mrs. Pérez, another combined group of military and security forces raided the apartment where Paty lived with our children, located in Colonia Roma of San Salvador. According to witnesses living in the same building, armed men in army uniforms arrived in several trucks, entered the apartment without forcing the door, searched the place and then proceeded to confiscate personal belongings, requiring several trips.

On the day of Paty's capture, the director of the school where her children attended had phoned her aunt, Mrs. Consuelo Cuéllar, to ask that someone from the family come to pick up the children because Patricia had not come for them. Doña Consuelo then contacted Paty's father, who picked up the children and carried them to the aunt's house to await the eventual arrival of their mother. In the course of that afternoon, Don Mauricio and Doña Consuelo spent several hours calling friends and family trying to locate Paty. When their efforts failed, Don Mauricio left the children with Doña Consuelo in the hope that Paty would pick them up at any moment and return to his home. But Paty did not appear.

The children, already in a state of bewilderment and increasing fear, slept that night at their aunt's house. The following morning, Consuelo called her brother, Mauricio, to ask him to take them to school since Paty had not appeared, but her brother did not answer the phone. Already worried about Paty, Doña Consuelo called another of her brothers, León Enrique Cuéllar, asking that he go to the home of Mauricio to see whether he was there, but when he arrived at his brother's house, León Enrique found the door open, the interior of the house in disarray, the telephone line torn from the wall and Mauricio absent. He also noticed that his brother's vehicle was not in the parking lot.

Mauricio Cuéllar, an economist and business administrator, was general manager of the Salvadoran Association of Industrialists (ASI in Spanish), a well-known organization defending the interests of the country's industrial business sector. Mauricio had scheduled a press conference that morning, and when he hadn't arrived, ASI staff proceeded to file a kidnapping complaint, and León Enrique informed them of the disappearance of Paty as well.

🐦

I learned about the apparent kidnapping of Paty and her father on the afternoon of the 29th when a mutual friend with whom Paty and I had worked in Christian youth groups came to pick me up at the Central American University, "José Simeón Cañas" (UCA) where I worked as a researcher and analyst at the Center for Information, Documentation and Research Support (CIDAI). The friend wanted to know if I had seen

Paty and I replied that I had not, nor had we spoken by phone recently. He told me that Doña Consuelo had called him and told him about the disappearance of Paty, Don Mauricio, and his domestic worker, Mrs. Pérez; he also told me that Don Mauricio's and Paty's homes had been searched and ransacked and that both Don Mauricio's car and Paty's VW, were nowhere to be found. When I asked him about the children, he explained that Maite, Javier and Gaby were fine and that they were at Doña Consuelo's house.

At that moment, I was unsure about what to do. I was bewildered, shocked, and terrified to think what Paty and her father could be suffering. I was also anguished at not knowing how our children were. I thought that Maite and Javier would be more affected than Gaby since she, at that time, was only eight months old and probably less aware of what was happening. Over the years following their mother's kidnapping and disappearance, however, I have seen that the absence of their mother in their lives affected everyone equally and severely.

I was also deeply confused about the reasons for Don Mauricio's disappearance. Although he was a high-level executive in the private sector and close to the government, he was not part of the country's political opposition, so his capture made no sense.

Paty's case was easier to understand. She had worked from a young age in defense of human rights alongside people who were motivated by Liberation Theology with its preferential option for the poor, placing her on the radar of the repressive forces of the country. Most recently, she had worked with Socorro Jurídico Cristiano, supporting Christian Base Communities and other organizations of the Catholic Church, supporting families displaced from their communities of origin by scorched earth strategies and indiscriminate bombardment by the Armed Forces.

Paty knew (we knew) that she was exposed. The situation in the country was becoming more treacherous each day. The peasant population was being massacred by military operations, and in the cities, hundreds of students, professionals, trade unions and religious leaders were being killed, captured, tortured and disappeared. In El Salvador, political prisoners were not officially recognized until 1983, as a result of the U.S. Congress beginning to condition the approval of economic and military assistance to the government of El Salvador, demanding greater control of the security forces and death squads through advances in the respect for human rights.

On several occasions, Paty had noticed that she was being watched, and a day before her disappearance, she reported that several unknown individuals had been chasing her. Each time, she had managed to outmaneuver her pursuers and evade capture, but we always knew that there was a lot of risk. I never thought, however, that the military would go to the extreme of disappearing her, much less her father and his domestic worker, Doña Julia Perez.

Days after the disappearance of Don Mauricio and Doña Julia, I still clung to the hope that the authorities would release them upon verifying their identity. In Paty's case, I was also hopeful that she would eventually be released or at least accused and sent before a judge, but that was wishful thinking in a country like El Salvador in the 1980s.

With many lingering doubts and fears about what was happening, I returned to my office at the UCA and spoke with the director of CIDAI, who communicated with the university authorities and the Society of Jesus and later informed me that the Jesuits and the university would be following this case closely. They offered me support and protection, but that night and many nights afterward, I didn't sleep at home for fear that I might also be captured.

On the morning of July 30, I went to the offices of the Archdiocese of San Salvador to speak with Monsignor Ricardo Urioste, with whom Paty and I had collaborated in previous years, providing talks and workshops on national reality in parishes in and around San Salvador.

That same morning, two detectives from the National Police also arrived at the archdiocese to question me about Patricia's disappearance. They wanted to take me to their headquarters, but Monsignor and his legal assistant objected, insisting that I be interviewed in the offices of the archdiocese. In addition, we were all beginning to perceive that the police, in an effort to hide the truth, intended to treat Paty's disappearance as a domestic problem, as they often did in cases of disappearance.

That afternoon, I spoke with a special envoy from the U.S. Embassy, who I think was one of the FBI agents that the Embassy had summoned to help them investigate Patricia's disappearance since she was a U.S. citizen. Finally, on the same day, I met with the legal assistants of Socorro Juridico Cristiano and Tutela Legal to report the disappearances.

Socorro Juridico Cristiano's lawyer prepared a Habeas Corpus that was presented to the Supreme Court and published the next day in the local press. The following week, Socorro Jurídico Cristiano sent a letter to the U.S. Congress denouncing the illegal capture of U.S. citizen Patricia Emilie Cuéllar and requesting the intervention of President Ronald Reagan's government to investigate and pressure its Salvadoran counterpart to release Patricia, Mauricio and Julia Pérez immediately.

In the following days, Socorro Jurídico Cristiano remained in communication with the U.S. Embassy in El Salvador, but as time passed without news of Paty, her father, or Mrs. Pérez, our certainty grew that they had all been tortured and murdered and, in the cases of Paty and Julia Pérez, probably raped.

A confidential 1983 U.S. State Department document titled "Situation of Murdered American Citizens in El Salvador" reported that nine U.S. citizens had been killed under different circumstances in El Salvador and that, in the case of Patricia Cuéllar, it was likely that she had been murdered.

The day that Paty, her father and Doña Julia disappeared, Maite María was three years old, Javier Ernesto was two years old, and Ana Gabriela was eight months old. For the next seven years, for reasons of safety, well-being and family, our daughters and son would live with their great-aunt Doña Consuelo. Not living permanently with my daughters and Javier since my marriage to their mother failed was a harrowing experience that left me profoundly depressed and filled with anxiety. But under the present circumstances, things got worse. Watching the sad faces and searching for ways to explain their mother's absence took me to the depths of despair. Since they were so young and we all clung to the hope that Paty would one day come home, Paty's aunt, Consuelo, suggested at first that I not tell the children about the kidnappings. But one fearful day, I found the necessary strength and the courage to tell them the truth.

I don't know exactly what must have gone through their heads and hearts at that precise moment. To my surprise, the immediate reaction was not one of tears or exorbitant sadness. Perhaps their own self-defense mechanisms prevented them from processing the full details of this horrible truth, I don't know. But for me, it was perhaps the most difficult moment of my life, and it still brings tears when I think about it.

I feel in some ways responsible for the fact that my children have lost the loving presence of their mother, her laughter and her singing, among a thousand other joys. I am sorry that they no longer had their maternal grandfather who took them for walks to eat ice cream around the corner from the house or to play in the park. I feel responsible for how much they have suffered, not only from a very young age but also as adults. I am so sorry.

I can't change the past, but the least I can do is continue to investigate, write and hope that one day, the truth about the case will be known and that justice will be done. State propaganda since the end of the war has tried to make us forget. Those responsible for serious war crimes have remained hidden and have escaped punishment with impunity. But the process of forgiving requires first the clarification of crimes and the identity of their intellectual authors, so that is my continued demand.

I tried to build a new home with my children, and the four of us finally lived under the same roof in El Salvador, then in Mexico City, where I married my beloved Irish partner, Pauline, who gave birth to our son, Pablo. And we finally settled in the United Kingdom, where we continue to reside today.

For forty-one years, the Salvadoran state made no advances in the investigation of the forced disappearances of Paty, Mauricio and Mrs. Pérez. This was due, on the one hand, to the ineffectiveness of the judicial system during the twelve years of civil war. Then, during the post-war period of transition and national reconstruction, a "General Amnesty Law for the Consolidation of Peace" was enacted in March 1993, benefiting those responsible (on both sides) for the crimes committed during the war.

On March 28, 2003, we filed a complaint with the Attorney General of the Republic requesting his intervention in the disappearance of Paty, but nothing was done. On October 23, 2004, almost a year and a half later, through the Human Rights Institute of the UCA (IDHUCA), we filed a complaint with the Inter-American Commission on Human Rights (IACHR) in Washington, DC, against the State of El Salvador for the forced disappearance of Patricia Emilie Cuéllar Sandoval, Mauricio Cuéllar, and Julia Orbelina Pérez. In addition, on this same occasion, we requested that the complaint against the State of El Salvador be admitted for the violation of fundamental human rights contained in the American Convention on Human Rights and that a "friendly settlement" process be convened.

On December 15, 2004, the IACHR reported that the petition had been registered and that it would be studied in accordance with its procedures. From this moment on, an exchange of formal correspondence was established around the case between the IACHR, the State of El Salvador and the representation of the relatives that continued for another 20 years until the hearing of the Inter-American Court of Human Rights (IACHR-Court) on November 22, 2023 in San José, Costa Rica, in which I provided testimony.

What is relevant about the reconstruction of the period is that it provided us with a historical-political perspective that shows that the persecution, capture (possibly torture and rape) and subsequent murder and disappearance in the main case of Patricia Emilie Cuéllar was the result of systematic, far-reaching military intelligence work and that it was carried out by combined security forces, state intelligence agents, and the Salvadoran army. This implies that, through the chain of command existing at that time, different civil servants and military agents of the State were involved, directly or indirectly, in the process.

Thus, the capture and subsequent forced disappearance of my ex-wife and mother of our three children was not an accident nor an improvised operation. As the Report of the UN Truth Commission for El Salvador has pointed out and documented, in the military and paramilitary operations of annihilation of that period, the interrelationship between the security forces, the army and the so-called death squads of the ultra-right was indistinguishable.

Unfortunately, the governments of El Salvador at that time, as well as the Reagan administration, were direct or indirect accomplices, as exposed by different sources during the period and confirmed by documents recently declassified by the United States. The capture and subsequent forced disappearance of Mr. Mauricio Cuéllar, at that time general manager of the Salvadoran Association of Industrialists (ASI), and his employee, Mrs. Julia Orbelina Pérez, on the other hand, was incidental, insofar as they never participated or were involved with any type of political organization, human rights, humanitarian or religious organizations that, by virtue of the doctrine of national security and anti-communist ideology, were categorized as "subversive".

The authoritarian military state of that period directed generalized violence and repression primarily against peasants who participated in emerging organizations in the rural sector (cooperatives, grassroots ecclesiastical communities and trade unions) and against citizens who participated in or worked in student associations, trade unions, human rights organizations, humanitarian aid NGOs, the media (national and international) and others.

One of the targets systematically and quantitatively most affected in this period were diocesan priests, the most horrendous being the assassination of the archbishop of San Salvador, monsignor Oscar Romero, and several nuns of the Catholic Church. It is worth remembering also the kidnapping, rape, and murder of three North American nuns and a lay missionary perpetrated by agents of the (defunct) National Guard. Of equal significance, Jesuit priests suffered multiple bombings, as well as the assassinations of six eminent academic priests of the Central American University (UCA) and two of its workers.

By the end of 1980, "the Catholic Church counted 28 priests killed (including Archbishop Romero) and 21 arrested, 14 bomb attacks, 41 machine-gun attacks, 15 robberies, and 33 church takeovers." To all of this must be added two disappeared priests (Fr. Abrego and Fr. Cosmo Spessotto) along with thousands of catechists (men and women) murdered throughout the country. This phenomenon confirms that, from very early on, the Catholic Church, with its Liberation Theology, grassroots communities and popular church, was a special and hard-hit target of counterinsurgency and national security activities under the cover of anti-communism.

There are thousands of families who, as in the case of Paty, Mauricio and Mrs. Pérez, have been victims of the madness of state terrorism. Were

Patricia and I naïve idealists? I think so, at least in part. In the seventies and eighties, we believed that it was possible to change the world together with the weakest and most needy members of our society.

We held tightly to the idea of a common project of change that gave meaning to our lives. The unity and strength of our community of young friends, combined with Archbishop Romero's persistent commitment to the poor, were fundamental to our lives. The work of the priests and nuns we met was also a great example for us and for many other young people of the time.

We grew up with the idea that it was not possible to change reality without changing ourselves in an integral and spiritual way. We could never be indifferent to pain and injustice, and it was this that made Paty such a special person, brave and consistent always in her commitment. She knew that she was working and giving her life for a better future for Maite, Javier and Gaby, for her future grandchildren (Lukkas and Olivia) and for those who are on the way, people that she loved until the last seconds of her life.

Forty-one years after the fatal and tragic events that changed the course of our lives, my family and I continue to suffer from the emptiness left by the disappearance of Paty and Don Mauricio. The pain that their absences have caused and continue to cause in our sons and daughters is like a permanent nightmare. To this day, Patricia, Don Mauricio and Doña Julia continue to be disappeared, and this has meant that our families have not been able to give a dignified burial or observe the normal process of mourning that our loved ones deserve.

(Note: This testimony is a brief summary of the testimony of its author given on November 22, 2023 in San José, Costa Rica, during an audience with the Interamerican Court for Human Rights).

Ana del Carmen[1]

A saint asked us to do it

In this country, injustice had its principal base of operations. Its principal characteristic was the imposition of a brutal system of military repression that resulted in the imprisonment, torture, disappearance and death of thousands of people. The Constitution was conspicuous for its absence. The government, headed by General Carlos Humberto Romero, had no popular support. There was no consensus, and in order to govern, they had to do so through terror. The situation was unsustainable for Salvadorans.

Fear, like a poisoned mist, permeated the hearts of all people. At dusk each day, there was an overwhelming sense of anguish, given the uncertainty of knowing if one would still be alive the next day. The death squads, like hungry reptiles, would begin to crawl through the neighborhoods where workers, teachers, students, priests and seminarians lived, where they kidnapped those to be sacrificed that night. There was terror, horror, anguish, tribulation and affliction.

In view of these facts, Monsignor Oscar Arnulfo Romero, archbishop of San Salvador, was concerned about the lack of truth in the mass media and said, "It is necessary and urgent that we do something to confront the seriousness of this situation. The people must know what is happening. They must know the truth in order to decide and organize their social action."

1 Reprinted, with permission, from her book *Ecos del Silencio*, 2003, Self-published, San Salvador. ISBN 978-99961-2-239-7

Monsignor came to the Central American University (UCA) to present a plan to remedy this situation. He had YSAX radio, but he didn't have the people to build and operate a serious news program that would tell the truth. The major print, radio and television media were part of the power block, so they shared its ideology and, above all, they shared the madness of the oligarchy and the military in their fear of communism. So, he asked the Dean of the UCA at that time, Román Mayorga, to help him develop the program. The university could create a team made up of professors and specialists of all of the career areas being taught, to write the editorials and comment on the news. Other people could write the news, record it, and air the program. Everything would be done under the name of the Archdiocese of San Salvador....

Those who were involved in the program wanted change for El Salvador, recognizing that it was urgent to work in all areas to turn this nation into a democracy and ensure that justice was carried out. It was necessary to listen to the cries of the Salvadoran people, victims of the brutal repression that prevailed, in order to put an end to their ordeal....

The first broadcast aired in early 1978. One Saturday, working as a radio announcer, I was handed a piece of news to report with a strong comment on the actions of certain members of the military. I argued that it should not be read because it was the kind of text that would attract the bombing of our radio station. However, on the following Monday, because there was not much material for the program of that day, the delicate commentary was aired. The following night, a bomb destroyed a large part of the radio's facilities. Monsignor ordered spare parts from Miami, and two months later, we were back on the air.

The program continued to air for about a year and a half after that but then suffered six bomb attacks, totally destroying its installations and equipment, so archbishop Romero decided to curtail programming, pointing out that if we insisted on re-establishing the radio, the right would simply destroy it again. He also said, however, that "The radio had already fulfilled its mission" and that we must now "think of another way to communicate truth to the people on what is happening in the country so that they can make their own decisions about what is best for them."

In my own case, since I had worked as an announcer on Archbishop Romero's radio program, an attempt was made to assassinate me by placing a bomb in my car that would explode while I was driving it. A gardener overheard the discussion about my death and went to a close friend of mine with the news, who, of course, came to me, so I didn't use my car again. That's when the National Guard decided to dynamite my house. If I had been there, I would have been instantly killed.

After the bombings, those of us who had worked on the radio began to receive threats or close calls like the bombing of my house, so it was no longer safe for us to remain in El Salvador. Hence, many of us went into exile to different countries to save our lives and those of our families....

When asked in later years why we worked on the news program, knowing the dangers, we answered: "We did it because we wanted to contribute, through that program, to building a democratic country, good for all, and because a saint asked us to do it."

The one with the machete wound

The war in El Salvador was rooted in the injustice and oppression that have always existed in our country. This reality forced more than a million people to leave the country as refugees. One of the countries that served as a destination for people in exile was Costa Rica, where I had a profoundly moving experience:

> The woman standing before us was petite, dark-skinned and small of stature, and it seemed at first glance that she would have nothing of interest to say. Nevertheless, she moved with confidence to the center of our group and, after a brief silence, began to speak with a strength and conviction that shocked us all. And this was her story:

> > We are from San Miguel and live in the countryside. We made our living from a small store selling religious objects. We sold rosary beads, holy cards, Bibles, the "Magnificat", photos of Archbishop Romero and medals of Jesus, the Virgin and several saints. The Magnificat is a prayer, she explained, to which Salvadorans attribute magical properties to such an extent that they believe that the bearer of the prayer is protected from all danger. Thus, we were defending ourselves. Remember that we were at war, and life was very difficult.

One day, the Army arrived and began searching our house. When they found the photos of Archbishop Romero, they became very angry and began to insult us. Without a thought, they killed my husband right there, in front of me. I had my 13-year-old daughter with me, and they raped her, also in front of my face. She was raped by about ten soldiers. Then, they took out their machetes and cut her to pieces. After that, it was my turn. They raped me repeatedly and gave me several chops to my back with their machetes. Then they shot me and left me for dead, soaked in my own blood.

As she spoke, she uncovered part of her back to show the scars left by the machete blows. Then she unbuttoned the front of her dress to show us a round scar surrounded by rays, like a sun on her collarbone. The soldiers, in their haste, did not aim at her heart as they had intended, and that saved her life.

That day, when she regained consciousness, she crawled to her parents' house, fainting at times and regaining consciousness until she arrived. Her parents gave her first aid; they washed her wounds and applied compresses of medicinal herbs that they use in the countryside. In the cities, that peasant wisdom has already been lost. Luck, or perhaps that God in whom they believe so strongly, saved her. Their two youngest children, who, luckily for them, were not in the house at the time of the crimes, stayed with their mother at the grandparents' house while she gradually began to heal.

When the woman was able to walk, she was transferred to a clinic run by nuns in San Salvador. The sister in charge quickly assimilated all that had happened. After assuring the parents that she was safe, she admitted the woman to the clinic and hid her from the authorities. There, they treated the wounds on her body, knowing that the emotional wounds would take much longer to heal.

When she regained her health, the sisters who ran the clinic gave her money to buy bus tickets for herself and the children to the port of Cutuco. There, they took the ferry to Corinto, a port in Nicaragua. They crossed all of Nicaragua and arrived at the Peñas Blancas border between Nicaragua and Costa Rica. At that border, the United Nations High Commissioner for Refugees (UNHCR) granted the woman refugee status.

In Costa Rica, UNHCR officials assigned her a monthly allowance to cover basic needs for her and her children. As a measure applied to all refugees, she also underwent a medical examination and learned that she was pregnant. Since she had a slight case of anemia, she was given blood transfusions and medical attention. When the time came, she gave birth to a girl whom she named María de Los Ángeles in honor of the Virgin and patron saint of Costa Rica.

When she finished her story, she said: "I thank God for having delivered me from so many dangers and for having brought me to this country where I will be able to raise my children in peace and freedom."

This woman is one of many who have left El Salvador fleeing repression, as they say, "with one hand in front and the other behind," that is to say, with nothing. However, despite the cruelty they have suffered, they have maintained great hope in life. As archbishop Romero said: "With people such as these, it is not difficult to be a good shepherd."

The Offensive, "To the End"

I studied literature at the UCA. El Salvador was at war, and because of my activities and those of my friends working on the radio program of the Archdiocese of San Salvador, I had been forced to go into exile. Some of my colleagues went to Mexico, others to Nicaragua. I went to Costa Rica. When I returned to El Salvador, the war was still going on, and I was hired as a professor to teach the subjects of Communication and Language.

The years went by, and the war continued. The professors of the UCA were all profoundly aware of national reality since the university conducted constant forums and workshops, with lectures given by economists, political scientists, political leaders, sociologists, etc. It was known that the guerrillas, the government and the military were talking in an effort to end the war. The dialogue meetings took place in Costa Rica, Mexico, Venezuela, Switzerland and, later, in the United States, among other countries. However, the agreement of the FMLN to seek peace through dialogue and negotiations was perceived by many in the military to be a sign of weakness and exhaustion on the field of battle, offering the opportunity to the Armed Forces to win the war without concessions. So, for a period of time, they withdrew from the negotiating table and concentrated on harsh military offensives with incursions and bombings deep into the territories under the control of the guerrillas.

In response, on November 11, 1989, the FMLN initiated its own guerrilla offensive, "Hasta El Tope" (to the end), carried out at the national level. The war was taken to San Salvador and all of the other important cities of the country to demonstrate its strength to the Salvadoran Armed Forces and its North American partners.

The next day, I asked my son to go for a walk around the UCA to see if they were still working despite the offensive. However, the university was surrounded by the army, and we couldn't get in. Faced with this situation, I decided to go to Rosales Hospital, where the wounded were being brought in, to see if I could be of any help.

On Thursday, November 16, as I was preparing again to go to the hospital, I received a phone call from one of the Jesuit priests who gave me the horrible news of the murder of Fathers Ellacuría, Montes, Martin-Baró, Amando, Pardito and López y López.

The Ides of November

When I arrived at the university, what I saw was horrifying. A horrible smell flooded the atmosphere, and a black shroud of flies partially covered the corpses. Scattered around the heads were clots of blackened blood, pieces of bone, and pieces of brain mass. Outside, there were only four bodies: Ellacuría, Montes, Martín-Baró and Amando López. Father López y López was there at the time of the massacre by chance, since he resided outside the UCA, but was probably woken by the sound of gunfire and came to see what was going on only to be killed along with his comrades. The gardener's wife and domestic worker of the Jesuits, Julia Elba, and her daughter Celina were sleeping in a small room near the priests' residence that night and were also killed.

The faces of the priests could not be seen because they were face down on the grass of the garden. The corpse of Father Moreno had been dragged into one of the rooms, leaving a macabre trail of blood. It was the room of Father Sobrino, who was in Thailand and escaped his own murder. I saw Father Moreno's face flaccid with nothing to sustain the skin since his facial bones had all been shattered. When the soldiers moved a bookcase to make room for his body, a book had fallen from one of the shelves and was lying on the floor beside the corpse, leaving the title visible, "The Crucified God", soaked with Father Moreno's blood.

I felt enormous pain and profound sadness. I couldn't pray, I couldn't think, I couldn't do anything, just cry. After a while, Father Ormaechea said to me: "Madam, what are you doing here?" and I replied: "Accompanying the dead and the living." That was my answer: a prayer of accompaniment. It seemed like a nightmare to me and I hoped that I would soon awake, but it was real.

It was the most horrific event I had ever witnessed. Later on, I was thinking to myself that all was lost, that our dream of changing our country was just a dream, that we would all be killed sooner or later. It was the end for El Salvador. This country no longer had salvation.

This gruesome event was the fulfillment of a plan that was born many years earlier. Father Montes was right when he told me in a conversation that we once had: "The military gave Archbishop Romero three years; they have given us thirty, but they will be our end."

It all began with the Second Vatican Council of October 11, 1962, which eventually led to a new theology of liberation in Latin America, concretized in the Medellín conferences of August 26, 1968, with the preferential option for the poor. As Father Sobrino said: "It is the point of praxis where God reveals himself in history." This would become the axis for the life of Catholics and would permeate all aspects of their lives.

In El Salvador, Father Ellacuría and a group of Jesuits enthusiastically embraced the task of putting the council's teachings into practice. Working for social justice had always been an imperative in the teachings of the Church, so priests began to work for social justice in El Salvador. They were called liberation theologians, meaning liberation from hunger, misery, injustice and exclusion. Father Sobrino sums it up as follows: "Liberation theology starts from the poor as a place of understanding of the faith that allows us to attain mercy from the victims." It was 1973 when the Jesuits began to implement changes in the education they provided at their school, Externado de San José, so that students would know the reality of their country and, in the future, be able and willing to implement the policies that El Salvador needed to begin the path to democracy...

According to the indictment of the Central Court of Instruction No. 6 of the National Court of Spain, "the direct order to assassinate the Jesuits was given during the afternoon of November 15, but it was the result of prior discussion, planning and authorization." President Alfredo Cristiani was housed in the quarters of General Staff during the guerrilla offensive, but it is not known if he attended the meetings that took place there... It is not known if the military decided on the assassination on their own and did not consult the president or if the president agreed with what happened....

It is not known if the priests who were slain said anything before they died. A neighbor, whose house adjoins the property where they were killed, says that she heard a psalmody; it seemed that the priests had prayed before presenting themselves to their Creator. They did not resist their death, they understood that it was useless. Only Father Martín-Baró expressed his indignation, shouting to his executioners, "This is an injustice; you are carrion"!

The assassination of the Jesuit priests marked the end of the war. This brutal crime caused the United States to eventually cease its military aid of more than a million dollars a day to sustain the war, and an investigation into the Jesuit murders was initiated by a special committee headed by Congressman Joe Mockley.

The death of the Jesuits, because they were internationally known intellectuals, was a wake-up call for the world. They were good men who only wanted justice and peace for the country. They worked tirelessly to achieve that end, but for it, they paid an enormous price, added to the almost 80,000 deaths of innocent Salvadorans, offered so that their country would finally have the opportunity to start on the path to democracy.

Promise of Hope: January 16, 1992

The day dawned splendidly. A cobalt blue sky covered the city of San Salvador, and a fresh breeze blew from the east, which made the flags unfurled in the Plaza Barrios, in the National Palace, and in La Cathedral wave energetically. Banners were unfurled as well, flooding us all with their messages:

The Front: Present,
Long live the martyrs of the revolution,
After 11 years of the political-military effort, we have fulfilled our promise
END – FMLN,
Thank you, UN, for your contribution to peace: FEDECOPADES,
The people and COPAZ: guarantee for peace,
INDC: we won peace,
UCA: Present for peace.

Little by little, the square filled with people and the space was quickly insufficient to contain all the feeling and emotion that overwhelmed us.

When the Peace Accords were signed, many Salvadorans understood the importance of this first step, but we met with skepticism the promise of its complete and faithful implementation. Twelve years of declared war and fifty years of repression shaped us in such a way that "until we see, we don't believe", as the popular saying goes. But when we arrived at the square and saw the National Palace with the blue and white flag of El Salvador on the right and the red and white flag of the FMLN on the left, with a gigantic banner with the portrait of Farabundo Martí on the façade of the Cathedral, then we began to believe that now, perhaps, it was possible for the agreements to be fulfilled. The people needed to see "sacraments", visible signs of change, because they were tired of the words of the groups in power, empty of content and with promises that had never come true.

On the stage, in front of the Palace, musical groups performed. The songs were followed by slogans chanted with enthusiasm by all:

We won the peace, let us defend the Accords,
The conquest of peace is everyone's task.
The war is over, let's build peace,
The people united will never be defeated

Mixed in with the audience, young people were seen with red handkerchiefs and FMLN flags. I found it incredible and exciting what was happening around me. My memories came back, and I heard in my mind a song that I often sang to myself in exile when it seemed to me that returning to my homeland was an impossible dream:

I'll walk the streets again
Of what was the home of my bloodied people,
And in a beautiful liberated hovel,
I will stop to cry for those who are absent.

And I cried for the absence of so many, remembering my son among them. I saw him so young and so enthusiastic about going off to fight so that others could have the same opportunities that he had. I saw him smiling and cheerful, playing his guitar and singing of love. I saw him with eyes full of tears, moved by the poverty of the people. I heard his voice when he told me: "Courage, Mom, the day of triumph will come, and we will hug and sing in some square of San Salvador." I made it that day, but he couldn't. He died somewhere lost on this earth, defending his ideals through his work with the clandestine radio, Radio Farabundo Martí. Many others, like him, were also absent. Their faces passed quickly in my thoughts, and I saw Monsignor Romero, Father Ellacuría, Nacho, Amando, Pardito, Montes, Quique, Michel, Tolo, Ethel, Pedro... I saw them all pass by: young idealists, guerrillas and soldiers, workers and peasants, children and old people who gave their lives to make this day a reality.

The miracle was really happening, and little by little, we began to believe in the foundation of a new homeland. "A new heaven on a new earth." Symbolically, a dove landed on the hand of the statue of General Gerardo Barrios as a sign that, in this new society, we civilians will decide how we want to live and under what laws we will organize our society. No more money for weapons, but for food, medicine, schools, housing and culture.

My memories took me to another time and another reality filled with searches, prisoners, tortured, disappeared, shootings, bombs, and my house dynamited. I saw myself at the airport with a child in my arms and a suitcase. I left my land with a broken heart, and in my thoughts, I carried all the words of love that I wanted to say but didn't, all the hugs that I wanted to give but didn't give, all the friends that I wanted to see and couldn't...But I was there, in that square, fulfilling a promise I made to myself, to my children, to my friends.

It was twelve o'clock in the afternoon, and the bells were ringing joyfully on this historic morning. Tears were coming to everyone's eyes.

We all had someone to cry for, and we all had someone to rebuild this country for. We hugged friends and strangers; we were all united in pain, joy and the firm purpose of making El Salvador a new homeland built on truth, justice and forgiveness.

Brian

I am just one of thousands of internationalists from around the world who made the journey to El Salvador in the 1980s and early '90s – and for many years after – to accompany Salvadorans in their struggle for justice, equality and peace over those many years. My experiences were no more dramatic than others and certainly much less heroic. But they remain among the most important in my life, as are the relationships that I built during that time.

The fact is that the popular struggle in El Salvador that unfolded in the late 1970s into the early 90s captured the imagination of the world. There was a time when silk screen posters of Monsignor Óscar Arnulfo Romero were as common as those of Che Guevara in the headquarters of people's movements and social justice organizations around the world. And Romero remains an inspiration to millions even today, almost 45 years after his assassination in 1980.

What was it about El Salvador – what is it about El Salvador – that keeps us coming back to attend its experiences and lessons? Why is it so important to recuperate and nurture the historical memory of this long struggle?

One answer lies in the fact that the events in El Salvador during this period took place at a critical moment in a widening global struggle for authentic democracy and economic justice. In this context, the Salvadoran people and the Salvadoran popular movements were an inspiration to other movements around the world. And they continue to be so, just as the struggle for justice in El Salvador itself continues.

In taking their agency and activism to the outside world, in building global networks of solidarity and mutual support, Salvadorans were part of a radical transition in the strategies and methods of social movements and citizen political social action globally. In their instinct toward self-organization, they ultimately sparked fundamental transitions in the methods, governance and mandates of the formal international humanitarian regime. Most particularly, they had a significant impact on norms of refugee protection and human rights in general – in ways that still reverberate today.

As I reflect on this now, my mind goes back to late March 1992. I found myself in San José las Flores, a community to the east of the city of Chalatenango on the road towards Nueva Trinidad and Arcatao. January of that year had seen the signing of peace accords between the FMLN and the government, and the February 1st ceasefire was now several weeks old.

I was traveling with two Salvadoran companions. The three of us were good friends after many years of collaborating in support of social movements in Central America, particularly organizations formed by refugee and internally displaced communities. On this trip we were investigating the preparations for the FMLN demobilization that had just begun, in support of which we were campaigning for physical security and material support from the international community.

That morning, we met up with Germán Serrano, the FMLN comandante for Chalatenango Province. After many years commanding a guerilla force in war, he was now leading his troops in the dangerous transition to peace and civilian life. He had agreed to brief us on the challenges facing the demobilization process. Sitting together, drinking strong, sweet coffee in the kitchen area of a small, low-slung adobe bungalow, Serrano laid out the logistic landscape that he and his team confronted.

The January agreements had specified that the FMLN would gather their troops in fifteen 'points of concentration' after the ceasefire had been secured. Over the next nine months, the estimated 1,300 women and 7,500 men in the regular army of the FMLN would be disarmed and demobilized. The concentration of troops had already been delayed. Instead of strict concentration in fifteen points, there were at that moment forty-seven. The first demobilization of 1,700 combatants was scheduled for May 1, but the delay in providing adequate food, shelter and services had put this first critical target in doubt, threatening the schedule for implementation of the peace accords themselves.

The comandante explained that not even minimal conditions had yet been provided for the health and dignity of his troops, which was the responsibility of the government and the international guarantors of the peace process. Sanitary conditions were primitive and dangerous. There was little tenting or bedding, let alone building materials. There was only the barest allotment of beans, corn and water. The first significant delivery of food arrived only on March 20, seven weeks after the cease-fire, delivered by the relief agency CARITAS from borrowed government food stocks. These supplies were dwindling quickly.

Serrano acknowledged that the troops were getting discouraged and impatient, but he expressed faith in the discipline and goodwill of his soldiers – although things would have to change very soon.

I found out later that Germán Serrano, whose legal (birth) name was José Ricardo Ruiz, died a few short months after our meeting with him while the demobilization process was still unfolding. He was only 32 years old. He had mentioned to us the severe headaches that he sometimes suffered and that he hoped to soon take care of them once the war was over. Sadly he did not get that opportunity. José Ricardo Ruiz had joined the guerrilla and revolutionary work at the age of 13. It was clear in our visit and in the remembrances after his death that those he led loved and respected him very much.

We spent the next few days visiting some of the demobilization concentration points in the region. I had traveled in the Salvadoran countryside often over the previous decade, but this was my first visit to El Salvador in peace and my first to the conflict zones in security and safety.

What we see is moving, not for the terrible conditions, but for the spirit and generosity of the ex-combatants as they use the experience of their twelve-year struggle to survive these new conditions with humor and dignity. What they have, they share with us, and we talk of the war, and the peace, and the future. Time and again, they pull folders out of knapsacks with pictures of children, parents, the homestead, and the hearth. Time and again, they ask if the world outside El Salvador knows or cares what is happening to them now that it is peace rather than war that determines their fate.

Around noon on the second day, near the community of San Antonio Los Ranchos, we walk through the scrub bush to a concentration of more than 300 ex-combatants. Conditions are basic: hammocks strung from trees and thin blankets on the ground. A rudimentary pump for groundwater had been built just a few days earlier with emergency funds secured from the Canadian government. We share their lunch of watery soup and tortillas, and we talk of the war, the peace, and the future.

And it is this that strikes me most – these exhausted young people (and most of them are very young!) are not dwelling on the past, not telling us stories of the war and what they have endured in the last years; they are talking about the future, about what they hope will come out of their long struggle, for their country, and for themselves. They ask us questions about how the peace process is being received in the world and whether we think it can be a real peace, with justice and opportunity for all. Their hopes are not theoretical; they enthusiastically talk about what they will do when they are back home, about their families, about maybe going back to school, of starting normal lives with jobs. "And parties!" – *¡Bailar!* – someone gasps, while others laugh, and a few do a brief but extravagant shimmy, uninhibited by the frayed remnants of their camouflage cargo pants and tank tops.

Eventually, we got back to San Salvador, compared notes, and got down to the task at hand, working through Consejería en Proyectos, an institution based in the region supported by an international consortium of voluntary organizations from several countries – including my own, the Canadian social justice organization, Inter Pares.

In close collaboration with local Salvadoran organizations, our goal was to secure food, clothing, latrines and health care, as well as educational programs for the former combatants. We would soon also be seeking funds for the reconstruction of war-damaged communities that would have to follow the demobilization and return to peace and normal life. In the end, over the intervening months and years, we were able to bring significant resources to that purpose, one small contribution among many international efforts.

I think back to those times today as I write this contribution to a book on history and memory in El Salvador. I think about those young people we met in those days, those courageous kids who gave themselves to a struggle – a struggle whose success could never be guaranteed during the war nor after the peace. And it occurs to me that perhaps few of them could have fully realized how their struggle was seen in the outside world and how it contributed to developments in the wider world outside of El Salvador, during the war, and since.

The most dramatic example from the perspective of my work was the monumental impact of the refugee return process and repopulation movement that unfolded between 1986 and 1989. Consejería en Proyectos – known by its English-language acronym, PCS – was intensely involved from the outset of the process through its on-the-ground support and accompaniment of CRIPDES, CORDES, and several other community-based popular organizations that emerged in this period. At the same time PCS was collaborating with these organizations to promote the Salvadoran popular sector's capacity to engage in and influence the course of the various multilateral negotiations underway at the time.

This process – conceived and implemented by the Salvadoran popular movement – ultimately transformed the way the apparatus of international humanitarian assistance engaged and assisted communities uprooted by civil conflict. The impact was felt first in El Salvador, then elsewhere in Latin America, in Guatemala, then in Colombia and Peru, and now is evident in every conflict on every continent in the world today.

An indication of the significance of the self-organization of Salvadoran refugees and internally displaced populations in fomenting and negotiating the return process of those years is found in the fact that, more than three decades later, the process and its influence is still being studied and elaborated. An excellent example is a recent study authored by McGill University researcher Megan Bradley, "Realizing the Right of Return: Refugees' Roles in Localizing Norms and Socializing UNHCR", in the journal *Geopolitics* (2023).

Bradley explains how the large-scale return movements of the late 1980s in Central America had a major impact on how voluntary repatriation was perceived in the region and internationally. Understood as a more lasting ("durable") solution to displacement, it was ultimately embraced by the International Conference on Central American Refugees (CIREFCA), a 5-year inter-governmental process under the auspices of the United Nations.

Bradley describes her research this way:

> Through the lens of the mobilization of thousands of refugees who repatriated from Honduras to El Salvador in the mid-to-late 1980s, this article examines how refugees themselves have influenced the governance of return as norm entrepreneurs who socialized UNHCR to rethink and support broader interpretations of the right of return. Salvadoran refugees 'localized' this norm by developing their own conceptualization of the right of return as a collective and deeply political process of asserting citizenship rights... They strategically built on codified law and leveraged their experiences as refugees to lend political and moral weight to their interpretation. They also demonstrated their ability to take direct action to implement this right (even at great personal risk), notwithstanding government opposition, by planning massive repatriation movements that compelled UNHCR and the governments of El Salvador and Honduras to adjust, however grudgingly, to their vision.

In her conclusion, Bradley writes:

> [The] refugees involved in these movements had outsized influence on local as well as international and institutional imaginaries of the right of return as the cornerstone of repatriation movements, and the role of refugees and UNHCR alike in advancing this right. Through years-long processes of persuasion and pressure, the refugee leadership socialized UNHCR to accept and defend key elements of their normative interpretation and provided practical support for their implementation efforts ... this movement inspired return claims made by other refugee populations and influenced the approach to the right of

return particularly in the CIREFCA process, which in turn shaped UNHCR's efforts to support voluntary repatriation in other regions. Its implications thus reverberate across the daily lives of thousands of returnees and their descendants, and the evolution of UNHCR as the central international institution in the refugee regime.

Another recent major study, "'Tangled times': Central American refugee perspectives on the long Cold War," by Mary Todd, published in 2024, underscores the contemporary relevance of the recuperation of the memory and wide dissemination of the experience of the Salvadoran struggle.

Todd, a Professor at Montana State University, writes: "Adopting a transnational social historical approach allows us to see this Cold War-era 'refugee crisis' as the peasants saw it – as part of much longer historical patterns of dispossession and resistance." She explains that her essay, "explores how, rather than submit to conventional portrayals of refugees as pawns or passive victims, Salvadorans identified as citizen-activists who harnessed displacement as an opportunity to continue progressing toward long-standing goals of building a more just and equitable world."

Todd writes,

> In this hidden history, refugees were active protagonists. They created their own organizations, insisted on their inherent dignity and rights as humans and as citizens of El Salvador, and mobilized national and international laws, conventions and other resources in support of their claims. They set standards for their own government as well as aid agencies, and they made it known when these groups failed to meet expectations. As they did all this, they contested their literal and figurative erasures – from law, territory, nation, and history. …

Todd's article also usefully brings us forward to present times, examining how the experience of struggle from the 1980s and early '90 did not end there. She writes, "Despite the many positives, however, historic patterns of exclusion continued...Former refugees clearly connected these post-war problems to long-standing inequalities in international relations." As an example of how they used their long experience of organizing to continue to be engaged in political action, she describes the actions of the 'water defenders' movement in the repopulated zones of Chalatenango and Cabañas who carried out a massive anti-mining campaign beginning around 2006 and continuing to the present day. In that work, Todd writes,

> Taking advantage of post-war mechanisms for community participation, they organized popular referenda, resulting in municipal ordinances prohibiting mining and increasing pressure on legislators to take similar action on a national level. In late 2016, to everyone's surprise, the Tribunal decided in El Salvador's favor, and a few months later, the Legislative Assembly of El Salvador made the country the first in the world to ban metallic mining.

Writing about this, I think of the young folks that we met in our brief encounters back in 1992 visiting those FMLN demobilization camps. Some of them would have continued in civilian life to engage in the life and action of these popular movements.

My visits to El Salvador over those years leading to 1992 and for many years after the war ended were always a highpoint in my work. But I knew – and my Salvadoran colleagues knew – that the most important contribution of my organization, and the international organizations with whom we collaborated, was to carry out public engagement and political advocacy actions in our own places to build international support for Salvadorans struggling to bring justice and peace to their country and communities.

One of the most ambitious and successful public education actions that we took in Canada was the art exhibit *Disrupted Lives, Children's Drawings from Central America*. This was a project conceived and coordinated by Linda Dale, sponsored by Inter Pares in coordination with CUSO, with the assistance of PCS.

Linda was a trained child educator and museum curator who, on a voluntary basis, was also involved in Central American solidarity. In 1983 she came across examples of drawings from children residing in refugee camps in Honduras. She immediately saw their potential to engage the Canadian public in the lives and circumstances behind those depictions and raised the idea of an exhibit with me and a few others in our circle. In visits to Central America in 1984, she reached out to local organizations and others working with refugees and displaced people to test her ideas for the exhibit and sought their collaboration. People in the region and in Canada were enthusiastic about the idea. Inter Pares agreed to sponsor and house the project, in close collaboration with CUSO, and financial and logistic support from a host of other Canadian NGOs and faith-based organizations.

As the project developed, Linda ultimately was able to collect over 900 drawings, mainly by Salvadoran children but also including drawings by Guatemalan children in camps in Mexico. It was an intensive process relying on the collaboration of local refugee organizations and a network of committed solidarity activists. The process of selecting the drawings to be included and curating them into a coherent exhibit was arduous. The goal was to build an exhibit that met the standards of public galleries and other public spaces while at the same time creating educational tools that could easily be brought to schools, community halls and church basements by local educators and activists.

From the beginning, Linda professed that the drawings were not artifacts to be exploited, but were in themselves art, children's art, and should be presented and explained this way, bringing the children's experience, expression and voice directly to an audience without mediation or manipulation, whether in a gallery, a classroom, or a church hall. And as it developed, that is what happened. Between January 1986 and December 1987, the exhibit appeared at many of the most prominent public art galleries across Canada. The world-renowned National Film Board of Canada commissioned a 14-minute adaptation of the exhibit, called 'Of Lives Uprooted," which was made available publicly. For a period, it even appeared as a 'short' film in advance of main features in public cinemas.

The project also included a scaled-down traveling exhibit, using the same interactive material as the formal institutional exhibit, that could be carried or transported to communities across the country and placed in the hands of teachers in schools and educators in church groups and other community organizations. This transportable exhibit was packaged up and sent by train and bus all over the country.

In the making of this success, there were hours, days, and months of dogged work, working with folks across Canada and Central America to help bring the exhibit and the community education outreach to reality. For those of us involved as the project developed and came closer to fruition, it really had the feel of a community effort, an engagement beyond solidarity – an experience of international common cause.

Something that Linda shared with me in a note a few years ago perhaps captures this spirit. Referring to that period when we were developing the exhibit, she wrote:

> One of my favorite memories relates to the translation of the text which was quite a daunting task for all kinds of interesting reasons. While we were in the throes of doing this, a delegation from El Salvador arrived to do a tour and engage in a series of political meeting – very serious stuff. So it was with some trepidation that I asked if they could spare a few minutes to look at some of the text. To be frank, I worried that this would seem a bit trivial in relation to their other priorities. However, they responded with great enthusiasm, carefully viewing the drawings and text, reading it out loud to properly express the meaning and having many debates with each other over what that child wanted to say. They did this over lunch time but then cancelled the lunch saying this was much more important. For me it was a lovely experience.

Disrupted Lives had a significant impact on awareness and understanding in Canada about what was happening in El Salvador, generating important public support for the solidarity action of Canadian NGOs, unions, faith-based organizations and other institutions, and our Salvadoran counterparts. The project overlapped the period during which the repopulation movement and refugee return process in El Salvador was being planned and initiated. In so doing, it helped Canadian civil society in our conversations with the Canadian government to encourage its proactive support of these processes led by the Salvadoran popular movements.

The widening public awareness and concern about the conflicts in Central America also generated public pressure on the Canadian government. In response, Canada increased its diplomatic engagement in the geopolitical arena to assist in creating conditions for a permanent and just negotiated peace in El Salvador and, subsequently, in Guatemala.

Following the gradual winding down of the project, the children's drawings and other resources of the exhibit were repatriated to El Salvador in 1994 as a contribution to the historical memory process of the communities that had assisted with the project. A few of the original drawings are included in an exhibit in the Museo Regional en Santa Ana, in an exhibit simply called "Imborrables" ("Indelible"), which also includes a memorial to the signing of the peace accords. The remainder of the exhibit materials are archived in the Museo de la Palabra y la Imagen.

Some of the material was also later made available in support of a process in El Salvador in 2017 marking the anniversary of the beginnings of the organized return of Salvadoran refugees from Honduras. Named "Surviving Memory in Postwar El Salvador," that process continues today as a popular education and collaborative research initiative involving several international university-based research institutions. In El Salvador the collaborators include the University of El Salvador; the Central American University; ACISAM–Association of Training and Research for Mental Health; Asociación Sumpul; CCR–Association of Communities for the Development of Chalatenango; Centro Arte para la Paz; the Committee of Surviving Historical Memory in Arcatao; CRIPDES–The Association for the Development of El Salvador; Museo de la Palabra y la Imagen; Pro Vida–Salvadoran Association for the Humanitarian Aid; Tutela Legal "Dra. Maria Julia Hernández"; and the Salvadoran municipalities of San José Las Flores, Las Vueltas, Arcatao, Nueva Trinidad, and Suchitoto.

As deceased Buddhist monk Thích Nhat Hanh wrote, and this book attests to, "The path of return continues the journey."

EPILOGUE

Hopes for a New Nation and a Durable Peace

Hopes for a New Nation and a Durable Peace

From the moment of its birth as a republic, the history of El Salvador has rarely seen an absence of conflict. The country has suffered for centuries from a structural reality dominated by conflict and generated by injustice, inequality and the imposition of an economic model benefiting the elite and excluding the majority of the Salvadoran people.

This history of exclusion was exacerbated in the twentieth century when the power of the state fell into the hands of the military supported by one of the most powerful oligarchies in Central America. For almost half a century, the country was governed by a military dictatorship, first under General Maximiliano Hernández Martínez (1931-1944) and then institutionalized in the Armed Forces (1944-1979). During this period, the history of El Salvador suffered through coups d'etat, electoral fraud, the systematic violation of basic human rights and the absence of civil liberties.

In the 1960s, the country experienced one of the most impressive rates of economic growth in Central America. Paradoxically, however, the same period witnessed an alarming rise in poverty, clearly demonstrating that economic growth alone, in the absence of a more inclusive economic model, does not produce well-being.

In this context, the seventies were particularly critical due to the enormous growth of social organization and the growing demands for social justice and participatory democracy in the face of ever-increasing state-sponsored repression, as recounted in Part One of this book. In that same period, clandestine armed groups emerged that later formed the Farabundo Martí National Liberation Front (FMLN).

This complex chain of events led to a war that was seen by some as the final option for overcoming centuries of injustice and oppression in the wake of decades of failed attempts through non-violent means. This is not a matter of making an apology for war. Wars have their causes that can explain them, but the suffering they produce is always unjustifiable. Only those who have lived through a war understand the pain that it causes, frequently affecting the innocent bystanders more than the direct protagonists.

The armed conflict of the 1980s in El Salvador came to an end with the signing of the Peace Accords in 1992. Those highly important agreements have been disqualified by some in recent years in an effort to erase from the public mind one of the most important periods in El Salvador's history. Nevertheless, it is clear that they have played a fundamental role, both in ending the war and in defining the path for the future of El Salvador as a more just and democratic nation.

Much has been written about the Peace Accords, both within and outside the country. At the national level, analysts have recognized their enormous importance for the profound hope that accompanied their signing as well as for their undeniable impact on strengthening democracy and respect for human rights, while internationally, they have served as a model for resolving conflict in other parts of the world.

It will seem odd to some that this final section of our book is being written at all since it covers a theme that many people already know, but many are still not aware of or have forgotten how profoundly the Peace Accords changed the face of El Salvador. At the same time, others have begun to believe a different narrative that maintains that the war itself, as well as the Peace Accords that brought that war to an end, were nothing more than a "farce".

The successful signing and then implementation of the Peace Accords in El Salvador was possible due to several key factors. The most important among these was the enormous level of consensus generated by the universal longing for peace. Twelve years of war, more than 75,000 dead (most of them civilians), nearly a million people displaced, more than 8,000 young people disappeared, and a country whose social fabric had been torn to pieces and whose economy was in shambles was more than enough reason to wish for an end to the war.

At the same time, social movements had grouped together at the beginning of the 1990s in the Permanent Committee for National Debate for Peace in El Salvador and were exerting enormous pressure, together with the Catholic Church, for a negotiated settlement.

The desire for peace also transcended El Salvador's frontier, involving countries around the world. In this regard, the intervention of nations in solidarity with the Salvadoran people, like France, Mexico, Canada and Spain, made it possible for the international community represented in the United Nations system to focus attention and provide full support to the attainment of this sacred goal.

A second factor was the decision of the Armed Forces of El Salvador, the gendarme of the wealthy elite, to abandon its historical mission of maintaining the "status quo", a move which opened the door for the oligarchy to step forward and take power in defense of its own interests. The person chosen for this new role was Alfredo Cristiani, a millionaire businessman with diverse investments, including the favorite of the oligarchy at that time, coffee. The vehicle for this transition was the Nationalist Republican Alliance (ARENA), a far-right political party that had been founded in 1981 by Major Roberto d'Aubuisson (also founder of the death squads and responsible for the assassination of Monsignor Oscar Arnulfo Romero) to defend the interests of the oligarchy.

Cristiani won the elections in 1989 and immediately began to search for ways of ending a war that was seen by him as a key obstacle to economic recovery. The guerrilla offensive of that same year and the assassination of the Jesuits by members of the army battalion, Atlacatl, were the necessary ingredients for revealing the inhumanity of the military and of the war itself and for completing the task of building national will as well as international support. A delegitimized Armed Forces was put against the wall and pressured to finally sit down and seriously negotiate.

An obvious stalemate in the war also produced a change in the FMLN's position on a negotiated settlement. Although the guerrilla offensive in November 1989 had demonstrated the ability of the FMLN to put the army in checkmate, it also revealed weaknesses that prevented a definitive victory through military means. The FMLN's original revolutionary agenda that would have radically turned the country upside down ceded to more pragmatic aspirations of democratic transformation, leaving behind the utopian dream of socialism. This change in the FMLN's position, like that of ARENA and its military, helped to facilitate the negotiation process and move it towards peace.

A final factor, externally, that contributed to the signing and successful implementation of the Peace Accords was the new geopolitical scenario evolving in the world around the fall of the Berlin Wall and the subsequent end of the Cold War, modifying the geopolitical priorities of the United States.

The Peace Accords that ended the 12-year war in El Salvador resulted from a long and difficult process of dialogue and negotiation filled with starts and stops and constantly threatened by the war itself and the intentions of its protagonists to attain a definitive victory through military means. If the first meetings between the government and the guerrilla organizations of the FMLN are taken into account, the formal negotiation process lasted more than seven years, from 1984 to 1992, although the final stretch that led to the signing of the Accords took less than two years.

The final document of the Accords has nine chapters that include six key areas:

1. Reform of the Armed Forces
2. Creation of the National Civil Police
3. Changes to the judicial system
4. The defense of human rights
5. Modification of the electoral system
6. Adoption of socio-economic measures for a more equitable society

The passage of time has provided the opportunity for a more leisurely and reflective assessment of the significance that each of these areas had on national life at the time of signing, as well as their legacy for future years. It is also clear, nevertheless, that temporal distance can be – and in fact has been– utilized to disqualify these Accords a posteriori, commonly from an anachronistic and self-interested position. Nevertheless, anyone unable or unwilling to comprehend the enormous influence that these Accords have had on the institutional reality and political life of El Salvador, as well as their transcendence in the world at large, is simply ignoring history prior to the war and during the last three decades.

Three principal elements explain why the Peace Accords are of such great importance historically, why they proved so significant at the moment of their signing and why they are perceived as being of such great importance for the future.

The **first element** is the simple fact that the Peace Accords generated a level of consensus – perhaps the first and only agreement based on consensus that El Salvador had experienced since its independence – necessary for bringing the war to a halt. Only those lucky enough to have avoided the twelve-year conflict in El Salvador, who were not touched physically or emotionally or are incapable of feeling empathy with those who suffered, cannot understand what peace meant for the country at that moment.

The **second element** is the fact that the Peace Accords were successfully implemented, and their respective objectives were attained in their entirety, with a few exceptions, producing a clear impact on national reality (discussed in more detail in the following paragraphs).

A **third element** pointing to the historical importance of the Peace Accords is the fact that, up until the present moment in El Salvador, the peace attained through dialogue and negotiation (considered by the United Nations to be the most successful peacebuilding initiative in its history) has been stable. And, to the degree that the Peace Accords demonstrated the possibility of resolving conflict through dialogue and negotiation, they became a model for conflict resolution in other parts of the world. This was the case, for example, in Colombia, where warring parties learned from the lessons of the Salvadoran experience in their efforts to bring to an end the longest guerrilla war in Latin America.

In a meeting in Geneva in April 1990, during the negotiating process, agreement was reached on four key objectives for assuring a sustainable peace in El Salvador:[1]

1. To end the armed conflict by political means in the shortest time possible
2. To promote the democratization of the country
3. To guarantee unrestricted respect for human rights
4. To reunite Salvadoran society.

Three out of four of these objectives were attained to a satisfactory degree, and the fourth object saw some gains. In the case of the first three interrelated objectives, it can be said that complete compliance was attained, although with delays in some cases. FMLN guerrillas gradually

---

1 Government of El Salvador, Peace Accords, commemorative edition on the fifteenth anniversary of its signing. January 2007. P. 6

demobilized and were reintegrated into the social and political life of the country, the Armed Forces were reduced quantitatively and qualitatively, and security forces most responsible for the violation of human rights during the conflict (National Guard, Finance Police, National Police) were disbanded.

Important constitutional reforms were approved and ratified related to open and free elections, including the legalization of the FMLN as a political party and the establishment of a Supreme Electoral Tribunal (TSE). Measures were also taken to create an institutional presence capable of assuring transparency, ethics and honesty in government and to strengthen the separation of powers.

Constitutional reforms were approved and ratified, redefining the mandate, size and doctrine of the military, limiting its role to the defense of national sovereignty and territorial integrity (Art. 212 Cn) while leaving public security in the hands of a new National Civil Police (PNC) (Art. 159 Cn), an institution which had been militarized during the dictatorship. New institutions were also formed, such as the Office of the Ombudsman for the Defense of Human Rights (PDDH), as well as other initiatives in the pursuit of institutionalizing justice.

Full implementation of these objectives was a key concern for FMLN combatants, its leaders and political activists in student, peasant and worker organizations since the degree to which democratization and the respect for human rights were attained for opponents of the regime, other sectors of the population could feel more secure about their own protection. Compliance was also an indication of the overall direction of the country as it attempted to leave the systematic abuses of power in the past and assure respect for the rule of law.

Only the fourth objective – the reunification of Salvadoran society – remained unmet in its entirety. The victims of the war, on both sides, were clearly given little consideration during the negotiating process. Nor were they included in the implementation phase of the Peace Accords.

In an attempt to resolve this situation, the parties meeting in Mexico on April 27, 1991, during the negotiations agreed to the creation of a Truth Commission composed of three neutral personalities appointed by the Secretary General of the United Nations. The Commission was charged with "the investigation of serious acts of violence that have occurred since 1980, whose impact on society demands with greater urgency the public knowledge of the truth." (Peace Accords, p.18).

This Commission was formed in 1992 and carried out the mission entrusted to it by collecting information from a significant sample of cases of serious human rights violations committed during the period of the war. The Commission's final report, entitled "From Madness to Hope: The Twelve-Year War in El Salvador", was published on March 15, 1993.[2]

Five days after the report was published, however, the ARENA-dominated Legislative Assembly approved the "General Amnesty Law for the Consolidation of Peace," which, in practice, meant the burial of the UN report and the legalization of impunity for crimes committed during the war. Supporting this position, President Cristiani spoke of turning the page, of wiping the slate clean and of forgiveness and forgetting as conditions for achieving national reconciliation. Amnesty was applied unconditionally and absolutely for all crimes, and, in this way, the historic opportunity to do justice to victims of the war was lost.

Years passed, with ARENA followed by the FMLN in government without anything being done to rectify this injustice. The amnesty law was in force for more than 23 years until July 13, 2016, when the Supreme Court declared it unconstitutional. Despite this, however, little has changed in the country regarding the fate of the victims and, over the years, a blatant disregard for the guidelines and recommendations established in the report of the UN Truth Commission curtailed further efforts at reparation and justice.

Related to this same objective of reuniting Salvadoran society is the challenge of resolving deep-rooted inequities that were clearly one of the central causes of the conflict from the 1960s. With this goal in mind, the Accords contemplated the creation of a Forum for Economic and Social Concertation whose task was to continue a process of dialogue and negotiation designed to resolve the threat of continuing unrest around

---

2 The commission received direct testimonies on 7,000 victims, in addition to 23,000 complaints filed by other institutions and organizations, and obtained information on another 8,000 victims from secondary sources. From that accumulation of cases, the commission drew up a list of more than 13,500 cases and, of those, selected 32 because they were considered representative of the atrocities committed by three parties involved in the war: the Armed Forces, the FMLN guerrillas and the Death Squads.

social and economic issues with the hope of transforming El Salvador into a more just and inclusive country for all. A lack of political will and a lack of action on the part of the government, however, led to the incompliance of this component.

A final element affecting the impact of the Peace Accords regarding the fourth objective of reuniting Salvadoran society has been neoliberalism. At the end of the war, when El Salvador most needed a robust state to face the challenges of the post-war period, the neoliberal recipe, adopted by ARENA in 1989 in pursuit of economic growth, was strengthened through growing privatization (telecommunications, the distribution of electricity, banking, commercialization of coffee and sugar) leading to the increasing concentration of wealth in the hands of a few, a situation incompatible with democracy.

As alluded to earlier, the profound significance of the Peace Accords for El Salvador has not always been valued in its proper dimension. One of the most common errors when it comes to weighing this issue is the tendency to understand them only as a point of arrival and not also as a point of departure. Applying the wisdom of Winston Churchill, the Peace Accords were not simply the end, or the beginning of the end, but rather the end of the beginning.

The Accords clearly marked the end of a long and difficult path of dialogue and negotiation leading to the end of the war, with its ups and downs, starts and stops, obstacles and crises. From this perspective, bringing the war to an end was the clearest proof of the significance of the Accords for El Salvador, appreciated especially by combatants on both sides of the conflict and by the population in general, exhausted by an unending bloody fratricidal confrontation.

The process of dismantling the guerrilla army and its transition to civilian life, the reduction of the Armed Forces, the elimination of security forces guilty of violating human rights and the dismantling of counterinsurgency battalions (BIRIs) established by U.S. military advisors were carried out successfully. These measures, along with the constitutional reforms necessary to redefine the mandate of the Armed Forces and the creation of a new National Civil Police under civilian control, undoubtedly provided a new face for the nation that was more democratic and more respectful of the lives and rights of the population.

The Accords, in this regard, represented a new beginning involving fundamental change. The most decisive change was the emergence of a country from the shadows of military dictatorship into the light of an incipient democracy based on citizen participation, transparency and respect for human rights. This transition made it possible for the country to turn the page on electoral fraud, repression and the systematic viola-tion of citizen rights by the country's security forces that for decades had acted contrary to the law. In the words of Geoff Thale, ex-director of the Washington Office on Latin America (WOLA),

> El Salvador went from being a country where opponents of the government feared for their lives, hid or took up arms to protect themselves and advance their views, to a country where political disagreements were openly expressed, where politicians with very different visions for the country could campaign without fear of reprisals, and where investigative journalism – print and online – grew dramatically (Thale, 2021).

As already stated, El Salvador emerged from the war without having adequately addressed the chronic problems of poverty and inequality that had led to conflict in the past, and the country once again became fertile ground for the emergence of other types of violence, such as gang warfare, theft, kidnapping and blackmail. The gangs grew to unimag-inable levels, causing, once again, pain and suffering to the poorest sectors of the population and led these sectors to distrust the solutions put forth in the Peace Accords, including the incipient democracy that they had engendered. This, in turn, led to the rejection of traditional political parties who had shared extended periods in power over the previous decades and opened the door to broad-based acceptance of any government or leader who could convince the majority of their ability to resolve the nation's problems, regardless of the type of government that was implemented.

The deepest levels of disenchantment and anger could be found among former FMLN militants who spent the war years fighting on the frontlines, risking and sacrificing their lives for the revolutionary dream. The words of Isaías Sandoval Alas (pseudonym, Felipe Ardilla), former guerrilla commander and postwar mayor of Suchitoto, present a clear example of this sentiment:

> By laying down our arms and joining the political process, our intention was to continue our struggle for a more just and democratic country by applying the same principles that had guided us during the war. The objective was to come to power through elections in order to implement the transformations that our country needed. But what hurts me the most after so much sacrifice, effort and suffering on the part of our people and those of us who walked in the war fronts, is that, soon after taking power, things took a different course.
>
> Our top leaders of our party began to forget about the people, about social organization, about our historical political base…. The party became focused only on elections and our leaders became arrogant and anti-democratic, refusing to listen when we presented criticisms. The system absorbed them. They forgot the principles for which we had fought. They…turned the party into a traditional party, just like the right-wing parties throughout our country's history, in some cases even worse…, the same that has occurred with so many popular revolutionary struggles throughout time.

There is much to criticize on the part of governments and political leaders that have administered El Salvador in the last three decades and the powerful sectors of the economy that have been accomplices, passively or actively. Corruption has been rampant in all of them, economic growth has been slow and limited, and inequality has continued to grow. But to blame the Peace Accords for the problems that governments and politicians have failed to solve during this postwar period would be simply absurd.

The challenges of the coming generations in El Salvador will be centered on defending the new institutional reality of their country created through the Peace Accords over thirty years ago. They will also be challenged to defend the historic memory of men and women, young and old, who pursued the utopian dream of building a more just and democratic nation during one of the most important periods of El Salvador's history. Finally, they will be challenged to confront the issues of a new millennium, including the defense of natural resources, especially water, with a rights-based focus and a clear goal of always moving forward, of never going back to where the madness lurks in waiting.

About the Author

Andrés (Drew) McKinley was born in the United States but has worked for over 50 years in programs for sustainable development, environment and human rights in Africa, Latin America and the United States. He has worked for the past 48 years in Central America, residing in El Salvador. He possesses a masters degree in Health Administration and is the author of six books, including his memoirs from El Salvador, *For the Love of the Struggle*, published by Daraja Press in 2021.

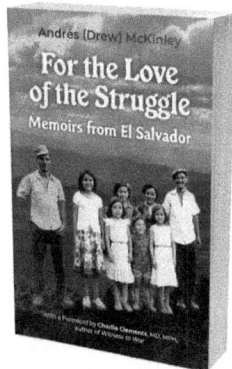

For the Love of the Struggle follows Andrés McKinley's remarkable journey from the comfort and security of a picturesque New England town to a stirring and heroic engagement in common cause with the struggle for peace and justice in El Salvador. The story is marked by terror, adventure and courage, by trials and tragedy redeemed by the beauty and transcendence of people in struggle. As the memoir closes, the author reflects on his choice to stay in El Salvador over the past 43 years, and the country as he finds it in these changing times.

www.ingramcontent.com/pod-product-compliance
Lightning Source LLC
Chambersburg PA
CBHW071736270326
41928CB00013B/2696